GATHERING THE LIGHT

GATHERING THE LIGHT

A JUNGIAN VIEW OF MEDITATION

V. Walter Odajnyk

Gathering the Light
A Jungian View of Meditation

Copyright © 1993, 2011 by V. Walter Odajnyk
Revised Edition
ISBN 978-1-926715-55-1 Paperback

Previously Published by Shambhala as
Gathering the Light: A Psychology of Meditation

Published simultaneously in Canada and the United States of America by Fisher King Press. For information on obtaining permission for use of material from this work, submit a written request to:

permissions@fisherkingpress.com

Fisher King Press
PO Box 222321
Carmel, CA 93922
www.fisherkingpress.com
info@fisherkingpress.com
+1-831-238-7799

Many thanks to all who have directly or indirectly provided permission to reprint their work, including: Excerpts from *The Collected Works of C.G. Jung* by C.G. Jung, vol. 13 © 1967 by Princeton University Press and vol. 14 © 1970 by Princeton University Press, reprinted by permission of Princeton University Press. Diagram on page 62 from *Zen: Dawn in the West* by Philip Kapleau © 1979 by Zen Center, Inc. Used by permission of Doubleday, a division of Bantam Doubleday Dell Publishing Group, Inc.

Every effort has been made to trace all copyright holders; however, if any have been overlooked, the author will be pleased to make the necessary arrangements at the first opportunity.

Front cover image © is from an original painting by Rebecca Gomez, www.rgomezart.com

FOR KATHY AND ALEXANDER

Meditation preserves the one who meditates, it gives one long life, and endows one with power, it cleanses one from faults, it removes any bad reputation and gives one a good name, it destroys discontent and fills one with content, it puts an end to all fears and endows one with confidence, it removes sloth filling one with zeal, it takes away lust and ill-will and dullness, it puts an end to pride, it breaks down all doubt, it makes the heart peaceful and the mind gentle, it makes one glad, it makes one grave, it gains one much advantage, it makes one worthy of reverence, it fills one with joy, it fills one with delight, it shows one the transitory nature of all compounded things, it puts an end to rebirth, it obtains for one all the benefits of renunciation.

—*Milindapanha 139-40*

CONTENTS

ACKNOWLEDGMENTS

I want to thank Margaret Ryan, who edited chapters 3 and 5 when they first appeared in *Psychological Perspectives*. Emily Hilburn Sell was brilliant in organizing these initially disparate chapters into a coherent whole. Kathy Willner Odesmith, my wife, read and corrected the rough draft and provided friendly advice and loving support. Kendra Crossen, managing editor of Shambhala, goaded me on with questions and arguments. Her incisive intelligence and attention to detail transformed the raw material of a manuscript into a book.

Thomas Moore was unstinting with his kindness and generosity in writing a Foreword for this new edition of *Gathering the Light*. Appreciative of the value of the book for future psychotherapists, Allen Koehn, my colleague at Pacifica Graduate Institute, regularly brought it to the attention of his students. Rebecca Gomez was gracious in letting me choose a cover illustration from among her remarkable paintings. Pacifica Graduate Institute provided the academic and financial support that enabled me to organize a new edition of the book. And finally, I am most grateful to Mel Mathews, publisher of Fisher King Press, for his enthusiastic commitment to this project, making *Gathering the Light* available to a new generation of readers.

FOREWORD

by Thomas Moore

In its basic forms meditation is simply something that human beings do. We stop before a beautiful sunset and take it in as a deep aesthetic experience. We hear bad news and stop and think through all its implications and feel its impact on our emotions. We walk in a forest and can't help but get quiet to be part of the natural world around us. We think through our problems and wonder about our future and consider the past.

Spiritual traditions offer ways to make these simple, primal ways of meditating more formal and more effective. More sophisticated ways of meditating take us deep and have an even greater impact on our emotions, worldview and sense of self. They calm us not just by quieting the body and the mind, but by cleansing the impurities of our psychological and spiritual condition, a point made by that well-known champion of meditation and the dark night of the soul, John of the Cross.

If you have read C.G. Jung's memoir, *Memories, Dreams, Reflections*, you will have eavesdropped on a remarkable man who, perhaps more than any other 20th century person, used many methods, internal and external, to explore his soul. Many readers are surprised to find what they thought was an autobiography to be slight on facts and heavy with internal images and experiences. Jung explored and mapped and named the inhabitants of the inner world with a ferocity of imagination rarely seen. All the while, he connected his discoveries and inventions to the discipline of psychology and to the religious, occult, and spiritual traditions of the world.

So it makes sense to relate our efforts to meditate with Jung's writings, especially with his notions of Self, his alchemical studies, and his special method of active imagination. Having not worked this idea through for myself, after studying Jung intensely for many years, I was surprised and happy to see it done so enthusiastically and intelligently in this remarkable book by V. Walter Odajnyk.

When contemporary psychology confronts meditation, it often moves in a reductive direction, like telling us that certain parts of the brain are lighting up when a person enters deep focus. But Jung was not your typical psychologist. He had a vast and detailed interest in religious and spiritual issues and for the most part didn't reduce the spiritual to the psychological. Or, if he did come close to it on occasion, generally he tried to elevate psychology through an enthusiastic appreciation of religion and opened up the meaning of religious rites and imagery with his own rich brand of psychologizing. As a former member of a Catholic religious order, I found his writings on the Mass and on the Virgin Mary enlightening and enriching.

This book also makes interesting comparisons between psychotherapy and transcendent forms of meditation. There is much to learn here about the two processes, one sorting out the psyche and the other reaching into transpersonal realms. In my own favored language, I would say that there is a spiritual form of meditating that takes us beyond ourselves and a soul meditating that remains close to life and personality, using art, images, ritual, and nature as aids to contemplation.

Jung tells a fascinating story of his discovery of alchemy and its usefulness to his own life and to his work. In the first relevant dream he found himself in a wing of his house he didn't know existed. It contained a library of esoteric books. Then he found himself locked up in the 17th century, the time when European alchemy flourished. I find it an exciting and fruitful idea to use alchemy as the basis for a special kind of meditation, and you have the fundamentals in this book.

Alchemy provides us with particular images for the materials, processes, and phases of soul work. Jung began with the *The Secret of the Golden Flower,* and so it's appropriate that it is the focus of this book. Today especially, a time of thorough materialism in science and psychology, we have to extract the soul from the many literal and purely physical ideas we have about human life. You might say that a primary purpose of meditation is to

—— *Thomas Moore*

recover our souls from being lost and stuck and covered over with ideas that are too thick for the subtleties of soul work.

Most people who know a little about Jung are familiar with the notion of the psychological complex and the archetype. These are essential elements in a Jungian therapy that helps a person get freed from the dominance of a particular complex or archetype. Professor Odajnyk makes the important point that meditation is an effective way to contact the complexes and to reach the archetypal level of experience. I can imagine it having a useful role in the therapeutic analysis of the psyche. I might even go so far as to say that at times therapy itself is a kind of meditation. Dream work, for instance, takes you deep into reflection on images that are full of interest and relevance because they shed so much light on the underworld of our daily experience.

I welcome the re-appearance of this book because generally people focus on the technical aspects of meditating and not so much on the processes and fantasies of the psyche that are involved. I wouldn't recommend a purely Jungian style of meditating, but Jungian ideas can enrich the experience and importantly bring the deep psyche into the picture. Sometimes people become so focused on their spiritual progress that they neglect the deep soul.

As you read this subtle, carefully thought-out book, you might draw simple lessons for yourself that you can apply to your meditations. You might expand your very notion of what meditation is and how to go about it. In a more general sense, you might begin to reconcile soul and spirit in your life, achieving one of the primary goals of alchemy. Imagine this book lying open in a warm, shadowy and mysterious laboratory of the soul. It offers you guidance and a few recipes for becoming a deeper and more soulful person.

Thomas Moore ———

INTRODUCTION

At the beginning of the Christian era, the entire Mediterranean world was caught up in the throes of a spiritual ferment—not unlike that of our day. The Roman Empire had completed the eastward expansion begun by Alexander the Great and brought together the ancient cultures of the Near East and the younger cultures of the West. A cosmopolitan, secular, Hellenic civilization and a common language unified the entire region. The various indigenous traditional religions lost their hold on the religious feelings of their adherents. A merging of the gods and cults of different regions took place, and something like our New Age movement developed. That movement combined Oriental mythologies, astrology, Iranian theology, elements of Jewish biblical and occult traditions, Christian salvation-eschatology, the mystery religions of Isis, Mithras, and Attis, Platonic terms and concepts, and alchemical imagery. Christianity itself was only one among many new religions of the time that held a radically dualistic view of the nature of reality along with an otherworldly goal of salvation. In ancient Rome, as in the United States today, every conceivable religion was represented, and many people wandered from sect to sect in search of novelty and transcendent experience. It was even possible to travel to India and China in that quest.

Today, the religions of East and West have met once again. One of the significant results of that encounter is a renewed interest in meditation. I say "renewed" because meditation is not new to the West. Both Christianity and Judaism have a rich contemplative tradition. But beginning with the Renaissance, that tradition slowly began to recede as Europeans turned their attention toward the outer world—exploring the newly discovered American continent, studying different cultures, and pursuing an objective inquiry into nature. Thus, when the Eastern religions gained popularity in the West during the late 1960s and early 1970s, many Christians and Jews initially encountered meditation through Eastern teachings. Daniel Goleman, in the introduction to his book *The Meditative Mind,* describes the situation at the time. He states that when he wrote the first version of the book in 1977, meditation was new to the West. (This is not quite true; rather, meditation in the West had disappeared from common religious practice.) Goleman became intensely interested in meditation and as a graduate student in psychology went to Asia to study the meditative traditions in their original setting. He writes:

> Those of us who were drawn to the meditation teachings of the East were confronted by a panoply of techniques, schools, traditions, and lineages. Suddenly we heard talk of strange states of consciousness and exotic states of being—"samadhi" and "satori," Boddhisattvas and tulkus.
>
> It was new and unfamiliar terrain to us. We needed a Baedeker, a traveler's guide to this topography of the spirit. I wrote *Varieties* as such a guide, an overview of the major meditative traditions that were then finding so many eager students. . . .
>
> Now, more than a decade later, things have changed. Meditation has infiltrated our culture. Millions of Americans

_____ *Introduction*

have tried meditation, and many have incorporated it into their busy lives. Meditation is now a standard tool used in medicine, psychology, education, and self-development. . . . People meditate at work to enhance their effectiveness; psychotherapists and physicians teach it to their patients; and graduate students write theses about it.[1]

During the 1970s, and even more so today, a good number of believing Jews and Christians who were exposed to Eastern meditation began to look to their own traditions to rediscover and revitalize the practice of meditation in a Christian or Jewish context. Rabbi Aryeh Kaplan, for example, made such an attempt with his book *Meditation and the Bible,* published in 1978. In a later book, *Jewish Meditation,* he noted that "as many as 75 percent of the devotees in some ashrams are Jewish and large percentages follow disciplines such as Transcendental Meditation. When I speak to these Jews and ask them why they are exploring other religions instead of their own, they answer that they know of nothing deep or spiritually satisfying in Judaism. When I tell them there is a strong tradition of meditation and mysticism, not only in Judaism, but in mainstream Judaism, they look at me askance."[2]

Nevertheless, Kaplan admitted that even many rabbis and scholars were not aware that such a tradition exists. For since the Enlightenment, reference to meditation disappeared from mainstream Jewish literature, and even from Chasidic literature, where it once played a central role. Kaplan had to undertake a difficult scholarly task to rediscover the tradition of Jewish meditation, for most of the important texts on Jewish meditation had never been published and existed only in manuscript form stored in libraries and museums in different parts of the world. The manuscripts first had to be located, copied, and their often obsolete scripts deciphered. And even then, much of the material would have been incomprehensible to someone who had had no experience with meditation.

Although the once numerous and thriving monasteries of the Catholic Church are gone or stand empty, at least the classic texts on meditation have always remained available. Among these are *The Cloud of Unknowing* by an anonymous fourteenth-century author; *The Ladder of Perfection* by Walter Hilton; *The Dark Night of the Soul* by Saint John of the Cross; and *The Interior Castle* by Saint Teresa of Ávila. The monasteries on Mount Athos, too, stand mostly empty, but the Eastern Orthodox Church has maintained a lively, if diminished, tradition of meditation with the so-called Jesus Prayer. The tradition is preserved in the *Philokalia,* a collection of writings by early Church Fathers. The Jesus Prayer (known in the West as Hesychasm) is associated with Hesychius of Jerusalem, a fifth-century teacher who stressed the value of repetitive prayer as a way of stillness and repose leading to a vision of God. The prayer consists of the unceasing repetition of the Publican's plea: "Lord Jesus Christ, Son of God, have mercy upon me, a sinner." The shortened version of the prayer is simply *Kyrie eleison,* "Lord have mercy." (The technique is similar to the Hindu practice of *japa,* or holding the object of one's devotion constantly in mind through the ceaseless repetition of a divine name or a mantra.)

In spite of these still extant Christian meditative traditions, many contemporary Christians were led back to these pursuits by way of an exposure to Eastern meditation. One notable example is that of John Main, a practicing Catholic, who was taught mantra meditation by an Indian teacher in Malaya. He decided to become a Benedictine monk, and when he described his way of meditating to his novice master, he was told to stop. Instead, he was asked to undertake the more intellectual forms of meditation—discursive, conceptual, and imaginative. Then one day he read John Cassian, the teacher of Saint Benedict and Saint Thomas

Aquinas, and recognized that Cassian's *meditatio* was essentially identical with what he had been taught by his Indian teacher. He began to teach this form of meditation in 1976 and founded a worldwide network of small meditation groups.

The most popular Catholic exponent of the contemplative life in recent years was the Trappist monk Thomas Merton. His *Seeds of Contemplation,* which appeared in 1949, was a widely read book long before Eastern meditation made its incursion into the West. But eventually he, too, became greatly interested in Eastern, particularly Buddhist, meditation, and on his fatal trip to Asia in 1968 (during which he died accidentally from electric shock), he even toyed with the idea of working with a Tibetan guru. Merton had a life-long interest in Zen Buddhism and wrote a number of essays on the topic.

The newly revived interest in meditation, however, is not limited to religion. Many people meditate for purely secular reasons: to improve their concentration or to obtain a sense of equilibrium, clarity of mind, and a general feeling of well-being. Others use various meditation techniques to activate, explore, and sometimes restructure aspects of their psychology. Perhaps this broad interest in meditation is a presage of a Western cultural enantiodromia—a turning away from the preoccupation with outer reality toward an exploration of the inner world. But for the moment, the Western scientific approach is being applied to meditation as well. Different forms of meditation have been subjected to experimental studies both inside and outside a religious context. The psychological, physiological, and neurological (EEG patterns) changes taking place during and after meditation have been described. Research has shown, for example, that even the most elementary meditation practice, repeating a mantra or focusing on one's breath, tends to have a beneficial effect on the immune system and to improve such conditions as

Introduction ———

hypertension, angina and arrhythmia, high cholesterol, anxiety, stress, chronic pain, phobias, and addictions. (More recent studies have demonstrated that meditation is not unique in obtaining these results; any form of deep relaxation has the same effects.)

The states of consciousness experienced during meditation have been compared with other unusual forms of consciousness, such as those induced by hypnosis or psychedelic drugs. Many of these early studies were published in *Altered States of Consciousness* (1969), edited by Charles T. Tart. *The Journal of Transpersonal Psychology*, founded in 1969 by Anthony Sutich, a close collaborator of Abraham Maslow, has been particularly receptive to research and essays on the physiology and psychology of meditation, and on mysticism and other religious experiences. Interestingly enough, research in both subatomic physics and astrophysics has led to a perception of the universe that in essence parallels the often paradoxical descriptions of the nature of reality in Eastern mysticism. The theoretical physicist Fritjof Capra has documented and illustrated these similarities in *The Tao of Physics: An Exploration of the Parallels between Modern Physics and Eastern Mysticism* (1975). Since the 1960s a number of widely read psychologists and humanists have sought to integrate Eastern and Western psychology, among them Alan Watts, especially in *Psychotherapy East and West* (1961); Erich Fromm in *Zen Buddhism and Psychoanalysis* (1970), coauthored with D. T. Suzuki; Roberto Assagioli in *Psychosynthesis* (1971); and Abraham Maslow, particularly in his posthumously published book *The Farther Reaches of Human Nature* (1971).

Charles T. Tart, in *Transpersonal Psychologies* (1975), a survey of nine major Western and Eastern mystical traditions, acknowledges that the Western scientific approach has failed to deal adequately with the realm of spiritual experience: "The 'enlightened rationalism' and physicalism [the notion that ultimate reality consists of the interaction of matter and energy in time and space and exists independently of our perception of it] that have been so successful in developing the physical sciences have not worked very well in psychology. . . . Orthodox, Western psychology has dealt poorly with the spiritual side of man's nature, choosing either to ignore its existence or to label it pathological."[3] He therefore proposes the creation of "state-specific sciences," specific to different states of altered consciousness. Just as there are specially trained scientists in such areas as chemistry and biology, there would have to be specially trained scientists dealing with the observation and analysis of the experiences and states of consciousness characteristic of, say, hatha yoga, Zen meditation, telekinesis, LSD, and so on. The difference, of course, would be that the state-specific scientist would have to experience these conditions and observe them from "within," rather than from the outside, as is the case with the natural sciences. Jung faced this issue in the early decades of this century and simply opted for empiricism, the observation of experiential facts without regard to theory.

In a series of books, among them *The Spectrum of Consciousness* and *The Atman Project* (first published in 1977 and 1980 respectively), Ken Wilber has developed a theoretical framework that seeks to integrate the developmental and ego psychologies of the West with the spiritual and transpersonal psychologies of the East. The most recent effort in this vein, and one that purports to offer a "full spectrum" model of human development, is *Transformations of Consciousness: Conventional and Contemplative Perspectives on Development* (1986) by Ken Wilber, Jack Engler, and Daniel P. Brown.

I don't know whether Wilber is familiar with Jung's use of the color spectrum as an analogy for the range of psychic functioning. On the infrared end of the spectrum, Jung places the biological instinctive psyche, which gradually merges with its chemical and physical conditions. On the ultraviolet end, he places the archetypal images, which merge with the invisible-to-us realm of spirit. Thus: "In archetypal conceptions and instinctual perceptions, spirit and matter confront one another on the psychic plane. Matter and spirit both appear in the psychic realm as distinctive qualities of conscious contents. The ultimate nature of both is transcendental, that is, irrepresentable, since the psyche and its contents are the only reality which is given to us *without a medium*."[4] Wilber's spectrum is similar, for he places what he calls the preverbal, primary processes that are bound to the instincts at the initial state of the human life cycle, and of human evolution in general, and the transpersonal, archetypal consciousness at the most evolved end of the life cycle, and of human evolution. Although, like Jung, Wilber recognizes the limits of consciousness at the primary process level, he does not seem to acknowledge the limits of consciousness at the archetypal end of the spectrum.

With the current interest in Eastern thought and meditation, it is surprising how seldom Jung's contribution in this area is acknowledged. Jung played a major role in introducing a number of important Eastern texts to the Western reader: *The Secret of the Golden Flower; The Tibetan Book of the Dead; The Tibetan Book of the Great Liberation;* D. T. Suzuki's *Introduction to Zen Buddhism;* and Richard Wilhelm's translation of *The I Ching or Book of Changes.* He sought to make these texts comprehensible by translating their basic philosophical concepts and religious images into psychological language and by drawing parallels with similar Western ideas and religious experiences. As early as the 1930s, he attempted to integrate Western and Eastern psychology, particularly with his notion of the Self as a central, mandala-like psychic structure with transpersonal characteristics. For his efforts in this regard, and because, unlike Freud, he refused to ignore religious and parapsychological phenomena, he was labeled a mystic and dismissed by mainstream psychologists. Today, Jung's work is more readily acknowledged, and yet his psychological theories are mentioned only in a peripheral way in the most recent studies of meditation and altered states of consciousness. It appears that Jungian psychology is a "state-specific science," and only someone who has undergone a Jungian analysis and training is able to apply Jung's theories in a meaningful way.

This book is an attempt to do just that. It seeks, first, to bring to light the immense contribution that Jung has made to the comprehension and appreciation of Eastern religious thought and practice. Second, it applies the insights and discoveries of Jungian psychology to the study of meditation.

Chapter 1 chronicles Jung's encounter with Eastern thought and his attempts to make the Eastern worldview understandable in Western religious and psychological terms. A major part of the chapter is devoted to a discussion of the Jungian definition of *projection* and the relation of projection to the experience of enlightenment or Self-realization.

Chapter 2 describes the psychological processes that take place during meditation. By directing psychic energy inward, meditation activates the complexes and the archetypes, with different forms of meditation activating different archetypes and giving rise to different experiences and results. The topics covered include attention; concentration; "deautomatization," the freeing up of psychic energy that normally flows into our habitual responses; the role of the ego complex during meditation; the loss of body sensations; visions of light; and the psychological limits of enlightenment.

Chapter 3 discusses Zen meditation, which seeks to activate what Jung called the uroboric archetype of the Self, that is, the transcendent potential world of being that contains all the archetypes before they separate out and take on manifest form. In Zen this archetype is defined as Pure Consciousness or Formless Form. I apply the insights of Jungian psychology to the interior developments that take place in the course of Zen meditation: the effects of the posture and the focus on breathing and counting; the work with a *koan;* alterations of the ego complex; and the nature of *satori.* During the course of the discussion I introduce the concept of a "meditation complex" to account for the psychic structure and energy that appear when the ego gives up its unifying role of consciousness and before that role is taken over by the Self. (I use the term *complex* in the neutral way that Jung did, as a "feeling-toned cluster of psychic energy.")

Chapter 4 explores Jung's reservations about the practice of Eastern meditation by Westerners. He argues that there is a vast cultural and psychological difference between Easterners and Westerners, and that Westerners ought to widen their consciousness on the basis of their own psychology. He feels that psychotherapy is the appropriate Western method for the pursuit of this goal, and proposes active imagination as the meditation technique that best leads to the integration of the personality and the expansion of consciousness.

Chapter 5 delves into the relationship between meditation and alchemy. Without a knowledge of alchemical symbolism, certain Eastern meditation texts, like *The Secret of the Golden Flower,* are not fully comprehensible. Jung discovered that alchemy describes in prepsychological language the evolution and development of consciousness. Western alchemy, with its extraverted bias, projected this entire process onto the interactions of matter. Eastern alchemy, with its introverted focus, projected this development of the internal flow of energy within the body. The chapter concentrates on the final alchemical operation, *coniunctio,* in which the previously separated-out and "purified" opposite elements or energies are reunited and the goal of the opus is achieved. The product of this final union is described as the philosophers' stone or gold in Western alchemy and as the golden flower or the elixir of life in Eastern alchemy. Jung tended to see the symbolism of alchemy as analogous to the process of individuation and the goal of alchemy as the attainment of psychological wholeness. I revise his emphasis somewhat and demonstrate that alchemical symbolism also describes the psychological processes that take place during the course of meditation, and I view the goal of alchemy as the attainment of Self-realization or enlightenment.

Two appendixes follow the text. The first outlines Ken Wilber's criticism of Jung's concept of "archetype" and in response provides a fairly extensive description of what Jung meant by the term. The second examines a recently published translation of *The Secret of the Golden Flower* by Thomas Cleary. It compares the relative merits of Wilhelm's and Cleary's translations on several crucial points. In his notes to the translation, Cleary is highly critical of Jung's treatment and interpretation of the text. The chapter summarizes his concerns, responds to them, and, in turn, subjects Cleary's approach to a critique. Because Cleary has no real knowledge of alchemical symbolism, he does not realize the importance that the body and the emotions play in the meditation technique described by the *Golden Flower;* he thinks it consists primarily of mentally focusing inward toward the source of consciousness. A translation that does justice to the alchemical aspects of the book, therefore, has yet to appear.

As a psychoanalyst with an interest in meditation, I am often asked if I incorporate meditation in my therapeutic work. The answer is that I have been able to incorporate Jung's active imagination, which is a form of meditation, in my work, but not Eastern meditation. In active imagination, people are able to engage their complexes and troublesome affects in a direct way and obtain immediate therapeutic results. This does not happen with most Eastern meditation techniques, which require a period of arduous training and consistent practice before any significant psychological results become evident. Also, Eastern meditation, with some exceptions, does not deal with psychological or relationship problems in a direct way. People who come for psychotherapy are usually not interested in learning a meditation technique that may have a beneficial effect on their life in future years, because they are now seeking relief from psychic tension or pain that makes their present life difficult. In addition, not everyone is motivated by the aim of Eastern meditation, namely, a religious relationship with archetypal images, or, conversely, their demystification, or the experience of the ultimate ground of consciousness and being. Eastern meditation, therefore, is not an aid to psychotherapy; rather, it is the other way around: psychotherapy can help a person overcome the psychological obstacles and personal problems that interfere with the successful practice of meditation.

CHAPTER ONE

JUNG, MEDITATION,

AND THE WEST

We must get at the Eastern values from within and not from
without, seeking them in ourselves, in the unconscious. We shall
then discover how great is our fear of the unconscious and how
formidable are our resistances. Because of these resistances we
doubt the very thing that seems so obvious to the East, namely,
the *self-liberating power of the introverted mind*.

—*C. G. Jung*

When C. G. Jung began his
study of Eastern religions in the late 1920s, hardly anyone in
the West was interested in the topic. He could, he states,
point only to "a handful of orientalists, one or two Buddhist
enthusiasts, [and a] few sombre celebrities like Madame
Blavatsky and Annie Besant with her Krishnamurti."[1] But
already then, he felt that these tiny scattered islands of
interest in Eastern thought were in fact "peaks of submarine
mountain-ranges" that would in time rise to the surface.[2]
Most educated people believed, for example, that astrology
had been disposed of long ago "and was something that
could safely be laughed at. But today [1928], rising out of the
social deeps, it knocks at the doors of the universities from
which it was banished some three hundred years ago. The
same is true of Eastern ideas; they take root in the lower

levels and slowly grow to the surface."[3] Today, Jung's words seem almost prophetic.

Jung was struck by the historical irony that just at the time of the French Revolution, when the Goddess of Reason was enthroned in the Cathedral of Nôtre Dame, a Frenchman, Anquetil du Perron, was living in India and translating the Upanishads. His Latin translation was published in 1801–1802 and gave Western scholars their first glimpse of the Eastern mind. In the United States the Transcendentalists, notably Emerson and Thoreau, popularized the Eastern point of view, and in Europe Schopenhauer and Nietzsche did the same.

Jung himself has played a major role in the dissemination of Eastern thought in the West. In 1928 he contributed a psychological commentary to Richard Wilhelm's German translation of *The Secret of the Golden Flower: A Chinese Book of Life*. The book, an unusual amalgam of Taoist, Buddhist, Confucian, and alchemical ideas, is an instructional manual in meditation. Jung hoped to make the text comprehensible to the Western reader through a psychological interpretation of its basic concepts. His goal, he writes, was "to attempt to build a bridge of psychological understanding between East and West."[4] He continued this task in his 1935 psychological commentary on *The Tibetan Book of the Dead* edited by W. Y. Evans-Wentz. (The book, Jung writes, "caused a considerable stir in English-speaking countries at the time of its first appearance in 1927."[5] It became his constant companion, he adds, and he owed it "not only many stimulating ideas and discoveries, but also many fundamental insights."[6]) Four years later, in 1939, Jung wrote another psychological commentary, this time on *The Tibetan Book of the Great Liberation*, a text dealing with the goals of Buddhist meditation. In the same year, Jung contributed a lengthy foreword to D. T. Suzuki's *Introduction to Zen Buddhism*. Again, he sought to make the fundamental concepts of Zen comprehensible to the Western reader by drawing parallels with Western mystical thought and by trying to define the experience of *satori* in psychological terms. And in 1950 Jung composed a foreword to Richard Wilhelm's German translation of *The I Ching or Book of Changes.* In this case, he could not draw on Western parallels and had to content himself with illustrating and exploring the Chinese view of the meaningfulness of connections among events happening at the same time, for which he coined the term *synchronicity.*

During much of the 1930s the study of Eastern thought was one of Jung's major areas of interest. In the autumn of 1932, Professor J. W. Hauer, a specialist in Indian studies, was invited to offer a seminar in *kundalini* yoga to the members of the Jungian Psychology Club in Zurich. (*The Serpent Power* by A. Avalon—pseudonym of John Woodroffe—was published in 1931 and may have sparked the interest.) Jung again provided the psychological commentary, drawing a parallel between the process of development envisioned in *kundalini* yoga and the process of individuation. In 1933 he lectured for the first time at the international scholarly Eranos meetings in Ascona, Switzerland. The theme of the conference was "Yoga and Meditation in East and West." Heinrich Zimmer, another noted Indologist, participated in the meeting with a lecture on *tantra* yoga. Jung spoke on the "Empirical Basis of the Individuation Process." The lecture, after much revision and enlargement, became "A Study in the Process of Individuation," a commentary on and an interpretation of a series of remarkable mandala pictures that vividly depict a process of individual transformation culminating in what can be described as Self-realization or wholeness.

The theme of the 1934 and 1935 Eranos conferences was "Symbolism and Psychologic Methods in East and West." Professors Zimmer and Hauer again participated, as did Martin Buber with a presentation on the "Symbolic and

Sacramental Existence in Judaism." Jung lectured on "Archetypes of the Collective Unconscious" and on "Dream Symbolism of the Individuation Process"; the latter eventually evolved into part 2 of *Psychology and Alchemy*. By now Jung was deeply immersed in his study of Western alchemy, always looking for Western parallels to Eastern symbols as they relate to psychological transformation.

By 1936 European interest in yoga had become widespread enough for Jung to write the brief essay "Yoga and the West." He spoke of the uninterrupted four-thousand-year-old history of Eastern religions and contrasted that with the Western religious experience, with its splits between instinct and spirit, faith and rational knowledge. Within the religious tradition of the East, yoga is "the perfect and appropriate method of fusing body and mind together so that they form a unity."[7] Many Westerners are attracted to yoga because it seems to be a combination of religion and science, holding out the promise of healing the cleavage between the two. In the Western context, however, it is almost impossible to approach the practice of yoga in the right spirit and it becomes either a form of psychophysiological training or a religion accepted on faith. Yoga was originally a natural process of introversion with many individual variations that, in the course of time, became organized into distinct schools (*hatha, raja, tantra,* etc.). The West, Jung concludes, will eventually develop its own yoga, its own method of uniting body and mind, conscious and unconscious, science and knowledge. That method, too, will grow out of the individual practice of introversion by Westerners and reflect their particular psychology and religious tradition.

The topic for the 1936 and 1937 Eranos conferences was the "Formation of the Idea of Redemption in East and West." Jung's talks were "The Idea of Redemption in Alchemy," which became part 3 of *Psychology and Alchemy,* and "Visions of Zosimos," about a fourth-century alchemist, whose striking visions of the process of transformation were subjected by Jung to a psychological interpretation.

During the winter of 1937–1938, Jung took a three-month trip to India. He was invited to attend the Indian Science Congress in Calcutta, held as part of the celebrations connected with the twenty-fifth anniversary of the University of Calcutta. No doubt he was pleased by the opportunity to visit India, given his interest in Eastern thought. Upon his return he wrote two highly subjective and impressionistic essays, "The Dream-like World of India" and "What India Can Teach Us." Both appeared in the magazine *Asia* early in 1939.

During the following two years, while the political tensions in Europe were rising, Jung lectured on various Indian texts at the Zurich School of Technology (the ETH, or Eidgenössiche Technische Hochschule), where he held a teaching position. He became particularly interested in interpreting a tantric text, the *Shri-Chakra-Samghara Tantra,* and comparing its symbols with those of alchemy. He continued to lecture on Eastern texts until June 1940 and then devoted some time to the Spiritual Exercises of Saint Ignatius of Loyola as a Western example of his general theme of active imagination and meditation (which I shall discuss in chapter 4).

Having studied and assimilated a good deal of Eastern philosophy and religious thought during the decade of the thirties, Jung now turned his attention almost exclusively to alchemy. In the early forties, *Psychology and Alchemy* was published, and he wrote several extensive essays: "Paracelsus as a Spiritual Phenomenon," "The Spirit Mercurius," and "The Philosophical Tree." He did, however, give a lecture titled "The Psychology of Eastern Meditation" in 1943. He also edited Heinrich Zimmer's *Der Weg zum Selbst* (Zurich, 1944), on the Hindu sage Ramana Maharshi, and contributed an introduction entitled, "The Holy Men of India."

In "The Psychology of Eastern Meditation," Jung voiced his opposition to an uncritical admiration and acceptance of Eastern modes of meditation on the part of Westerners. The lecture was presented to the Society of the Friends of East Asian Culture, and for the occasion Jung spoke on the "Sutra of Meditation on Amitāyus" (*Amitāyurdhyāna Sūtra*), a Buddhist text dating from A.D. 424. The sutra offers instructions for a series of sixteen meditations that gradually become more and more complex, detailed, and intense, culminating in *samadhi,* a state of intense inner absorption and illuminated awareness. I think Jung deliberately chose this particular text to demonstrate to Western partisans of Eastern meditation that the task they envision for themselves is alien to their sensibility and beyond their psychological capacity. For example, one of the first meditations is to " 'form the perception of a lotus flower on a ground of seven jewels.' The flower has 84,000 petals, each petal 84,000 veins, and each vein possesses 84,000 rays *'of which each can clearly be seen.'* "[8]

Jung goes on to say that this text is not a literary museum piece but a living reality, in this and other forms, in the psyche of every Indian and that the images to be visualized are not just metaphors but must be actually, concretely seen. He proceeds to interpret the major symbols that form a part of the meditation and in this way attempts to connect the meditations with Western understanding. He also uses the text to support his discovery that behind the world of personal fantasies and instincts lies a deeper layer of the unconscious, characterized by a "concentric or radical order which constitutes the true centre or essence of the collective unconscious."[9] Because of this agreement between the insights of yoga and the results of his psychological research, he chose the Sanskrit term *mandala* for this central symbol. (Eventually, he preferred the term *Self,* which has the advantage of being a Western concept that with some extension corresponds closely to the Eastern notion of the Self as the divine core of one's being.)

The Buddhist sutra assumes that the meditator can simply dip into the collective unconscious and engage its archetypal symbols and energies in active imagination. It skips over the problem faced by Westerners when they first try to empty the mind and open it to the world of inner fantasies: they immediately become overwhelmed by subjective fantasies that are far removed from the religious images described in the text. This is the reason why, Jung argues, "we in the West have never developed anything comparable to yoga, aside from the very limited application of the Jesuit *Exercitia.* We have an abysmal fear of that lurking horror, our personal unconscious. Hence the European much prefers to tell others 'how to do it.' That the improvement of the whole begins with the individual, even with myself, never enters our heads. Besides, many people think it morbid to glance into their own interiors—it makes you melancholic, a theologian once assured me."[10]

Another criticism, sometimes heard today, is that such self-examination is narcissistic and self-indulgent. Moreover, the argument goes, all one seems to come up with are fantasies, and fantasies are distortions of reality ruled by wish-fulfillment. Yoga, Zen, and certain other Eastern meditation practices concur with this negative evaluation of fantasies. These disciplines seek to suppress the disorderly and chaotic instinctive forces that give rise to fantasies—and any fantasies that do appear are to be ignored and dismissed. The Spiritual Exercises of Loyola pursue the same ends. Both the Eastern and Western meditation techniques seek to shut out the world of personal fantasy by giving the meditator an object on which to concentrate and contemplate. In a religious context, such methods may succeed in their aim. But outside the religious context, Jung insists, the results are questionable and may cause serious problems:

Jung, Meditation, and the West ———

By throwing light on the unconscious one gets first of all into the chaotic sphere of the personal unconscious, which contains all that one would like to forget, and all that one does not wish to admit to oneself or to anybody else, and which one prefers to believe is not true anyhow. One therefore expects to come off best if one looks as little as possible to this dark corner. Naturally anyone who proceeds in that way will never get round this corner and will never obtain a trace of what yoga promises. Only the . . . [person] who goes through this darkness can hope to make any further progress. I am therefore in principle against the uncritical appropriation of yoga practices by Europeans, because I know only too well that they hope to avoid their own dark corners. Such a beginning is entirely meaningless and worthless.[11]

Toward the conclusion of the essay, Jung contrasts the Buddhist and Christian images of the goal of meditation. Having attained *samadhi,* the sutra states, "Thou wilt know that *thou* art the Buddha." A Christian, on the other hand, says with Saint Paul, "Not I, but Christ liveth in me." The Christian, Jung writes, "attains his end *in Christ,* the Buddhist knows *he* is the Buddha. The Christian gets *out of* the transitory and ego bound world of consciousness, but the Buddhist *still* reposes on the eternal ground of his inner nature."[12] For the Christian, only Christ could say, "I and the Father are one." Whereas every Buddhist is able to say, "I and the Buddha are one." Jung does not discuss the difference between the two experiences, although his phrasing suggests a more positive view of the Buddhist way. Logically, one would expect, Jung continues, that for contemporary Christians, Christ would still appear at the center of the mandala, as was the case in the Middle Ages. But modern mandalas drawn by countless individuals with no preconceived notions or suggestions show no Christ figure in the center. (It would be interesting to learn what the spontaneously drawn mandalas of modern Easterners look like.) Mandalas of contemporary Westerners tend to be simply abstract circles empty in the center or sectioned into quadrants and other radial divisions. In this connection, Jung was struck by the predominantly circular images attributed to UFOs and subjected the entire phenomenon to a psychological examination in his book *Flying Saucers: A Modern Myth of Things Seen in the Skies*. He thought that the persistent rumors of circular or sometimes phallic UFOs indicated that the collective unconscious, by spontaneously projecting these unifying symbols in the skies, is seeking to heal the personal, social, political, and religious disorientation of our day. (Jung leaves open the possibility that there may be actual objects onto which these symbols are projected or with which they coincide; that would not change the nature of the myth that has evolved around the UFOs.) The UFO sightings, like dreams and visions, reveal the dynamics operating in the unconscious. By itself, however, the unconscious is limited in what it can do. The symbols through which it speaks must be consciously interpreted and applied. Otherwise the symbols fall like apples to the ground, where there is no one to pick them up and eat them.

THE SECRET OF THE GOLDEN FLOWER

From the earliest years of his encounter with Eastern thought and Eastern methods of spiritual development, Jung deliberately sought to find parallel Western concepts, experiences, and methods of spiritual and psychological development. In the process, he realized that his own psychological discoveries and his form of analytical psychology were a major contribution to this endeavor. In the conclusion of his commentary to *The Secret of the Golden Flower*, for example, he included ten illustrations of mandala-like paintings done by his Western patients.[13] These pictures were a part of a larger series presented at a 1930 seminar in Berlin and eventually published in a 1950 essay, "Concerning Mandala Symbolism." He begins the essay by contrasting a typical Tibetan man-dala—a *yantra*, which is ritually used as an instrument of contemplation—with spontaneously produced mandalas by people in the course of analysis. Such mandala drawings tend to appear mostly in situations of psychic disorientation or panic, which was how Jung came upon the mandala himself.

During the last years of the war, in 1918–1919, while he was in command of the camp at Château d'Oex, every morning he would sketch a small circular drawing that somehow, he felt, reflected his state of mind. Thus he could observe his psychic condition as it changed from day to day, and that in turn helped him maintain his psychic equilibrium. In his memoirs he says that he no longer remembers how many of these circles he drew, but there were a great many. Initially he had only a dim notion of what exactly he was doing. But the drawings seemed highly significant, and he guarded them like pearls: "I had the distinct feeling that they were something central, and in time I acquired through them a living conception of the self. The self, I thought, was like the monad which I am, and which is my world. The mandala represents this monad, and corresponds to the microcosmic nature of the psyche."[14] It was during these years, he contin-ues, that he began to understand that the goal of psychic development is the Self. "There is no linear evolution; there is only a circumambulation of the self. Uniform development exists, at most, only at the beginning; later, everything points towards the center. This insight gave me stability, and grad-ually my inner peace returned. I knew that in finding the mandala as an expression of the self I had attained what was for me the ultimate. Perhaps someone else knows more, but not I."[15]

When in 1928 the Sinologist Richard Wilhelm sent him the manuscript of *The Secret of the Golden Flower,* Jung was thrilled to find in it an Eastern confirmation of his discovery that the goal of personal development is symbolized by a mandala. By then, he had already become aware of various Christian mandalas (for example, the many medieval pictures with Christ at the center and the four evangelists or their symbols at the cardinal points) and had begun to collect mandala pictures drawn spontaneously by his patients. Thus he was in a position to see the similarity between this basic Eastern and Western symbol. This and other analogies, he thought, permitted Westerners to understand the Eastern mind without sacrificing their own psychological standpoint. He felt very strongly that "the widening of our consciousness ought not to proceed at the expense of other kinds of consciousness; it should come about through the development of those elements of our psyche which are analogous to those of the alien [Eastern] psyche."[16]

Thus, in his psychological commentary on the meditation practice described in *The Secret of the Golden Flower,* namely, the "circulation of the light" through fixed concentration on the central white light, Jung again turned to a spontaneous parallel experience of a modern Western individual. I think Jung was pleased to find such contemporary and spontaneous experiences because they proved that the archetypal core of the psyche is universal and that Eastern meditation practices are not the only means of achieving such experiences. The account Jung gives is that of Edward Maitland, a collaborator of the Theosophist Anna Kingsford.[17] One day, while reflecting on an idea, Maitland found that other related ideas came up of their own accord in a long series stretching back to their source. He decided to perform an experiment: by concentrating on the series, he was going to try and see if he could penetrate to their core. He writes:

I was absolutely without knowledge or expectation when I yielded to the impulse to make the attempt. I simply experimented on a faculty . . . being seated at my writing-table the while in order to record the results as they came, and resolved to retain my hold on my outer and circumferential consciousness, no matter how far towards my inner and central consciousness I might go. For I knew not whether I should be able to regain the former if I once quitted my hold of it, or to recollect the facts of the experience. At length I achieved my object, though only by a strong effort, the tension occasioned by the endeavour to keep both extremes of the consciousness in view at once being very great.

Once well started on my quest, I found myself traversing a succession of spheres or belts . . . the impression produced being that of mounting a vast ladder stretching from the circumference towards the centre of a system, which was at once my own system, the solar system, the universal system, the three systems being at once diverse and identical. . . . Presently, by a supreme, and what I felt must be a final effort . . . I succeeded in polarizing the whole of the convergent rays of my consciousness into the desired focus. And at the same instant, as if through the sudden ignition of the rays thus fused into a unity, I found myself confronted with a glory of unspeakable whiteness and brightness, and of a lustre so intense as well-nigh to beat me back. . . . But though feeling that I had to explore further, I resolved to make assurance doubly sure by piercing if I could the almost blinding lustre, and seeing what it enshrined. With a great effort I succeeded, and the glance revealed to me that which I had felt must be there. . . . It was the dual form of the Son . . . the unmanifest made manifest, the unformulate formulate, the unindividuate individuate, God as the Lord, proving through His duality that God is Substance as well as Force, Love as well as Will, Feminine as well as Masculine, Mother as well as Father.[18]

Maitland noticed that while he was in the midst of this concentrated effort, his breathing seemed to become suspended (a phenomenon also alluded to in the *Golden Flower*). He felt that his ordinary breathing had stopped and was replaced by some kind of a "distinct personality within and other than the physical organism."[19]

Even though expressed in his own terms, this experience of Maitland's is an authentic experience of enlightenment, whether defined as the *unio mystica, samadhi, Tao,* or *satori,* and it contains all the essential symbols found in the text of the *Golden Flower.* Jung adds a word of caution: even though such experiences are undoubtedly genuine and may have profound psychological effects, the conclusions or convictions drawn from the content of these experiences are not necessarily valid. The content of such experiences is conditioned by the psychological makeup of the individual in question and by that individual's cultural heritage and expectations. Only a comparison of the experiences of different individuals, at different historical periods, and in different cultures can provide a more or less valid picture of the content of such enlightenment experiences.

The central vision of light described in the *Golden Flower* and by Maitland in his account is common to many mystics. As a further Western illustration of this particular phenomenon, Jung again chooses a "natural" or spontaneous experience of such a light. He quotes the report of Hildegarde of Bingen (1098–1179), a Catholic nun who from childhood experienced visions, prophecies, and revelations, and who, incidentally, composed a number of remarkable mandalas.

> Since my childhood I have always seen a light in my soul, but not with the outer eyes, nor through the thoughts of my heart; neither do the five outer senses take part in this vision. . . . The light I perceive is not of a local kind, but is much brighter than the cloud which supports the sun. I cannot distinguish height, breadth, or length in it. . . . What I see or learn in such a vision stays long in my memory. I see, hear, and know in the same moment. . . . I cannot recognize any sort of form in this light, although I sometimes see in it another light that is known to me as the living light. . . .

While I am enjoying the spectacle of this light, all sadness and sorrow vanish from my memory.[20]

Jung goes on to say that he knows other people who have had a similar experience. He thinks these experiences result from a heightened sense of consciousness, paradoxically both intense and abstract or "detached," that brings into awareness psychic contents that are usually unconscious. The "suspension of breathing" and the loss of general bodily sensation he ascribes to the fact that consciousness, in such instances, is withdrawn from everyday reality and its energy transferred to this process of heightening the clarity of consciousness. The text of the *Golden Flower* states that the central white light dwells in the middle of "the square inch field of the square foot house."[21] The square-foot house, we are told, is the face, while the square-inch field is the seat of consciousness ("the heavenly heart") located between the eyes.[22] This is not to be taken literally, of course. The face represents the core of our identity, while the "third eye" symbolizes the source of our consciousness. The emphasis on the square is important: the square represents the boundaries and limitations of material existence. The central white light found in the middle of the square inch, on the other hand, is circular and symbolizes the limitlessness of eternity. Jung considers this visualization of the central "creative point" a depiction of psychic "intensity without extension," while the field of the square inch is a symbol for all that which has extension.[23] "The two together make the Tao. Human nature (*hsing*) and consciousness (*hui*) are expressed in light symbolism, and therefore have the quality of intensity, while life (*ming*) would coincide with extensity. The one is yang-like, the other yin-like."[24] And once more, Jung finds a mandala, drawn by a patient of his some thirty years before he read this text, that "shows in its centre a spring of 'Primary Force,' or life energy without extension, whose emanations clash with a contrary spatial principle—in complete analogy with the basic idea of our Chinese text."[25]

Assuming that these experiences of the central point and source of consciousness have at least psychological validity, what conclusions are to be drawn from the characterization of that point as a paradoxical union of "intensity without extension" and extension with apparently reduced intensity? Jung returned to this question in one of his letters, where he speculated that the conclusion one can draw from these reports is that "the brain might be a transformer station, in which the relative infinite tension of intensity of the psyche proper is transformed into perceptible frequencies or 'extensions.' Conversely, the fading of introspective perception of the body explains itself as due to a gradual 'psychification,' i.e., intensification at the expense of extension. Psyche = highest intensity in the smallest space."[26]

In her book *Projection and Re-collection in Jungian Psychology*, Marie-Louise von Franz, relying largely on Jung's correspondence, seeks to summarize the ontological characteristics of this psychic center, which Jung called the Self. As one approaches this central area of the unconscious, the multiplicity of archetypes seems to be suspended or nullified, and the psyche "behaves as if it were *one* and not as if it were split up into many individuals."[27] Also, time and space become increasingly relativized until at the Self's core there is what could be called an omnipresent continuum, "an omnipresence without extension."[28] Then, "when something happens here at point A which touches upon and affects the collective unconscious, it has happened everywhere."[29] In Zen, this notion is expressed by the saying "When the bell sounds in Peking, the lecture begins in Korea." The great Japanese Zen master Dogen (1200–1253) attempted to convey the idea of the interrelationship between space, time, and all existence with the concept of "being-time." " 'Being-time,' " he writes in the *Shobogenzo*, "means that time is being. Every

Jung, Meditation, and the West ——————

existent thing is time. . . . In a word, every being in the entire world is a separate time in one continuum."[30]

Even though the practice of meditation aims to produce enlightenment experiences, the fact is they cannot be willed: they come and go of their own accord. When such an experience, however, does happen, its psychological effects are remarkable; for the moment, at least, it frees the person from all emotional and intellectual entanglements and creates a "unity of being which is universally felt as 'liberation.' "[31] This is not only a liberation from suffering, which is the Buddhist goal, but a general sense of being "free."

From what exactly is one liberated or freed? And what accounts for this sense of liberation and freedom? Psychologically, what accounts for it is the *end of projection*. Jung addresses this issue by citing another meditation text, *The Hui Ming Ching (The Book of Consciousness and Life)*, which stems from the same tradition as *The Secret of the Golden Flower*. (In his quotation Jung leaves out the first two lines, which I include because they describe the sense of infinity that accompanies the central enlightenment experience.)

> Without beginning, without end,
> Without past, without future.
> A halo of light surrounds the world of the law.
> We forget one another, quiet and pure, all-powerful and
>   empty.
> The emptiness is irradiated by the light of the heart of
>   heaven.
> The water of the sea is smooth and mirrors the moon in its
>   surface.
> The clouds disappear in blue space; the mountains shine
>   clear.

——— *Gathering the Light*

Consciousness reverts to contemplation; the moon-disk rests alone.[32]

The illustration that follows the verse in Wilhelm's edition of the text is that of an empty circle. This final state, Jung writes, depicts a consciousness that is detached from the world and withdrawn to a point outside it:

> Thus consciousness is at the same time empty and not empty. It is no longer preoccupied with the images of things but merely contains them. The fullness of the world which hitherto pressed upon it has lost none of its richness and beauty, but it no longer dominates. The magical claim of things has ceased because the interweaving of consciousness with world has come to an end. The unconscious is not projected any more, and so the primordial *participation mystique* with things is abolished. Consciousness is no longer preoccupied with compulsive plans but dissolves in contemplative vision.[33]

Participation mystique ("mystical participation") is the felicitous term coined by the anthropologist Claude Lévy-Bruhl to characterize the nature of primitive mentality, a condition in which there is little or no awareness of the difference between subject and object. In this condition, an unconscious identity prevails: the unconscious is projected onto an object, and the object is introjected into the subject and becomes part of his psychology. Plants and animals then behave like human beings, while human beings are at the same time animals, and everything is alive with spirits, gods, ghosts, and demons. In modern Western civilization we have withdrawn some of these projections and separated a good part of our psyche from the objective world. On the other hand, we are still often enough in a state of *participation mystique* with our parents all our life and also with our affects, biases, and prejudices, projecting our likes and dislikes onto other people. For example, we have a strong expectation that life should be fair. And we routinely single out people, groups, and beliefs that we find offensive, hateful, or evil, in contrast to other people, groups, and beliefs that we admire, love, and idealize. We hardly realize that these strong feelings are in fact projections of the dark and light sides of our own unconscious psyche, whether personal or collective. In these areas we are still afflicted with an unconscious nondifferentiation between subject and object and are "magically affected by all manner of people, things, and circumstances."[34] Thus we are beset by disturbing influences, both inner and outer, as much as "primitive" people and are therefore in need of just as many charms to ward off evil. We may no longer rely on magic, incantations, medicine bags, amulets, and animal sacrifices but we work with drugs, rational argument, will power, and various therapies or ideologies that we believe will rid the world of illness and evil.

Another major area of unconscious identification has to do with our instinctive drives, passions, and ego identity, and these, in turn, are connected to our talents, accomplishments, failures, dreams, and ideals. These areas are so close to home that the sense of *participation mystique* is particularly strong, for we feel that in owning and expressing these feelings, abilities, and ideals, we are most ourselves. And we consider it a severe blow to our sense of self should we be thwarted in the realization of these qualities. The same holds true of our identification with our family, with our ethnic, cultural, national, or religious group, and the realization of the desires and ideals of these collective entities.

In light of the strength and pervasiveness of the phenomenon of projection, one can appreciate the remarkable accomplishment of the Buddha. This accomplishment lies not in the fact that he attained enlightenment or Self-realization; aside, perhaps, from the depth and breadth of his experience, enlightenment was not a new or unique event in his time. Rather, he was the first person of historical record to describe

Self-realization in primarily psychological and nonreligious terms. Paradoxically enough, the state of mind he depicts as enlightenment is one in which there is no separation between subject and object. This state differs from the primitive absence of differentiation between subject and object in that one is conscious of the simultaneous interdependence or interpenetration of subject and object and recognizes the relative existence of both.

When one realizes that the Buddha achieved this psychological insight over twenty-five hundred years ago, when the vast majority of humankind was caught up in the worship of concrete tribal images (i.e., totally submerged in *participation mystique*), his attainment looms all the larger. (Although, from a psychological point of view, the fact that he had this experience and did not succumb to inflation is perhaps an even more remarkable achievement.) Even today, for believing Jews, Muslims, and Christians who are accustomed to praising and petitioning God in their prayers, the central prayer of Buddhism, the *Heart Sutra*, intoned daily by Buddhists monks and nuns in the manner of the Lord's Prayer or the Muslim and Jewish daily prayers, is a shocking thing:

The Bodhisattva of Compassion
> from the depths of prajna wisdom [the enlightened mind]
> saw the emptiness of all five skandhas [body, feeling,
>   perception, volition, consciousness]
> and sundered the bonds
> that create suffering.

Know then:
> Form here is only emptiness,
> emptiness only form.
> Form is no other than emptiness,
> emptiness no other than form.

> Feeling, thought, and choice,
> consciousness itself,
> are the same as this.

Jung, Meditation, and the West ———

Dharmas [all phenomena] here are empty,
all are the primal void.
None are born or die.
Nor are they stained or pure,
nor do they wax or wane.

So in emptiness no form,
no feeling, thought, or choice
nor is there consciousness.

No eye, ear, nose,
tongue, body, mind;
no color, sound, smell,
taste, touch, or what
the mind takes hold of
nor even act of sensing.

No ignorance or end of it
nor all that comes of ignorance:
no withering, no death,
no end of them.

Nor is there pain or cause of pain
or cease in pain or noble path
to lead from pain,
not even wisdom to attain,
attainment too is emptiness.

So know that the bodhisattva
holding to nothing whatever
but dwelling in prajna wisdom
is freed of delusive hindrance,
rid of the fear bred by it,
and reaches clearest nirvana [lit., extinction].

All buddhas of past and present,
buddhas of future time
through faith in prajna wisdom
come to full enlightenment.

Know, then, the great dharani [an extended mantra],
the radiant, peerless mantra,
the supreme, unfailing mantra,

———— *Gathering the Light*

the Prajna Paramita [Perfect Wisdom],
whose words allay all pain.
This is highest wisdom
true beyond all doubt,
know and proclaim its truth:

Gone, gone
gone beyond,
fully beyond.
Awake: Glory![35]

For Westerners, such a jarring insight into the ultimate nature of reality seems like a philosophical or psychological statement, but hardly a religious one. For there is no mention of God here, nor of heaven and hell or the saving of one's soul. Rather, it is a practical matter of becoming free of the psychological delusions that lie at the root of human suffering. Even the Buddhist notions of reincarnation and karma, although they focus on the consequences of "good" and "bad" deeds, are not expressions of divine judgment but function impersonally, like the laws of nature. There is no eternal soul or God to speak of: at the core of everything is only eternal Consciousness, the Enlightened Mind. And every human being has the capacity to realize this Mind and become a buddha—an awakened one. What makes this essentially psychological or ontological insight a religious event is the fact that it is usually accompanied by many of the feelings associated with religious experiences: a sense of awe, of personal transcendence, and of the harmonious unity of all existence. The Buddha's breakthrough into the heart of ultimate reality—an experiment since repeated countless times—is one of the most radical aspects of Eastern experience confronting Western religious consciousness. To put it metaphorically: having eaten of the Tree of the Knowledge of Good and Evil, Westerners are now invited to sit under the Tree of Consciousness itself and discover the realm that transcends the dichotomy of good and evil.

Jung, Meditation, and the West ———

In psychological terms, liberation from suffering is attained by overcoming the domination of the unconscious. In this respect, the practice of meditation is a prepsychoanalytic therapeutic method that can, for certain individuals, serve as an alternative means of self-development and individuation. When one pursues the work of dissolving projections, whether through psychoanalysis or meditation, the effects are highly therapeutic, and in time, the following development occurs, as Jung writes:

> The centre of gravity of the total personality shifts its position. It is then no longer in the ego, which is merely the centre of consciousness, but in the hypothetical point between consciousness and the unconscious. This new centre might be called the self. If the transposition is successful, it does away with *participation mystique* and results in a personality that suffers only in the lower storeys, as it were, but in its upper storeys is singularly detached from painful as well as joyful happenings.[36]

The creation and establishment of such a central structure that is conscious of but detached from the objective world and the subjective personality are symbolized in *The Secret of the Golden Flower* by the image of the golden flower. In other texts this psychic structure is described as the "holy fruit," the "diamond body," the "spirit body," or the "incorruptible" or "resurrection body." Jung thinks that the tendency to detach consciousness from the world and from the personal psyche sets in naturally after midlife and is a preparation for death. In this regard, *The Tibetan Book of the Dead* offers the following instructions to a dying person or one recently deceased: "O nobly born . . . listen. Now thou art experiencing the Radiance of the Clear Light of Pure Reality. Recognize it. . . . Thine own intellect, which is now voidness, yet not to be regarded as the voidness of nothingness, but as being the intellect itself, unobstructed, shining, thrilling, and

blissful, is the very consciousness, the All-good Buddha."[37]
If the individual is not able to hold on to this realization and
attain liberation, then other visions begin to appear. The
instructions continue:

> With every thought of fear or terror or awe for all
>   [apparitional appearances] set aside,
> May I recognize whatever [visions] appear, as the reflections
>   of mine own consciousness;
>
> . . . .
>
> When at this all-important moment [of opportunity] of
>   achieving a great end,
> May I not fear the bands of Peaceful and Wrathful [Deities],
>   mine own thought forms.[38]

In other words, the task of liberating oneself from unconscious delusions with their attendant feelings of desire, fear,
or awe remains the same even after death. The moment of
death apparently provides a supreme opportunity for realizing one's "true nature," but if that moment is lost, the world
of unconscious delusion reasserts itself. One then goes to
"heaven" or "hell," depending on the nature of one's attachments and on the nature of one's life and deeds on the earth.
In the Buddhist conception, however, the assignment to
heaven or hell is not permanent; when the effect of one's
karma has run its course, one is again reborn on earth. Only
the attainment of enlightenment, either in life or at the
moment of death, frees one from this endless cycle of death
and rebirth and from the inexorable operation of the law of
karma, which, incidentally, is fueled by projections stem-
ming from unconscious identifications and attachments.

PROJECTION AND MIRRORING

Even if one doubts or suspends one's judgment about these
metaphysical claims, the overcoming of delusions brought

on by projections is of utmost value; for it makes one more conscious and less neurotic, disturbed, and egocentric. In the Jungian view, however, projection is not limited to matters of psychopathology. One of the most thorough discussions of the Jungian concept of projection, the historical role of projection in primitive beliefs, its expression in modern science, and its relevance in psychological development is Marie-Louise von Franz's *Projection and Re-collection in Jungian Psychology*. Near the conclusion of this book, von Franz takes up an aspect of projection that is not concerned with the disturbances of adaptation to inner or outer reality or with the unconscious merging between subject and object. She calls this aspect of projection *mirroring*. Mirroring has to do with the imaginative or mental constructs that we make of material reality or of the unconscious psyche. In addition, Jung thought that a certain mirror-image relation existed between the unconscious and matter. In her discussion, von Franz focuses on four mirroring relations: "the mirroring of the ego by the Self, the mirroring of the Self by the ego, the mirroring of matter by the collective unconscious, and the possible mirroring of the latter in matter."[39]

The mirroring of the ego by the Self is most readily seen in dreams, where our conscious attitude or behavior is "objectively" mirrored by the unconscious. We may feel, for example, that in helping someone we performed a charitable or noble deed, but a dream depicting the situation may disclose an ulterior or egoistic motive behind the deed of which we were not aware. In this way, the Self holds up a mirror to us so that we can see ourselves from a point outside ego consciousness. Von Franz proceeds to say that "*what we see in the mirror held up to us by the Self is hence the only source of genuine self-knowledge;* everything else is only narcissistic rumination of the ego about itself."[40]

At the same time, the ego in the very act of this self-knowledge mirrors the Self by lifting it out of its unconscious, merely potential existence into the clarity of ego consciousness. To the extent that the ego picks up the knowledge or signals provided by the Self, it helps the Self attain realization in time and space. Thus, in a way, the Self can become aware of itself and realize itself only because it is mirrored in ego consciousness.

In his memoirs Jung mentions two dreams that illustrate the mirrorlike relation between the ego and the Self. The first dream came when he was trying to make sense of the worldwide sightings of UFOs, which he interpreted as projections of the Self onto unknown external phenomena. In his dream he saw a perfectly circular lens, like the objective of a telescope, with a metallic extension that led to a box, a magic lantern. The lens stood motionless in the air at a distance of sixty or seventy yards and pointed straight at him. He awoke with a feeling of astonishment, and while he was still half in the dream, the thought came to him: "We always think that the UFOs are projections of ours. Now it turns out that we are their projections. I am projected by the magic lantern as C. G. Jung. But who manipulates the apparatus?"[41] In the second dream, Jung sees himself walking along a road. He comes to a small roadside chapel and enters it. Instead of a statue of the Virgin or a crucifix, there is a flower arrangement on the altar, and before the altar, facing Jung, sits a yogi in the lotus position, in deep meditation. "When I looked at him more closely, I realized that he had my face. I started in profound fright, and awoke with the thought: 'Aha, so he is the one who is meditating me. He has a dream, and I am it.' I knew that when he awakened, I would no longer be."[42]

Actually, the situation is more complicated than the simple mirroring of the ego by the Self and of the Self by the ego. For the relationship between the ego and the Self is sometimes interchangeable, or rather there is an identity between the two. We know, for instance, that dreams will emphasize either the otherness of the Self or its identity with the ego, depending on the dreamer's conscious attitude. If a person sees the Self as "absolutely other," the dreams will stress its similarity with the ego; if the ego is too closely identified with the Self, then the Self will appear as "other." For example, some Zen practitioners report that at the moment of enlightenment, when they look at other people, all seem to have the practitioner's own face. Clearly this is a mirrorlike vision of the Self in the guise of the meditator's ego. The vision compensates the highly abstract and impersonal notion of the Self in Zen. Von Franz describes a recurring anxiety dream of a minister's son who saw God as too outer and as the unknowable "other." The dream recurred until his late forties. He would dream that he was walking through a vast wasteland. He'd hear steps behind him. He would walk faster and start to run, but the terror would pursue him. He'd come to the edge of a deep abyss and, looking down thousands of miles below, would see the hellfires burning. Then he'd turn around and see or sense a demonic face. Later the dream occurred exactly as before, but this time when he turned around, instead of the demon, he saw the face of God. When he was almost fifty, the dream occurred for the last time. This time panicky fear drove him over the cliff, and he fell into the abyss. As he fell, thousands of little square white cards floated down with him. On each card, in black and white, a different mandala had been drawn. The cards floated together into a kind of floor so that he didn't fall into hell but landed about halfway down. Then he looked back up to the edge of the abyss and there he saw—*his own face!*[43]

The third mirror relation is between psyche and matter. Our subjective ego consciousness is located between two apparently antithetical worlds—the external world mediated to us by the senses and the unconscious psychic realm that alone enables us to have any notion of the outer world. This psychic realm must be different from the external world, for if the two were absolutely identical, there would be no possibility of grasping the outer world. But everything we do know about the external world is a combination of the information garnered from our senses and shaped by the unconscious. A physicist, for example, makes hypothetical images of mathematical structures that he hopes will coincide with the behavior of the material universe. The remarkable thing is that our mental constructs do coincide or can be increasingly made to coincide with the behavior of the outer world. There is no reason why this should be, but the fact is that somehow we are able to correctly mirror in our minds the workings of natural phenomena. This is why Jung picked up Leibniz's view of the soul as "an active indivisible mirror" and spoke of the collective unconscious, again in Leibniz's words, as "a perpetual living mirror of the universe."[44]

The fact that our psyche can mirror the material world raises the question and the possibility of the reverse mirror-like relation: namely, do material events in the external world mirror conditions or events in the psyche? If so, concrete events in the external world could be seen as symbolic statements about unconscious psychic processes. The mirroring of these psychic processes by external events would then make it possible for us to become conscious of them. People have always suspected that there is a connection between external events such as accidents or chance meetings and one's psychic disposition. Primitive magical thinking, black and white magic, the power of prayer, visualization—all are based on this possible relationship between matter and psyche. Religious leaders frequently interpret outer events as reflections of inner events, either of the spiritual condition of people affected by the events or as signs and "acts of God." In any case, for the religious person, outer events, either positive in nature or negative, are messages that need to be heeded. For example, in ancient China, natural disasters such as earthquakes, droughts, and floods were seen as signs that the emperor or his government had somehow deviated from the Tao. The ruler then had to attone for past mistakes and change his attitude or behavior in order to restore the harmonious functioning of both nature and society.

The possible and as yet hardly understood connection between matter and psyche is suggested by such psychic phenomena as telepathy, in which an outer event seems to occur simultaneously within the psyche, or telekinesis and the poltergeist phenomenon, where a psychic condition seems to affect the behavior of matter. The occult powers that are sometimes said to result from the practice of meditation, such as levitation, might also be explained by this mysterious connection between matter and psyche.

Finally, there are meaningful connections between inner and outer events where one cannot say that either one caused the other—for example, the frequent reports of clocks stopping at the moment of someone's death. Jung coined the term *synchronicity* to describe such acausal meaningful events in which the only connection seems to be that they occur at the same time. Thus, in addition to the law of cause and effect, he proposed synchronicity as an "acausal ordering principle." He considered astrology and divination techniques such as the *I Ching* examples of the law of synchronicity. This concept then led him to the formulation of another hypothesis: the existence of "absolute knowledge" in the unconscious, an impersonal form of consciousness that exists "in a space-time continuum in which space is no longer space, nor time time."[45] This "absolute knowledge" is connected with the archetypal structure of the unconscious, for the archetypes have "a knowledge of themselves that is independent of both external causal and conscious influences and at the same time stand in analogous or equivalent, that is, meaningful, relationship to objective external occurrences that have no recognizable or even conceivable causal relationship with them."[46] This "absolute knowledge" is what a meditator experiences at the moment of a significant "breakthrough" into the realm of "pure consciousness." Von Franz concludes her discussion of the mirror relations between ego and Self and between psyche and matter by alluding, significantly enough, to Zen meditation:

> In Zen Buddhist meditation the master tries to teach his pupil how he can forever keep the inner mirror free of dust. To the extent that he lives in complete accord with the rhythm of psychic energy and with its regulator, the Self, he has no projections anymore; he looks at reality without illusion and more or less continuously reads the meaning of all the synchronistic events happening around him. He lives in the creative current or stream of the Self and has himself, indeed, become a part of this stream.
>
> If he remains, so to speak, always in contact with the succeeding currents of psychic energy that are regulated by the Self, he no longer experiences disturbances of adaptation, no longer projects, in the stricter sense of the word, but remains at the center of the fourfold mirror relation. Obviously, only a person with the most highly reflected concentration can achieve this.[47]

A dream reported by the Japanese Zen Master Hakuin (1685–1768) alludes to the mirrorlike nature of consciousness:

> In my thirty-second year I took up residence in a dilapidated temple. One night in a dream my mother handed me a violet robe. As I lifted it up I felt a great weight in both sleeves. I investigated these and found in each sleeve an old mirror about five or six inches in diameter. The reflection of the mirror on the right side penetrated to the bottom of my heart. My own mind as well as mountains and streams, yes, the whole earth, became alike transparently clear and bottomless. The whole surface of the mirror on the left had no focal point of light. The surface was like that of a new skillet not yet touched by fire. Suddenly there flashed a light from the

Jung, Meditation, and the West —————

mirror on the left that surpassed the light of the mirror on the right a millionfold. Now the vision of all things was like the beholding of one's own face. For the first time I understood the meaning of the words "The perfected one beholds the Buddha-nature in his eye."[48]

The two mirrors represent two different levels or aspects of enlightenment. The mirror on the right depicts a consciousness that is projection-free. The mirror on the left depicts a consciousness that has become one with itself, where the perceiver and the perceived are interchangeable.

RORSCHACH TESTS OF MEDITATORS

The fact that meditation leading to Self-realization alters the usual projection-dominated state of consciousness is illustrated by a study in which the Rorschach inkblot test was administered to practitioners of meditation. In this pioneering study by Daniel P. Brown and Jack Engler, the subjects practiced the Theravadin Buddhist form of *vipassana,* or mindfulness meditation.[49] Five groups were established according to the traditional division of the stages of practice: beginners, *samadhi* group, insight group, advanced insight group, and masters. The beginners' group showed little difference from typical responses to the test by nonmeditators. The outstanding characteristic of the *samadhi* group was the focus on the purely perceptual features (form and color) of the inkblot. It took conscious effort on the part of the members of the *samadhi* group to perceive images and produce associative elaboration of the images. Many of this group adopted a critical attitude toward the image: "it doesn't *really* look like that . . . I'm just projecting."[50] Still, most of the subjects of the *samadhi* group were able to report specific images for the majority of the cards; however, the images were fluid. The subjects complained that the images kept changing even as they were describing them; sometimes the image changed so rapidly that it was difficult to specify a single image. Their focus was less on the image and more on the process by which the image manifested itself in their stream of consciousness.

The insight group reacted almost the opposite of the *samadhi* group. These subjects' responses were characterized by increased productivity and richness of associative elaborations. Many claimed that their productivity per card was unlimited. They displayed an openness to the flow of internal associations and images; moreover, the associations were richly fabulized with a great variability and intensity of affect and much metaphoric use of color.

At first glance, the Rorschachs of the advanced insight group look like those of the beginners' group, although there are some references to the perceptual features of the inkblots and a high response to achromatic and shading variations. The most unusual feature of the group, however, is the degree to which the inkblots are perceived as an interaction of form or energy and space. The subjects viewed their own internal imagery, in response to the inkblots, as emanations of energy/space. For example: "I feel the energy coming from that, the whole energy of the picture . . . there's an intensity, a certain power of it, and everything else is just a dancing manifestation of that energy coming out."[51] Another characteristic of the advanced insight group's Rorschachs is a movement toward a central unifying point. For instance: "It's a natural source of energy, unfolding and extending to take certain forms, . . . I don't know if explosive is the right word. Let's say, such a strong source that it could come from that center core, that central orange, and go up into the blue and just push off just a little so that it could have its definite . . . shape and function."[52] In another instance, a subject saw several typical images on a card, such as dancing insects; then she began to see the card as color and form and noticed that the colors and forms seemed to be moving inward, concentrating themselves at the central blue region of the card. She saw all the forms and colors connected by a "unifying force" that made the seemingly separate images on the card flow back into the center region of "localized energy." Finally, she ended up seeing only the white background of the card as if all the colors and forms had become absorbed in it.[53]

The advanced insight group also gave responses referring to the activity of the molecules of the universe or the primal elements within the body, such as the energy of cell division or that of chromosomes dividing. All of the subjects made references to the main "center" of energy within the body: "I see the different colors . . . going up the different energy centers of the body, starting with the whole pelvic region . . . the abdomen, chest, and head, and each color respresenting the different energy in that part of the body."[54] All subjects in this group also made direct reference to sexual energy: "I see a vagina and ovaries or some kind of organs, internal organs . . . I see [something] very phallic . . . a lot of thrusting energy I get from it . . . I see like an energy flow between like, ah, the vagina and the penis . . . it's like one continuum, the flow of energy between them, sexual energy."[55]

In general, what characterized the advanced insight group's responses in terms of the interaction between space and energy or form and space is what the authors of the study call a *relativization of perception:* "No particular feature on an inkblot, or aspect of external reality, is compelling enough to suggest perception of solid and durable forms."[56] This is true even though the first responses of this group appear more like the Rorschachs of the beginners' group—identifying images with brief associative elaboration. When the subjects went beyond their first impressions, the above features came out. This characteristic accords with classical descriptions of enlightenment, in which one retains one's ordinary perception and experience even though the perspective is radically different and one may no longer react to one's perceptions and experiences with the usual emotional attitudes. There is a famous Zen saying that illustrates the developmental process depicted in the above study: "Before I began meditating, mountains were mountains and rivers were rivers. After I began meditating, mountains were no longer mountains and rivers were no longer rivers. Once I finished meditating, mountains were once again mountains, and rivers once again rivers." Thus for the advanced practitioners, Rorschachs were once again Rorschachs—and yet . . .

The masters' group, unfortunately, included only one person, so no comparison is possible with how other master subjects would respond to the test. In this subject's case, there were two major noticeable features. Whereas most subjects accept the "reality" of the inkblot and project their imaginings onto it, the master saw the inkblot itself as a projection of the mind. The second unusual feature, and an extremely rare finding, was the integration of all ten cards into a single associative theme. The master used each of the cards in a systematic discourse on the Buddhist teachings concerning the alleviation of human suffering. He did this without ignoring the realistic features of the inkblot, although he relied heavily on shading responses and on vague amorphously perceived forms. In other words, his projective mechanism no longer operated of its own accord; he was free to shape it to his own conscious needs.

As far as I know, this study provides the first documented empirical evidence for the fundamental changes that take place in the cognitive and perceptual operations of the psyche as the result of meditation. The study also raises the possibility of a cross-cultural validation of the psychological changes that occur at each major stage of meditation practice. The final characteristic of the changes a meditator undergoes is the ending of unconscious projection and of the associative cognitive and emotional attachments to the projected forms. Meditation breaks down the projected images, makes one aware of the process of projection, dissolves the images to their original energetic source, and frees one from a blind attachment to what we consider to be "reality." This freeing up of the psychic energy usually invested in projections is the reason for the feeling and experience of liberation that characterizes enlightenment.

CHAPTER TWO

WHAT IS MEDITATION?

One day a man of the people said to Zen Master Ikkyu: "Master, will you please write for me some maxims of the highest wisdom?"

Ikkyu immediately took his brush and wrote the word "Attention."

"Is that all?" asked the man. "Will you not add something more?"

Ikkyu then wrote twice running: "Attention. Attention."

"Well," remarked the man rather irritably, "I really don't see much depth or subtlety in what you have just written."

Then Ikkyu wrote the same word three times running: "Attention. Attention. Attention."

Half-angered, the man demanded: "What does that word 'Attention' mean anyway?"

And Ikkyu answered gently: "Attention means attention."[1]

There are essentially two types of meditation practice—fixed and discursive. Fixed meditation aims at focusing the attention on a specific object, either internal or external. The object can be an image or a statue, a part of the body or a bodily sensation, a feeling or an emotion, a word or a phrase, a tone or a chant, a statement or a question, silence or emptiness. Discursive meditation focuses the attention on a sequence of events: for example, reliving in one's imagination or through pictures the Passion of Christ; practicing some form of guided fantasy or Jung's technique of active imagination; observing the passing sensations, feelings, thoughts, and images in oneself; participating mindfully in a ritual, a dance, or some other activity, such as working or walking. There are also mixed forms of meditation, which begin by focusing the attention on a given object, allow the object to evolve or move, and then follow its evolution or movement; or the meditation may begin in a discursive way and periodically or finally fix the attention on a specific object. The common element in all these forms of meditation is the focusing of attention.

What is attention? From the psychological point of view, attention consists of the psychic energy that the ego is able to direct to an object or that an object is able to attract to itself. Consciousness is not attention. Consciousness is the psychic field in which objects manifest. Consciousness, too, requires psychic energy if it is to provide for the possibility of the awareness of objects. A common analogy is with light: consciousness is the light in which objects become visible.

Normally, our attention wanders from object to object. The course of this wandering is determined by our physical, emotional, and social needs and interests, by our temperament (our inherent likes and dislikes), and by our complexes. Since both the inner and the outer worlds are constantly changing, our attention, too, keeps flitting about with the changing kaleidoscope of the objects presented to it. Meditation is a deliberate attempt to arrest and direct this constantly shifting flow of objects that vie for our attention. The first aphorism of Patanjali's *Yoga Sutras* states: "Yoga consists of the intentional stopping of the spontaneous activity of the mind-stuff."[2] The focusing of attention can be accomplished in two ways: one can reduce the outer and inner images that enter the field of consciousness, or one can select a specific object or category of objects to which one will pay attention.

Meditation, then, is a deliberate and conscious attempt to focus the attention. By contrast, it is also possible for attention to become focused in a spontaneous or compulsive way. Plato reports that sometimes, and at the most unpredictable moments, Socrates would fall into a spontaneous trance.[3] And everyone is familiar with the power of obsessive-compulsive emotions, ideas, or behavior, which resist the efforts of reason, ego, and will to alter or free the attention directed to them.

The voluntary and conscious focusing of attention is a neutral psychological ability that can be applied to various ends. Work, study, art, prayer, and sport, for example, all require the conscious application of attention. What distinguishes meditation from these other forms of voluntarily focused attention is the ends it has in view. Characteristically, these ends include awareness of one's mental and emotional states (and of physiological states in the case of practices such as hatha yoga); mastery over one's instinctive, unconscious, and compulsive reactions; learning to live with full consciousness in every moment; insight into one's nature and into the nature of reality; exploration of religious themes, images, or feelings; and expansions of ego consciousness from an ego-centered to a "universal" or "cosmic" form of consciousness. Because religions are interested in these goals and their effects, meditation is usually associated with religious practice. Outside the religious context, meditation can be used simply as a method of relaxation or of enhancing physical and psychic well-being. In psychotherapy, meditation is sometimes used as a therapeutic aid in exploring and altering a person's psychic reactions and structure.[4]

CONCENTRATION

What exactly happens when one begins to meditate? The first observable effect is improved concentration: the ability to focus the attention on a specific object or task for an extended period of time. Given the natural tendency for attention to wander, the ability to concentrate is no mean accomplishment. Concentration, the ability to hold the attention steady, is the basic tool of every meditation practice. A corollary effect of concentration is the suppression or dismissal of stimuli competing for our attention. Concentration, therefore, gives the ego control over attention—over free-flowing psychic energy—and permits the ego to choose which inner or outer objects will become the focus of attention. The ability to concentrate, to freely focus one's attention, is already a form of "liberation." It means that we are able to free up a certain amount of psychic energy from the psychic and physical functions to which it is normally attached and place that energy at the disposal of the ego and of its self-reflective and choosing capacities. It means that at least a part of our psychic energy is no longer captured or held captive by the various and often arbitrary impulses and impressions that usually attract pyschic energy to themselves.

The next effect of meditation is that the more one is able to concentrate, the more psychic energy is released. Concentration can be likened to a water wheel, but one that grows bigger and more powerful with each turn, while at the same time the water rushing to meet it increases in volume and force. In practice, of course, this is not an ever-increasing phenomenon, because the strength of one's concentration is always waxing and waning.

There are times, however, when the process of concentration seems to be taken over by the autonomic nervous system so that little conscious effort is required. At that point a certain depersonalization takes place: the ego feels separate from the entire process and can observe it as if it were happening to another person.[5]

After long periods of meditation, the concentration continues subliminally and of its own accord even after one has stopped meditating. A woman who had been working on the koan *mu* at a Zen meditation retreat found that after several days her mind was concentrating on the koan even while she was asleep.[6] Clinically, one would refer to this state of mind as an obsessional neurosis or *idée fixe*. In Jungian terms, this is a deliberate attempt to create a complex—a cluster of feeling-toned energy that functions autonomously and more or less independently of the central control of consciousness.[7] Jung even speaks of the complex as "a small secondary mind," and in the case of a strong complex he notes that it "possesses all the characteristics of a separate personality" with its own intentions and will.[8] In many meditation practices a deliberate effort is made to submerge the ego within the artificially created complex. Psychologically this approximates a state of "possession." The American Zen master Philip Kapleau, for example, describes his work on the koan *mu* as follows:

> Threw myself into Mu for another nine hours with such utter absorption that *I* completely vanished. . . . *I* didn't eat breakfast, *Mu* did. *I* didn't sweep and wash the floors after breakfast, *Mu* did. *I* didn't eat lunch, *Mu* ate. . . . Once or twice ideas of satori started to rear their heads, but Mu promptly chopped them off. . . .[9]

From an energetic point of view, the emergence of the artificially created autonomous complex is an important development because it means that a portion of one's psychic energy is now permanently caught up in the process of meditation. This energy no longer "leaks" or reverts to its natural dispersal among inner and outer stimuli: a part of the psyche has been closed off, and an "alchemical container" for the production of the "philosophers' gold" is estblished. *The Book of Consciousness and Life* (*Hui Ming Ching*) states:

If thou wouldst complete the diamond body with no
    outflowing,
Diligently heat the roots of consciousness and life.
Kindle light in the blessed country ever close at hand,
And there hidden, let thy true self always dwell.[10]

The Secret of the Golden Flower likens this state to a brood-
ing hen, who, even while she may stand up and move about,
is ever concentrated on her task: "The hen can hatch her eggs
because her heart is always listening."[11] For the ancient
Chinese, the seat of consciousness was felt to be in the region
of the heart and not in the head, as it is with us. The book
also describes the process of concentration as "the circulation
of the light and the maintaining of the centre."[12] It states that
"the work on the circulation of the light depends entirely on
the backward-flowing movement [i.e., on introversion] so
that the thoughts . . . are gathered together."[13] It links this
work with careful attention to the rhythm of breathing.
Indian yoga, which influenced this Taoist work, also posits a
connection between breathing and the storing up and directing the flow of *prana,* of psychic energy. From a purely
organic perspective, deep inhalations increase the supply of
oxygen in the blood and provide the body with more energy.
In meditation, this energy is put at the disposal of the psyche
and thrown into the effort of concentration.

It was *The Secret of the Golden Flower* that inspired Jung to
undertake a study of Western alchemy. The book was sent to
him in 1928 by Richard Wilhelm and synchronistically con-
firmed Jung's own discovery of the Self, "the archetype of
orientation and meaning."[14] The alchemical aspect of the
book is clearly seen in the definition of the golden flower as
the elixir of life (*chin-tan,* literally, golden ball, golden pill).[15]
The goal of Western alchemy is similarly the production of
the *elixir vitae,* also defined as the philosophical gold or
golden glass. In the Chinese text, however, it is clear from

This sixteenth-century alchemical illustration of Saturn or Mercurius senex being cooked in the bath until the spirit or white dove ascends is analogous to the Taoist injunction to "diligently heat the roots of consciousness and life" until the "diamond body" appears. The cooking and heating refer to the accumulation of psychic energy and its transformation during meditation.

the outset that this goal is spiritual and not material. The opening paragraphs clearly state: "The Golden Flower is the light. . . . One used the Golden Flower as a symbol. It is the true energy of the transcendent great One."[16] The "transcendent great One" is the same as the Tao, that which exists through itself, the one essence, the one primal spirit that cannot be seen or named.[17] (I shall examine these themes in more detail in chapter 5.)

Another effect of concentration, particularly of fixed concentration, is that awareness of both the outer and the inner environment is held in suspension. This is a paradoxical state of mind: one can at any moment register a stimulus, but this capacity is held in suspension so that only "empty" awareness or "awareness of awareness" remains. Saint John of the Cross writes:

> Of all these forms and manners of knowledge the soul must strip and void itself, and it must strive to lose the imaginary apprehension of them, so that there may be left in it no kind of impression of knowledge, nor trace of aught soever, but rather the soul must remain barren and bare, as if these forms had never passed through it and in total oblivion and suspension.[18]

This state of suspension is accomplished either by the conscious refusal to entertain any stimulus, as in the *shikantaza* practice of Soto Zen, or by fixed concentration. Psychological studies have shown that continuous repetition of the same stimulus is the same as no stimulus at all: a constantly present stimulus stops being registered by the mind.[19] For example, if an image is made to remain constantly on the retina, the image disappears.[20] Similarly, if an observer is faced with a ganzfeld, such as a patternless and consistent field of vision—a green wall, say, or halved Ping Pong balls taped over the eyes—after about twenty minutes the observer reports an experience of *not seeing*.[21] It is not only a matter of seeing nothing, but of feeling that one does not see at all. The observer cannot tell if his or her eyes are closed or open and cannot even control the eye movements. In both cases, of the constant image on the retina and exposure to a ganzfeld, these blanked-out states of mind are correlated with increased alpha rhythm activity. (Electrophysiological studies of meditation have repeatedly shown that meditation is a high alpha state.)[22]

After some proficiency in meditation, most people report that upon their return to ordinary reality the world looks new—brighter, cleaner, more vivid and alive. William Blake probably referred to this phenomenon when he wrote in *The Marriage of Heaven and Hell:* "If the doors of perception were cleansed everything would appear to man as it is, infinite." This renewal or rebirth of the world is really a renewal or rebirth of the psyche. The feeling is as if one had just woken up after a good night's rest to a beautiful, sunny, crisp, clear day.

DEAUTOMATIZATION

The simplest nontechnical explanation of the above experience is that the conscious mind and the senses have had a rest and feel rejuvenated, much as the body and muscles do after a period of inactivity. A more sophisticated psychological explanation is based on the hypothesis of the *deautomatization* of the habitual reactions of the mind to inner and outer stimuli, a hypothesis that has been elaborated by Arthur J. Deikman.[23]

Normally, the psyche automatizes all repeated stimuli— this includes, for example, noises, patterns of events, learned activities, and all physical, mental, and emotional operations. Automatization "solidifies" set patterns and frees the psyche to give attention to new events. By refusing to permit or by remaining conscious of automatizations associated with all major stimuli, meditation reverses or interferes with the automatization process. To begin with, this is an exhausting and difficult task, and one has to fight the tendency to fall asleep or revert to habitual fantasizing. But with the automatization even of the practice of deautomatization, the task becomes easier, and instead of draining energy, meditation then releases the energy taken up by our other automatizations. The result is an enhanced state of consciousness in which every stimulus is experienced as new, not only because it receives conscious attention but also because it has been deautomatized, denuded of its previous psychophysiological associations.

During meditation, of course, no extraneous stimulus is given conscious attention, and the ability not to respond to distracting stimuli increases with practice. However, after meditation ends, the response to stimuli becomes more intense. Studies have shown that with accomplished yogis and Zen meditators, repetition of an external stimulus does not lead to the usual habituation or automatization. In one experiment, lay people and Zen monks were placed in soundproof rooms and subjected to a clicking sound every fifteen seconds. The lay people became quickly habituated to the sound. After the third or fourth click there was a decrease in the response of brain activity, and after habituation there was no response at all. The Zen monks' response to the click remained the same throughout a period of five minutes. There was no habituation: the response to the last click was the same as to the first. [24]

A further development of the deautomatization hypothesis speaks of the effects meditation has on entire psychological structures. Most meditation practices seek to inhibit the cognitive function—abstract categorization and thought. Such inhibition or deautomatization of the cognitive function forces the psyche to shift toward a developmentally earlier psychological functioning, "an organization preceding the analytic, abstract, intellectual mode typical of present-day adult thought."[25]

Those familiar with Jung's typology will notice that this statement, as well as the entire orientation of the argument, is biased in favor of *thinking* as the dominant and superior function. The fact is that there are many people whose psychological type emphasizes one of the other three functions: feeling (among them many musicians and psychotherapists), sensation (laboratory scientists, engineers), or intuition (businessmen, psychics).

The deautomatization hypothesis also states that "cognition is inhibited in favor of perception; the active intellectual style is replaced by a receptive perceptual mode."[26] In reality, it is not only the cognitive function that is inhibited. Certain meditation practices, such as *zazen,* also inhibit the affective function. In fact, in many meditation practices all four psychological functions—sensation, thinking, feeling, and intuition—through which we perceive and evaluate all stimuli, are inhibited or restricted to a single expression: staring at an image, holding on to one feeling or emotion, one thought or intuitive concept. Moreover, meditation does not only or primarily enhance the function of perception (an aspect of sensation). The notion that it does is probably influenced by the need to explain the vivid perception of the outer world experienced after meditation.

The deautomatization of our habitual responses is a valid description of an important meditation technique, but its aim is not to renew or restructure one's vision of reality. Deautomatization has two purposes: to free up the psychic energy that normally flows into our habitual responses and to give the ego and the conscious functions nothing to hold on to. The meditation requirement to sit still with unfocused or unifocused vision is directed toward the same ends.

What Is Meditation? ————

After some practice in meditation, one of the subjects in Deikman's experimental study (in which people were asked to focus their attention on a blue vase placed in front of them) reported that the vase disappeared and only a diffuse blue occupied her entire visual field. She felt merged completely with that diffuseness and then "had a sense of falling, of emptiness, of loneliness and isolation as if she were in a vacuum. Her sudden realization that there were absolutely no thoughts in her mind made her anxious and she searched for thoughts to bring her back. 'It was as if I leaped out of the chair to put the boundaries back on the vase . . . because there was nothing there . . . the vase was going and I was going with it. . . .' "[27] Had she overcome her anxiety and let herself merge with the emptiness, she would have had an enlightenment experience—and the fear would have turned to awe.

A frequently given instruction to meditators is to empty the mind of all contents and to become egoless. What is really meant is that the mind should ignore all ego-related contents and abandon its ego-based identity. The above person's experience demonstrates that concentration and deautomatization are techniques that accomplish this end. The content that then emerges is that of emptiness, of nothingness. The ego remains as a point of consciousness but with no reference to one's previous sense of identity; also, the usual dichotomy between subject and object disappears. The ego merges with the content of emptiness and feels as if it has ceased to exist. It is aware of its nonexistence, which sounds paradoxical but is an experiential fact.

Aside from the fear and anxiety brought about by the loss of conscious boundaries and the suspension of ego activity, one of the more familiar effects of meditation is "the dark night of the soul." The classic fourteenth-century meditation guide *The Cloud of Unknowing* states:

———— *Gathering the Light*

In the beginning it is usual to feel nothing but a kind of darkness about your mind, or as it were, a *cloud of unknowing*. You will seem to know nothing and to feel nothing except a naked intent toward God in the depths of your being. Try as you might, this darkness and this cloud will remain between you and your God. You will feel frustrated, for your mind will be unable to grasp him, and your heart will not relish the delight of his love. But learn to be at home in this darkness. Return to it as often as you can, letting your spirit cry out to him whom you love. For if, in this life, you hope to feel and see God as he is in himself it must be within this darkness and this cloud.[28]

Similarly, in Zen it is said that "the grand round mirror of wisdom is as black as pitch."[29]

The Dark Night of the Soul, of course, is the title of another work of Christian mysticism, by Saint John of the Cross (1542–1591). Saint John was a perceptive psychologist and gave an exhaustive description and analysis of this state of mind. Because this is a fairly familiar work, I will refrain from the temptation to quote him and the biblical texts to which he refers, with their lengthy and graphic depictions of this horrible feeling of alienation and despair. I do, however, want to point out that the "dark night" varies greatly in intensity and length: some people pass through it in a flash; others experience it as a balm, as cool and restful when compared to their former life's exertions; while still others are tormented and sick at heart, on and off, for years.

Viewed clinically, the dark night of the soul is a depression. In his "Two Essays on Analytical Psychology" in *Symbols of Transformation* and in his description of the *nigredo* in alchemy, Jung explores this state of mind from a modern psychological perspective. He thinks it is the result, first of all, of the ego's encounter with its shadow, with the repressed, despised, and unacknowledged side of the personality. Next, the very process of withdrawing psychic energy from conscious func-

What Is Meditation? ———

A seventeenth-century picture of an alchemist in the initial nigredo *state of meditation. The raven is a symbol of this dark night of the soul. The two angel-like figures depict the separation of the soul and spirit from the body. (See page 138.) The alchemist is at the center of a tension of opposites, expressed by the fire and water in the upper corners. The stars represent the separated-out and suspended archetypal energies of the Sun, Moon, Mercury, Venus, Mars, Jupiter, and Saturn.*

tioning and from our usual ego gratifications brings about a "darkening" of mood and spirit. And finally, his examination of the alchemical phase of the *nigredo* confirms the mystics' experience that the "divine spirit" or "the philosophers' gold" must be extracted by painstaking work on the *prima materia*—on our originally given "mind-stuff," which is described as "black blacker than black."[30]

Normally, the ego complex is an active center of consciousness and identity. During meditation, ego activity is suspended and the center of consciousness shifts to a content other than the ego; or, to put it in another way, the ego complex merges with another content or complex of energy—with the void, with *mu,* with an image, idea, or emotion. However, in its suspended state the ego remains as the link between one's former sense of self and the new experience. It is the thread that holds the two together. A person who asked a meditation instructor what happens to the ego when it seems to disappear and received no satisfactory reply dreamed that the ego becomes a ray of light, that it merges with the ray. I take that to mean that the ego becomes a carrier and a link between the personal and the transpersonal unconscious. Should the link snap, a psychosis could result. Those who engage in serious meditation practice would do well to develop a strong ego structure and maintain a firm hold on reality. Many of the long-term physical and psychological hardships that, for example, nuns and monks undergo serve to develop a resilient ego structure.

The idea of the ego as a link and a carrier between consciousness and the unconscious is also found in the Buddhist description of the psyche. Buddhism distinguishes nine forms of consciousness (see page 62).[31] The first six are sight, hearing, smell, taste, touch, and thought or intellect. In Jungian terms, the first five make up the sensation function, while the sixth, thought or intellect, encompasses the functions of thinking, feeling, and intuition. These six functions comprise our everyday consciousness, which, according to the Buddhist view, by interpreting and reacting to the data provided by the functions, creates the illusion of the subject "I" and the added illusion that the "I" is separate from the objective world. Moreover, consciousness is not always aware of the ego. Constant awareness of the ego occurs only in the seventh level of consciousness, *manas* (mind or spirit), which lies below the surface of daily consciousness. Besides being the source of persistent ego consciousness, *manas* acts as the conveyer of the "seed" essence of sensory experience to the eighth level of consciousness, *alaya-vijñana* (ideation store or

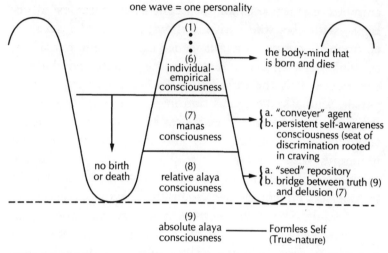

one wave = one personality

(1)
⋮
(6)
individual-
empirical
consciousness

→ the body-mind that is born and dies

(7)
manas
consciousness

{ a. "conveyer" agent
  b. persistent self-awareness consciousness (seat of discrimination rooted in craving

no birth or death

(8)
relative alaya
consciousness

{ a. "seed" repository
  b. bridge between truth (9) and delusion (7)

(9)
absolute alaya ————— Formless Self
consciousness   (True-nature)

Nine forms of consciousness. (From Kapleau, Zen: Dawn in the West)

"seed" repository). *Alaya-vijñana* records the essence of every action, feeling, thought, and sense impression and responds to them out of its own storehouse of "seeds," which are reconveyed by *manas* to sense consciousness. Philip Kapleau writes:

> In a sense the eighth level, or "storehouse" of experiences, is the basis of personality and character since it continuously seeds new actions, giving rise to different thoughts and varying behavior. But then these thoughts and behavior in turn change the quality of the repository consciousness as they are instantaneously impressed upon it to become new seeds of action.[32]

Below the eighth level of consciousness is the realm of Pure Consciousness or of the Formless Self, the source of all the other forms of consciousness. The experience of birth and death is associated with the first six forms of consciousness; at the seventh and eighth levels the notion of birth and death disappears or no longer applies.

In Jungian terms, the seventh level of consciousness, *manas,* appears to be the realm of the personal unconscious, where the complexes are located, including the ego complex. The eighth level, *alaya-vijñana,* then, is the collective unconscious, where Jung locates the archetypes. Pure Consciousness or the Formless Self is the archetype of the Self, the source of all consciousness and of all the archetypes and complexes. What are the "seeds"? They seem to be both pockets of energy and psychic structures in their most elementary and potential form. The Buddhist image of the seed, then, is what Jung calls the *archetype per se.* "The archetype in itself," he writes, "is empty and purely formal, nothing but a *facultas praeformandi,* a possibility of representation which is given *a priori.*"[33] The real nature of the archetype, he feels, is probably not capable of being made conscious; its existence and function become manifest only when the archetype begins to take on specific material or psychic energy and form. As pockets of energy, the archetypes are the *scintillae,* the "seeds of light" referred to by the Gnostics and the alchemists, that are scattered throughout nature.[34] "In the 'Water of the Art,' . . . which is also the chaos [the watery slime of the earth from which Adam was created, the *prima materia*]," writes an alchemist, "there are to be found the 'fiery sparks of the soul of the World as pure *Formae Rerum essentiales.*' "[35] Jung comments:

> These *formae* correspond to the Platonic Ideas, from which one could equate the *scintillae* with the archetypes on the assumption that the Forms "stored up in a supracelestial place" are a philosophical version of the latter. One would have to conclude from these alchemical visions that the archetypes have about them a certain effulgence of quasi-consciousness, and that numinosity entails luminosity.[36]

The archetypes, therefore, as the forms of "perception and apprehension"[37] and "the necessary *a priori* determinants of all psychic processes,"[38] are the "seeds" that consciousness

What Is Meditation? ————

conveys via the complexes to the archetypal psyche, which, in turn, responds with its own archetypal energy and form, conveyed again, via the complexes, to consciousness. One could say, therefore, that in its essence all life is an archetypal process.

Now, what about the ego complex? Even though it may wax and wane in strength and degree of continuity, from the Western point of view it is the central complex that organizes our consciousness and gives us our sense of identity. We are conscious of a psychic element only to the extent that it is related to the ego complex. Jung puts it this way:

> To us, consciousness is inconceivable without an ego; it is equated with the relation of contents to an ego. If there is no ego there is nobody to be conscious of anything. The ego is therefore indispensable to the conscious process. The Eastern mind, however, has no difficulty in conceiving of a consciousness without an ego. Consciousness is deemed capable of transcending its ego condition; indeed, in its "higher" forms, the ego disappears altogether. Such an ego-less mental condition can only be unconscious to us, for the simple reason that there would be nobody to witness it. I do not doubt the existence of mental states transcending consciousness. But they lose their consciousness to exactly the same degree that they transcend consciousness. I cannot imagine a conscious mental state that does not relate to a subject, that is, to an ego. The ego may be depotentiated—divested, for instance, of its awareness of the body—but so long as there is awareness of something, there must be somebody who is aware.[39]

Also, it seems to me that even in the Buddhist view of the psyche, the ego is not just an ephemeral illusion, as is repeatedly claimed. Its core rests in the *manas* consciousness, where supposedly there is persistent self-awareness. Not only that, but at its deeper levels *manas* consciousness is no longer affected by the phenomenon of birth and death. The clear implication, therefore, is that the archetypal essence of the ego complex is immortal and that potentially it is possible to maintain a certain form of ego consciousness even after death. That possibility, after all, is the assumption of *The Tibetan Book of the Dead,* while the development and perfecting of such postmortal consciousness is the aim of many Eastern meditation practices.

The Eastern theological attack on the ego gives rise to serious misunderstandings. The ego is seen as the most stubborn and entrenched seat of delusions about ourselves and the world; it is the "enemy" that must be annihilated if one is to gain insight into one's true nature. The Eastern religious goal, like that of most religions, is to reunite us with our original nature, from which we have become estranged. In the Judeo-Christian tradition, that estrangement is the consequence of the Fall. In the East, it is associated with the development of the ego. The idea is that the ego stands in the way of our return to the original egoless state of mind, which is seen as a more whole, complete, and true state of consciousness than that of the ego.

The problem is that the ego is now a psychic fact. Also, human beings did not consciously invent the ego. It evolved out of the Self. The ego cannot be destroyed without destroying the integrity of the psyche. Psychopathology amply demonstrates the devastating consequences that ensue when the ego is ill, maladapted, or deflected from its proper functioning. Moreover, one cannot return to an egoless condition without regressing to a childlike or even a womblike existence. That is not the intention or the goal of Eastern religious practice. The point is to break through to an insight into our original nature as mature adults and to integrate that insight in our conception of ourselves and of the world. This cannot be accomplished without an ego. In the Judeo-Christian cosmology there is the Garden of Eden at the beginning and the Kingdom of God at the end. The two are not the same. The Garden of Eden is the original pre-ego state of

What Is Meditation? ———

mind. The Kingdom of God is a return to our original condition but as ego-conscious individuals.

The sensation that Jung mentions above, in which one is no longer aware of one's body, is another common experience that occurs during meditation. The body seems to disappear or become "transparent," or it feels as if it were floating or levitating. *The Secret of The Golden Flower* describes these phenomena:

> As soon as one is quiet, the light of the eyes begins to blaze up, so that everything before one becomes quite bright as if one were in a cloud. If one opens one's eyes and seeks the body, it is not to be found any more. This is called: "In the empty chamber it grows light." Insight and outside, everything is equally light. That is a very favourable sign.
>
> Or, when one sits in meditation, the fleshly body becomes quite shining like silk or jade. It seems difficult to remain sitting; one feels as if drawn upward. This is called: "The spirit returns and touches heaven." In time, one can experience it in such a way that one really floats upward.[40]

At these times, one loses all awareness of outer reality: the senses shut down, and time and space evaporate.

The French philosopher Henri Bergson (1859–1941) argued that since potentially we can bring to mind all the details of our past experiences and perceptions, the primary function of the brain must be selective and eliminative. Were this not the case, we would be overwhelmed and confused by our remembered associations to every new event and perception and unable to act. Modern psychology tends to confirm this reductive and selective character of our sensory systems. The disappearance of the body and of outer reality, therefore, can be accounted for by the fact that meditation deliberately pushes the reductive and selective operations of the brain and the nervous system to such a point that they essentially shut down the entire sensory apparatus. Jung has another hypothesis to offer:

It might be that the psyche should be understood as *unextended intensity* and not as a body moving with time. One might assume the psyche gradually rising from minute extensity to infinite intensity, transcending for instance the velocity of light and thus irrealizing the body. . . .

In the light of this view the brain might be a transformer station, in which the relative infinite tension of intensity of the psyche proper is transformed into perceptible frequencies or "extensions." Conversely, the fading of introspective perception of the body explains itself as due to a gradual "psychification," i.e., intensification at the expense of extension. Psyche = highest intensity in the smallest space.[41]

In other words, loss of awareness of the body and of outer reality is the result of the "intensification" of psychic energy to the point where it exceeds the speed of light and passes beyond the realm of perceptible sense data and the notions of time and space. In a controlled experiment with psychedelic drugs, one subject reported the following:

I was experiencing directly the metaphysical theory known as emanationism in which, beginning with the clear, unbroken and infinite light of God, the light then breaks into forms and lessens in intensity as it passes through descending degrees of reality. . . . Bergson's concept of the brain as a reducing valve I now saw to be precisely true.[42]

Actually, the image accords more with Jung's than with Bergson's theory. Bergson refers only to memory and perception; he does not describe the psyche in terms of increasing and decreasing energy frequencies. Jung's notion also conforms with descriptions of meditation as involving the

What Is Meditation? ————

"creation," collection, and intensification of energy, heat, or light. After a meditation session a man dreamed: "I see Michelangelo's painting of God and Adam, and where God reaches out to Adam, light is born in between—intense, exploding light. Wonderful! I am so excited. He did that? He knew about that?" When the dreamer awoke, he realized that there was no such light between the figures in Michaelangelo's painting. In the dream he was so convinced that there was that he planned to buy a reproduction of the painting.

Marie-Louise von Franz, who has expanded on Jung's hypothesis with the use of dreams about death and with accounts of near-death experiences, writes that in these experiences "light" appears more often than any other image. She thinks that if Jung's notion of psychic reality lying on a supraluminous level of frequency is correct, "light" would "be the last transitional phenomenon . . . before the psyche fully 'irrealizes' the body, as Jung puts it, and its first appearance after it incarnates itself in the space-time continuum by shifting its energy to a lower gear."[43]

Jung's hypothesis implies that there is a threshold between the world of appearances and the world of the psyche per se. The division corresponds to the philosophical distinction between the world of becoming and the world of being or to Kant's phenomenal and noumenal realms. In terms of the structure of the psyche, there seem to be two or three thresholds: between consciousness and the personal unconscious; between the personal unconscious and the collective unconscious; and between the archetypal images of the collective unconscious and their purely formal or energetic manifestation, at which point there is very little difference between the collective unconscious and the psyche per se or the Formless Self. In every case, the threshold seems to be defined by the amount of psychic energy or psychic intensity needed to perceive the contents of the various levels. There is awareness of these contents only if they carry a sufficient energetic charge to register with the conscious ego complex. This is true of dreams, of complexes, of the archetypal images encountered by psychotics or deliberately activated through meditation, and of the purely formal manifestation of the archetypes via the numinous feelings, ideas, and visions described by mystics.

The vividness of the outer world that many people experience after meditation is therefore a combination of two things. On the one hand, the psyche becomes more energetically charged than is normally the case, and this extra charge is projected onto the external world. In the same way, during a depression, the lack of psychic energy is projected onto the world so that it appears bleak and lifeless. On the other hand, it is possible that during meditation the psyche has partially penetrated into the psychoenergetic basis of reality and that this vision carries over into the perception of the outer world. The depressed state of mind, "the dark night of the soul," is also a penetration into the psychoenergetic basis of reality. The difference is that in a depression one experiences the empty, cold, disintegrating, death-bearing aspects of reality, while during the enlightenment ecstasy one experiences the fullness, joy, oneness, and ever-living creative energy of being. In Hindu mythology this dual aspect of the universe is represented by the dancing god Shiva. In Freudian psychology the same duality is spoken of as the death instinct and the life instinct, Eros and Thanatos. One could argue that our preference for one over the other, for life over death, is really a human bias and that from an objective cosmic point of view both are equal and necessary aspects of existence. However, our bias for one over the other is deeply ingrained in the archetypal psyche. It seems that the creative spirit is in a "life and death" struggle with the destructive energy of the universe and seeks to engage us in that struggle on its side. That is the message, it seems to me, of all mythologies and religions.

What Is Meditation? ⸻

It is, of course, possible to claim that the various meditation experiences are the result of physiological and chemical changes in the brain. Lysergic acid diethylamine (LSD) and other hallucinogenic drugs seem to trigger all the usual "mystical" states of consciousness. Arthur J. Deikman argues that the visions of light and the sense of the oneness of the universe may be the result of the psyche's perception of its own internal electrochemical activity.[44] One can, in the same way, speak of love and other emotional responses as consequences of endocrinological and neurological processes.

Jung does not deny the role of the organism in psychic life. He thinks the situation is best described by a color spectrum. Physiology and instinct are dominant at the red end of the scale. Their influence gradually diminishes until at the violet end the psyche takes the lead and is more or less free of the determinism of the body. He also argues that ESP experiments and reports of "clinically dead" people, for example, provide evidence that at times the psyche operates independently of the body and even of the limitations of time and space.

LIMITS OF TRANSFORMATION

In the end, meditation is a technique for conserving, heightening, and directing the flow of psychic energy for the purpose of activating and bringing to consciousness psychic contents that normally elude our awareness. It reverses the normal flow of psychic energy, which streams from the "inside" toward the "outside" and is broadly disseminated among our complexes and objects of awareness. Meditation shuts off this natural flow of psychic energy, gathers it together, and focuses it on inner psychic processes. Meditation can be compared to a telescope in that it allows the perception of the invisible world of the psyche. The lens of the telescope is the ego complex, through which we experience and "see." The analogy breaks down when the ego and the Self merge and the "seer" and the "seen" become one, while at the same time a subtle distinction is maintained. If no distinction remained, no one who undertook this inner journey would be able to say anything about it. (See diagram.)

Different meditation exercises focus on different aspects of the psychic realm. *Kundalini* yoga, for example, seeks to energize the chakras, the psychic organs of the "subtle" or "etheric" body. Jung's active imagination seeks to activate and work with the personal complexes and their underlying archetypes. Religious meditations, such as the Spiritual Exercises of Saint Igna-

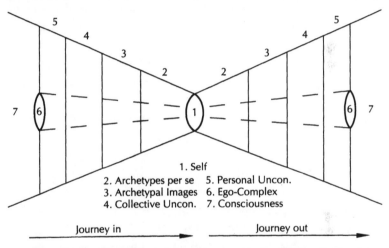

1. Self
2. Archetypes per se 5. Personal Uncon.
3. Archetypal Images 6. Ego-Complex
4. Collective Uncon. 7. Consciousness

Journey in   Journey out

During meditation the ego complex passes through the different levels of the unconscious. It can stop at any level and, by focusing on its contents, activate its images and consciously interact with them. In Zen, the meditator focuses on the core of the psyche, the Self, and, after a conscious experience of this central archetype, emerges with a radically altered psychological perspective. The entire journey is depicted by the statement attributed to the Chinese Zen master Ch'ing-yuan Wei-hsin (Jap. Seigen Ishin): "Before a man studies Zen, to him mountains are mountains and waters are waters; after he gets an insight into the truth of Zen, . . . mountains to him are not mountains and waters are not waters; after this when he really attains to the abode of rest, mountains are once more mountains and waters are waters" (Suzuki, Essays in Zen Buddhism, I, p. 22).

What Is Meditation? ⸺⸺

tius or certain meditation practices of Tibetan Buddhism, seek to enhance a person's religious sensitivities and to activate the archetypal images of the gods. Hinduism hardly leaves a corner of the psychic space unexplored and delights in the depiction of it all. Zen Buddhism, on the other hand, ignores all the complexes and archetypes and aims directly at the experience of the Self in its most abstract or energetic form, as Pure Consciousness or Formless Form. In this regard, the Zen type of enlightenment is the most universal and the least culturally conditioned. The Zen tradition arises out of Buddhism, but Zen may be compatible with any religion or with no religion. The archetypes that are usually activated through religious meditation can be defined as collective or cultural complexes. And the images that arise are those that, for whatever reason, are personally or collectively highly charged to begin with. This inherently given psychic charge of certain complexes and archetypes accounts for the spontaneous visions of religious figures and, nowadays, for the hallucinatory sightings of UFOs.[45]

In passing, I should mention that in Zen, the attainment of a state of mind characterized by serenity and bliss is considered a pseudo-emancipation and is described as the "cave of Satan." Psychologically speaking, such a womblike, oceanic feeling comes from the activation of and fall into an aspect of the archetype of paradise. That archetype, apparently, lies at the threshold of a complete experience of the Self. Because it has so many characteristics of the Self— reconciliation of opposites, wholeness, universality—and because its feeling tone is one of peace, happiness, and well-being, the ego is tempted to remain embedded in that archetype and consider its work done.

Meditation initiates the process of activating the images of the unconscious, but the inherent potential for such activation varies greatly with individuals. For some it requires very little effort, sometimes happening spontaneously. Others have to work at it very hard. Once these complexes and archetypes come to life,

-------- *Gathering the Light*

however, they develop a dynamism of their own and seek to bring the ego complex under their influence. Hence the dangers inherent in meditation. The ego can easily become "possessed" by a complex or an archetype, and then its freedom of choice is severely curtailed. In extreme cases, feelings of depression and suicide follow, or megalomania, fanaticism, and martyrdom, or a full-blown psychosis.

On the other hand, it is possible to have the most remarkable experiences via drugs, dreams, or visions, yet remain completely unaffected by them. Understanding and appreciation of these experiences are not vouchsafed by them. After all, the archetypes are mediated by the collective and personal complexes and by the conscious attitudes of the day. Besides, the capacity for a philosophical, religious, aesthetic, and moral understanding of such archetypal experiences also varies greatly with individuals. The full effect of such potentially transformative experiences is felt only if one is able consciously to integrate their message and meaning in one's daily life, behavior, and worldview.

To begin with, one never knows whether these experiences will lead to good or ill. It is important to remember that political and religious persecutions and wars, as well as the most wrenching psychoses and crimes, are all consequences of energetically charged complexes and archetypes. An enlightenment experience, no matter how profound, is no guarantee of reasonable, humane, and ethical behavior. "It is a fearful thing," writes Saint Paul, "to fall into the hands of the living God."[46] Jung is reported to have said that if God asked him to murder someone, he would refuse to do it, would interpose himself and die instead. In a letter he writes:

God wants to be born in the flame of man's consciousness, leaping ever higher. And what if this has no roots in the earth? If it is not a house of stone where the fire of God can dwell, but a wretched straw hut that flares up and vanishes?

What Is Meditation? ———

73

Could God then be born? One must be able to suffer God. That is the supreme task for the carrier of ideas. He must be the advocate of the earth. God will take care of himself. My inner principle is: Deus *et* homo. God needs man in order to become conscious, just as he needs limitations in time and space. Let us therefore be for him limitation in time and space, an earthly tabernacle.[47]

Meditation is a technique for encountering the "gods." During such encounters, and afterward, it is essential that the ego retain its sense of reality, its awareness of human limitations, and its commitment to ethical conduct.

CHAPTER THREE

THE PSYCHOLOGY

OF ZEN

I enter in a very focused way; then I go through it; then I go way beyond it.

One's art goes as far and as deep as one's love goes.

—Andrew Wyeth

In comparison with other meditation practices, Zen is unique in that it seeks an experience of the original state of Being. Jung defines this state as the uroboric archetype of the Self, the transcendental potential world of being that contains all the archetypes before they separate out and take on manifest form. The activation of the uroboric archetype of the Self is accomplished in Zen meditation through various exercises that produce particular psychological effects: the freeing up and accumulation of psychic energy, the creation of what I have termed a meditation complex, and the modification of the ego complex.

THE PHYSIOLOGY OF ZEN MEDITATION

Zen is an abbreviation of the Japanese word *zenna*, which is a transliteration of the Sanskrit *dhyana*, meaning contemplation, concentration, meditation. *Zazen* means "sitting Zen," or sitting meditation. The first instruction usually given to a Zen student is to sit still and watch the breath. The classic posture, which is held for from fifteen to thirty minutes, is some form of the lotus position, in which the spine is straight and the head aligned with the spine. The eyes are kept slightly open, lowered and unfocused. The straight spine, upright head, and open eyes are meant to keep one awake and alert. The muscular tension required to keep the body still and upright stimulates the proprioceptors and other sensory nerve endings in the body; these sensory signals are transmitted to the thalamus and then to the reticular formation—the wakefulness center in the brain. The wakefulness center, in turn, excites the muscles, keeping them tense, and the tension re-excites the wakefulness center so that a cycle is established, keeping one awake. There are two separate oscillatory cycles in the nervous system responsible for wakefulness. The other cycle involves the cerebral cortex. The cortical areas transmit impulses to the wakefulness center, exciting it and initiating impulses that return to the cortex and restimulate it.

The scientific investigation of meditation is still only in its initial phases. A number of studies have shown that the practice of meditation seems to have a restorative effect on the autonomic nervous system and may therefore be instrumental in alleviating a variety of psychosomatic illnesses and symptoms such as hypertension, insomnia, asthma, peptic ulcer, migraine, and tension headaches. There is also some evidence that meditation may be helpful in the treatment of allergies and even heart disease. Similarly, a number of psychological benefits accrue from the regular practice of meditation: improved concentration, greater emotional equanimity, "centeredness," and a general feeling of well-being. In psychotherapy, meditation techniques such as Jung's active imagination or various forms of guided imagery are sometimes used to explore and alter a person's psychic reactions and structure.

I know of no studies to date that have correlated what the psychologist Ernest Rossi calls the ultradian healing response (the need for a 20-minute rest period every 90–120 minutes to maintain excellence in performance, health, and well-being) with the practice of meditation.[1] However, beginning meditators are often instructed to sit for about 20 minutes at a time. More advanced practitioners usually sit somewhere between 35 and 45 minutes, approximately a double 20-minute period. It is possible that these 20-minute periods are an intuitive attempt to parallel the ultradian rhythm so as to obtain an optimal physiological response. Further evidence for the connection between meditation and the ultradian rhythms may be the fact that in psychological experiments in which an observer is faced with a ganzfeld—a patternless and consistent field of vision—it takes about 20 minutes before the observer reports an experience of "not seeing" (as discussed in chapter 2). Also, in an electroencephalographic (EEG) study of two Zen masters, it took about 20 minutes before the alpha waves characteristic of a typical meditative state changed to rhythmical theta waves.[2]

WATCHING THE BREATH AND COUNTING

In the Zen meditation exercise, the student is instructed to sit still so that the only discernible movement is breathing, which in the beginning is used as a focus for the mind. (Here is where the cortex receives its stimulation.) Watching the breath has a number of useful effects. Being aware of one's breathing keeps one connected to the body. In fact, the main purpose of this initial focus on posture and breathing seems to be to connect the meditator to the body. Zen is not

The Psychology of Zen   ———

interested in "head trips" or "out of body" experiences. Instead, one's center of gravity and concentration are localized in the lower part of the abdomen. Following the breath and the movement of the diaphragm makes it easier to keep the attention in the lower abdomen. The added advantage is that such a focus tends to make the breathing deep and measured, which has a quieting effect on the mind. Finally, the rhythmic quality of breathing provides a steady, repetitive pattern, so that when the attention wanders, the rhythm is there to bring it back.

The position of the hands on the lower abdomen also helps to keep the attention in that area. The left hand is placed in the palm of the right, the thumbs barely touching and forming an oval. The student is told to direct the flow of breath to the palm of the left hand. Since most people are right-handed, placing the left hand in the palm of the right and directing one's attention to it reverses the usual flow of psychic energy to the right hand. As the exercise is continued, the left palm gets hot, and that sensation stimulates the right side of the brain. Neurological research has demonstrated that the right hemisphere of the brain is associated with visual-spatial, artistic, intuitive, and mystical states of mind, while the left hemisphere (which controls the right side of the body) is related to the verbal, logical, analytic, and rational functions. For most people the right hand is the extraverted hand, associated with ego consciousness, will, activity, and relationship to the outer world. Symbolically, too, the right side represents the solar, masculine, outward-going, aggressive principle, while the left side is lunar, feminine, inward-looking, and receptive. Focusing the mind on the left hand and supplying it with energy may be a symbolic gesture as well as an actual stimulation of the psychic traits associated with the left and right hemispheres of the brain.

Once the student is able to sit still and direct the breath to the palm of the left hand, counting is introduced. The student is asked to count "one" with the first exhalation, "two" with the second, and so on, up to "ten," and then again back to "one." Few people manage to get past the first three or four counts without the mind beginning to stray. Whenever that happens, the student is told to begin again at "one." All thoughts, feelings, or bodily sensations are quietly observed (neither entertained nor actively resisted), as the mind's focus is continually brought back to the numbers. The counting adds another rhythmic pattern to the breathing and gives the mind something familiar (cognitive) to occupy it. For beginning students, changing the numbers with each exhalation and trying to get to ten keeps the mind alert and prevents boredom.

Numbers also have a deeper psychological significance. They are primary archetypes and in most cultures considered to be the basic principles from which the entire objective world emerges and according to which it functions. Each of the cardinal numbers has both quantitative and qualitative aspects of which the unconscious mind is aware. The deliberate concentrated repetition of the first ten cardinal numbers, therefore, stimulates the archetypes represented by these numbers and activates the deepest levels of the psyche. Also, numbers are the simplest universal concepts; as such, they lead the mind away from concrete, particular reality. Focusing the attention on numbers is a beginning step in bringing the psyche to an experience of the immaterial and universal form of reality.

Although there is no scientific evidence for the existence of the subtle-body energy centers known in Hinduism as chakras, it is interesting to note that the lower abdominal area is associated with the *manipura* chakra (see illustration). This chakra is the fire center or, in psychological terms, the center of desire, of emotional life. (The abdominal muscles are indeed engaged in any intense emotional expression,

The Psychology of Zen ———

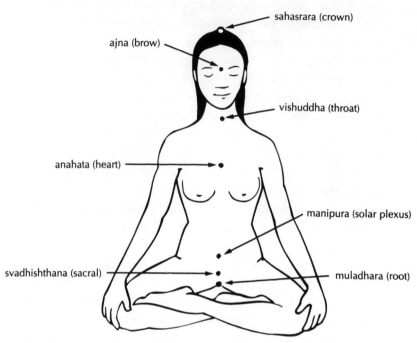

The Chakras.

whether crying, laughing, shouting, singing, or fighting, and, conversely, in deep sleep and relaxation.)

The *manipura* chakra lies below the *anahata* chakra, which is located in the area of the heart and lungs and associated with air (spirit) and thought. At the psychic level of the *anahata* chakra, conflict and self-reflection emerge because one is aware of both thoughts and emotions. With self-reflection comes ego consciousness as well as discernment, division, and separation of subject and object. Descartes's notion, "I think, therefore I am," is an expression of the *anahata* chakra. In the *manipura* chakra there are no thoughts, only emotions, and no separation from the emotions: every reaction is *total,* like that of an infant. One is identified with the emotion: I *am* angry. In the *anahata* chakra one is able to reflect on the emotion: I *feel* angry. Jung writes:

When you are in *manipura* you have no conflict, because you are the conflict itself, you just flow like water or fire; you can be exploded in ten thousand pieces yet you are one with yourself because there is no center from which to judge, there is nothing in between the pairs of opposites, For you are everything, you are also the pairs of opposites, you are this and that when you are emotional. It is not I who realize, it is the emotion that realizes.[3]

If one accepts the hypothesis of the chakras, then the Zen meditation practice of focusing on the lower abdomen has a number of important effects. The focus activates and energizes the *manipura* chakra. The chakra then unifies the meditator's being in a condition prior to the psychic split born of ego consciousness. And the chakra becomes the "fire" or the "cauldron" in which the psychic energy extracted from the instincts and emotions is reunited with them, *but in the subtle body*. In the *manipura* chakra,

things which were separate and contradictory are fused together, it is a melting fire; there is also the idea of the alchemical pot in which substances are mixed and melted together. So you can descend into the abysmal water to be healed, the baptismal water being the *uterus resurrectionis* where you are made whole again; or you can go into the fire. Therefore John the Baptist said of Christ: "He shall baptize you with the Holy Ghost and with fire." The two forms of baptism refer to the two lower centers [the *manipura* and *svadhishthana* chakras]; in the fire you can be made whole, and the water is still better because it is deeper down. . . . But the figurative death in the water, and the death . . . in the fire also mean regeneration, because in going back into any state where the ego consciousness is not, there is regeneration.[4]

Zen meditation, therefore, could be described as the process in which libido is extracted from the emotions, instincts, and consciousness. By refusing to act on emotional and instinctive drives, to entertain any fantasies charged by them, or to pursue any conscious thoughts, one enables the extracted libido to be transmuted into "pure," archetypal energy. This archetypal energy is then accumulated in and fused with the emotional subtle-body center. When enough energy is accumulated in this manner, the result, on the emotional level, is an ecstatic feeling of oneness and wholeness, and, on the conscious level, an intuitive vision of the unity of all being. In Zen, this enlightenment experience is not the end of the process, however, but only the beginning of a further psychospiritual development.

WORKING ON THE KOAN *MU*

Once the student is able to concentrate on the counting, she or he is asked to do *shikantaza,* literally "just sitting" with the mind empty, taut, and alert, or is presented with a *koan.* A koan is a logically baffling statement, question, or anecdote that points to or expresses an experience of ultimate reality. The student is asked to solve the koan and advised that the solution will not come from recourse to logical reasoning. Rather, the solution lies in awakening a level of the psyche in which the limitations of the discursive intellect are transcended. The koan traditionally assigned to beginning students is Joshu's *mu:*

> A monk in all seriousness asked the Zen master Joshu, "Does a dog have Buddha nature?"
> Joshu answered, *"Mu!"*

Mu is the Japanese transliteration of the Chinese *wu* and means emptiness, nothingness, the void. *Buddha nature* refers to the underlying nature of all existence; "divine nature" is probably the closest Western equivalent.

The question the Zen student is asked to answer is not whether a dog has Buddha nature, but "What is *mu?*" or

--------- *Gathering the Light*

"What is emptiness?" Conceptual answers and insights are not acceptable. Only an experience of emptiness will do. "Show me *mu;* show me emptiness," the Zen teacher will insist. Until one can adequately demonstrate an actual experience of emptiness, the koan has not been solved. Once the student can say what *mu* is, then she or he knows the answer to the monk's question about the dog and Buddha nature and, more important, understands why Joshu answered the question with *"Mu!"*

How does one work on this koan? One soon discovers that the solution does not come from contemplating or inquiring into the nature of nothingness. Rather, one must simply concentrate one's entire being on the syllable *mu,* voice it silently with every exhalation, periodically ask, "What is this *mu?,*" and ultimately merge with it—*become mu.* Then the answer will burst forth, of its own accord. To some it comes soon enough, while others work on it for years.

There is nothing special about this particular koan that is responsible for the breakthrough. Any other question, word, or syllable could serve as well. It is the intensity of one-pointed concentration that brings about an experience of emptiness. Sometimes a student is asked to answer the question "Who are you?" Or, as one of the koans puts it: "Think neither good nor evil [stop all dualistic thinking]. At this very moment, what is your original nature?" In Zen literature, the questions and koans used to effect the initial breakthrough experience are highly individual and varied. In the practice of *shikantaza,* by contrast, no question or syllable is used; the mind is simply kept empty and alert, and one awaits a breakthrough.

Keeping the mind empty or focused only on one point (which psychological experiments have shown to be equivalent to keeping the mind empty) is the chief characteristic of Zen meditation. The purpose of such one-pointed concentration is threefold: (1) to withdraw energy from consciousness

The Psychology of Zen

and from the complexes; (2) to accumulate this newly freed energy and hold it in suspension; (3) to intensify the accumulated energy. Normally our energy is dispersed among outer and inner objects and sensations. Sitting for extended periods of time without moving and deliberately ignoring all thoughts, sensations, and feelings, as well as any mystical states of mind, accumulates psychic energy (referred to in Japanese as *joriki*). This energy is then focused on the effort of concentration and maintaining a state of pure awareness. In the early stages of practice, the body and psyche are not accustomed to such a focused and suspended way of being. With further practice, it becomes easier to empty and focus the mind. This is especially true, once the meditation complex (described below) has been built up. At that point, an *abaissement du niveau mental* takes place: ordinary daytime consciousness recedes and one becomes aware of being within the unconscious. (In the Zen Oxherding Pictures this change is represented by the moon and the nighttime sky.) Now, concentration is intense and sometimes effortless for long periods. A still further stage is reached when one is able for brief moments to merge with *mu* or to become one with the void. This is a form of *samadhi* (Skt., lit. "putting things together" or union of the meditator with the object meditated upon).

A momentary contemplative merger with *mu* is not considered a solution to the koan, however. The attainment of this stage is seen as a prelude to the final effort, a breakthrough into the realm of the Absolute. Here methods differ between the two major schools of Zen Buddhism in Japan. The Soto school favors "gradual awakening," while the Rinzai sect pushes for "sudden" or "abrupt awakening." For a sudden breakthrough to occur, the psychic tension must be constantly intensified. Asking oneself, "What is *mu*?," helps to keep the tension, as do the admonishments of the teacher to keep probing ever deeper, to exhaust oneself in the effort.

———— *Gathering the Light*

But the techniques and admonitions alone will not suffice. The motivation of the meditator ultimately determines the outcome. For most meditators, the discipline and resolve required to accomplish the task, whether gradually or abruptly, call for a wholehearted desire for "enlightenment."

Particularly in the Rinzai method, one must be able to summon every ounce of physical and psychic strength and perseverance; one must be willing to extinguish ego consciousness and throw oneself completely—body, mind, and heart—into an unknown realm. The courage and stamina called for are illustrated by the Chinese story of a carp that swam against the current of an onrushing mountain stream and, upon coming to a waterfall, leaped up into the air with tremendous effort—and suddenly turned into a dragon.

THE MEDITATION COMPLEX

In chapter 2 I explored the psychological dynamics and effects of meditation, and proposed that meditation, by directing psychic energy inward, activates the complexes and archetypes. Westerners meditating on the koan *mu* actually create an artificial complex, for in the beginning there are no feeling associations with *mu* as there would be for Japanese Zen students. Yet by focusing the mind on the syllable and withdrawing energy from all other psychic contents, it is possible to create a powerful complex around it.

Although at first the syllable *mu* may elicit no personal associations, in time it does become the focal point of strong feelings and expectations; this seems to happen even though one is repeatedly told not to expect anything, to give up all desire for enlightenment, and simply to immerse oneself single-mindedly in the syllable. The meditator tries to do all that, but what keeps one at the task are the motivations that brought one to meditation in the first place. *Mu* simply gives voice to these motivations. Most people do come to meditation with a desire for enlightenment, or for a personal experience of transcendent reality, or because of some burning issue, frustration, or doubt. What is the point of my life? What happens after death? If Buddha nature pervades the entire universe, why is there so much injustice and senseless suffering in the world? How can I relieve my own suffering and find peace of mind? Indeed, any serious conflict, tension-producing situation, severe neurosis, or psychological trauma can serve as the basis for the meditation complex. Even though the personal motivations for meditation must be compelling, paradoxically, during meditation they must be forgotten. This is especially true when working on a koan such as *mu,* which may not directly address one's reasons for meditating.

The personal motivations behind the meditation complex are clearly apparent in Christian contemplative practice. The desire to experience the love of God or to attain to a living vision and knowledge of God serves as both the motivation and the content of meditation. The anonymous author of *The Cloud of Unknowing,* for example, writes: "This is what you are to do: lift your heart up to the Lord, with a gentle stirring of love. . . . Center all your attention and desire on him and let this be the sole concern of your mind and heart."[5] *The Cloud of Unknowing* describes a meditation technique that is essentially identical with the practice of *mu:*

> If you want to gather all your desire into one simple word that the mind can easily retain, choose a short word rather than a long one. A one-syllable word such as "God" or "love" is best. But choose one that is meaningful to you. Then fix it in your mind so that it will remain there come what may. This word will be your defense in conflict and in peace. Use it to beat upon the cloud of darkness . . . and to subdue all distractions. . . . Should some thought go on annoying you, demanding to know what you are doing, answer with this one word alone. If your mind begins to

intellectualize over the meaning and connotations of this little word, remind yourself that its value lies in its simplicity. Do this and I assure you these thoughts will vanish. Why? Because you have refused to develop them with arguing.[6]

The transcendent experience is the same for both Christians and Buddhists, but it is sought after and defined in different terms. There is no personal God in Buddhism, nor a personal soul. There is only the Awakened Mind, or what in my experience could best be described as Consciousness Being. For someone raised in the Jewish or Christian tradition, it is startling to see that the outstanding personalities of Zen were stirred not by love of God, but by questions and doubts about the fundamental nature of existence. Zen master Bassui (1327–1387), for example, spent years pondering the question "What is it within me which this very moment is seeing and hearing?" The koan *mu*, as well as such koans as "What was my face before my parents were born?" or "What is my own mind?," is concerned with philosophical or metaphysical issues. Instead of centering one's attention and desire on God, Zen Buddhists speak of generating the Great Doubt and building up a "doubt mass" in the mind. (The "doubt mass" is what I call the meditation complex.) A contemporary Chinese Zen master, Sheng-yen, explains:

> The "doubt mass" that accumulates can disappear in one of two ways. Due to lack of concentration or energy, the meditator may not be able to sustain the doubt, and it will dissipate. But if he persists until his doubt is like a "hot ball of iron stuck in his throat," the doubt mass will burst apart in an explosion.
>
> If that explosion has enough energy, it is possible that the student will become enlightened.[7]

Actually, as Sheng-yen's comment makes clear, the Great Doubt or "doubt mass" is a heightened state of psychic

The Psychology of Zen

tension. The term *doubt* is misleading, unless one understands it in an existential way. There is a direct parallel here with *The Cloud of Unknowing,* in which the Christian mediator is instructed to abide within the Cloud of Unknowing, empty of all thoughts, feelings, sensations, and images. In Rinzai Zen particularly, this empty state of consciousness must be accompanied by intense awareness.

The Japanese Zen master Hakuin (1685–1768) depicts the Great Doubt in imagery opposite to the "hot ball of iron" referred to by Sheng-yen. Describing his first spiritual break-through in a letter to a Zen nun, Hakuin writes:

> Suddenly a great doubt manifested itself before me. It was as though I were frozen solid in the midst of an ice sheet extending tens of thousands of miles. A purity filled my breast and I could neither go forward nor retreat. To all intents and purposes I was out of my mind and the "Mu" alone remained. . . . This state lasted for several days. Then I chanced to hear the sound of the temple bell and I was suddenly transformed. It was as if a sheet of ice had been smashed . . . and I returned to my senses.[8]

The contrast between the hot iron ball stuck in one's throat and Hakuin's being "frozen solid in the midst of an ice sheet" with a sense of purity filling his breast indicates that it is possible to experience the Great Doubt in strikingly different ways. (My conjecture is that Hakuin's experience of the unconscious as an ice sheet was a compensation for his generally passionate temperament.) Sometimes the experi-ence is also described as encountering an "iron wall" that one can't break through or a "silver mountain" on which one can't gain a foothold.

The hot ball of iron stuck in the throat refers to the gathering of one's psychic energy in the form of emotion and desire, then raising that concentrated energy to the *visuddha* (throat) chakra, where ego consciousness and desires are transcended and where one experiences oneself as an emanation of Mind or God. "Being frozen in the midst of an ice sheet" depicts a condition in which all desires and feelings are in a state of suspension; the image is analogous to the *albedo* (whitening) stage of alchemy and psychologically represents emotional equanimity, objectivity, and calmness. Hakuin's feeling of purity in his breast is his experience of this state of mind. The chest is associated with the *anahata* (heart) chakra where ego consciousness first appears. This means that at first his ego was still active, until, as he says, he was out of his mind and *mu* alone remained.

The image of the iron wall, like that of the iron ball, represents a psychic condition in which the unconscious and its energy have been unified into a single whole confronting the ego. In alchemy, "iron" is a synonym for the *prima materia*, the initially contaminated matter that needs to be purified; "silver" is already the purified essence of the "feminine" aspect of matter and only needs to be brought into a union with "gold" for the "philosophers' stone" to appear. The silver mountain consists of two images: "silver" standing again for the already purified, receptive emotional equanimity of the unconscious, and "mountain" for the Self, the experience of wholeness that the ego initially finds impossible to integrate. (In Zen, one does not ascend the mountain; at a certain point it simply collapses.) All these images refer to the meditation complex as the ego works to build it up and merge with it, and before it transforms into its archetypal core, the Self; when that occurs, the experience of enlightenment ensues.

All meditation practices, including Jung's method of active imagination (which I discuss in chapter 4), seek to activate various complexes and archetypes. Zen is unique in that it seeks to activate only the uroboric archetype of the Self in its most elemental, pre-image form—as Pure Consciousness or Formless Form. Hence comes the value of an abstract term such as *mu,* around which the meditation complex is formed: from the beginning the complex mirrors the quality of the Self that the meditator is striving to experience. (The same is true of *shikantaza* and of any other method of one-pointed concentration.) The Self, the archetype of wholeness and source of all being, can manifest itself and be experienced in many ways—from abstract mandala designs to personal encounters with the voice or vision of God. Zen eschews all these manifestations for an experience of the *fundamental creative energy of Being.* By unifying the entire psyche around the inner sound of *mu,* and by refusing to entertain any conceptual, feeling, or imaginal psychic contents, Zen meditation forces the Self to become the archetypal nucleus of the *mu* complex. When the two merge, an enlightenment experience occurs. However, to unite the entire psyche around the meditation complex is no easy matter, for one must first deal with the other complex whose function it is to unify all contents that enter its field of awareness: the ego.

THE EGO COMPLEX

The final aim of most meditation practices is to bring the ego into a conscious relationship with the contents that have been activated by meditation. During meditation, however, the ego complex must be "depotentiated," "denuded," and made "porous." By these somewhat psychologically imprecise terms, I hope to characterize the changes that the ego complex undergoes in the course of meditation.

The experience of meditators indicates that the ego is the most intractable of all the complexes. One is able, in time, to ignore the emotional pressures of all the other complexes; the complex that invariably remains is the ego. The author of *The Cloud of Unknowing* writes: "All else is easily forgotten in comparison with one's own self. See if experience does not prove me right. Long after you have successfully forgotten every creature and its works, you will find that a naked knowing and feeling of your own being still remains between you and your God."⁹

Jung hypothesizes the ego as an energetic emanation or projection of the Self into the three-dimensional world of the personality. (In the accompanying illustration, I have depicted the totality of the Self in two ways. The conelike form is a three-dimensional representation of the two-dimensional circle, showing that the transpersonal Self is at the same time the center, the circumference, and the source of all psychic contents.) Reflecting its origins, the ego possesses the chief characteristic of the Self: the tendency for integrating and unifying all psychic contents and experiences. The ego performs this function for consciousness; the Self, for the entire psyche. The development of the ego splits the original unity of the psyche and brings about an alienation of the ego from the Self. Adam and Eve's banishment from Paradise is the Judeo-Christian depiction of this psychological development.

Zen meditation seeks to bring about a *conscious* reunion of the separated ego consciousness with the universal conscious-

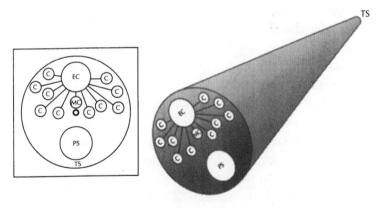

Two ways of picturing the Self. TS = transpersonal Self; PS = personal Self; EC = ego complex; C = complex; MC = meditation complex.

The Psychology of Zen ————

ness of the Self. (The alchemists, incidentally, sought the same goal in terms of a reunification of the spirit that had fallen into matter during the process of creation.) It is possible to bring about an *un*conscious reunion of the two realms by simply regressing the ego to its preconscious condition. The longing for this regressive union with the Self is expressed in various back-to-nature movements, childish fantasies, and certain addictions. The progressive union with the Self, by contrast, requires conscious effort in transcending ego limitations and is depicted by images such as the Kingdom of God and the alchemical philosophers' stone or gold, or experienced as the *unio mystica,* the mystical marriage between the soul and God.

Even though alterations of the ego complex take place more or less continuously and simultaneously during meditation, for the purposes of discussion I shall distinguish several distinct phases. To illustrate these phases, as well as the other psychological changes that take place during the course of Zen meditation, I use the diagrams and pictures on pages 94–95. The drawings, attributed to the Chinese master Pu-ming, represent the stages of Zen meditation with ten images of an ox and its herder. I use only six of the original ten pictures and translate each into psychological terms in the associated diagrams.[10]

In the beginning stage of meditation, the ego is responsible for focusing the attention and thus freeing up psychic energy from consciousness and from the complexes, and for directing the flow of this energy to the meditation complex. (See figure 1.) However, the ego cannot maintain the concentration past a certain point, especially since its own energy is also being channeled to the meditation complex. Once this complex has accumulated enough psychic energy to become autonomous and independent of the ego, it takes over the task of concentration and of drawing further psychic energy to itself. In later stages of meditation, the complex may even take on a voice and a partial personality, so that "*Mu* is calling *mu*," as some Zen teachers phrase it. As the meditation complex takes over the role of unification and concentration, the ego helps by observing the process and brushing aside interfering stimuli. (See figure 2.)

Next, the ego must "denude" or strip itself of all its functions and contents except for pure awareness—just being aware of being aware; it must become an "egoless ego," as one Zen teacher aptly describes it.[11] This means that the ego's sense of personal identity, its attempt to monitor and unify all psychic contents that enter its field of awareness, and its connection to temporal reality must all be dropped.

Once concentration is stable, the psyche quiet, and the ego denuded of its contents, its next task is to submerge itself within the meditation complex. This task can be conceived of in one of two ways: (1) as the energy of the ego complex penetrating or pouring itself into the meditation complex, or (2) as the ego holding itself in suspension and allowing the energy of the meditation complex to pour into it or penetrate it. The first is an active process, the second a receptive process; it is a matter of temperament which one prefers. (The Rinzai school emphasizes the active method; Soto, the receptive.) The task is difficult because a well-developed ego complex is a closed energy field that strives to maintain its integrity and resists penetration. This, then, is the final contribution of the ego to the meditation process that aims at a union with the Self: voluntarily to seek its own demise by dispersing its energy and opening its energy field, or by allowing itself to be displaced by the meditaton complex as the center of the psyche.

UNION WITH THE SELF

Once the meditation complex is firmly in place, the Self then serves as the archetypal nucleus of both the ego complex and

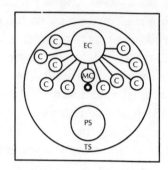

Figure 1. Discipline Begun: Beginning meditation.

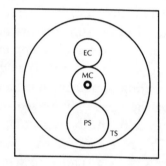

Figure 2. In Harness: The meditation complex as center.

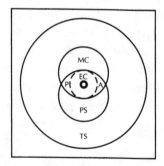

Figure 3. Laissez Faire: The paradise archetype.

EC = ego complex (ego awareness). MC = meditation complex. C = complex. PS = personal Self. TS = transpersonal Self. O = center of the psyche and of the transpersonal Self. --- = porousness of a psychic structure.

——— *Gathering the Light*

 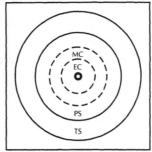

Figure 4. All Forgotten: Union with the personal Self.

 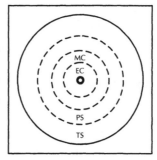

Figure 5. The Solitary Moon: Union with the transpersonal Self.

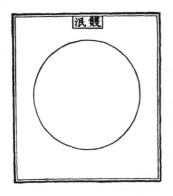 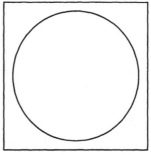

Figure 6. Both Vanished: Union with the core of the Self.

The Psychology of Zen

the meditation complex. The depersonalized ego carries the self-reflecting capacity of the Self, while the meditation complex performs the unifying function of the Self. In conscious life these two functions were both performed by the ego, but during meditation they are separated out. The reason for the separation seems to be that in its essence, the ego is not the unifying factor in the psyche. The ego is capable of unifying only the conscious part, and even that to a limited degree. Since the goal of meditation is to unify the entire psyche, both conscious and unconscious, this function is performed by the archetype of the Self. To begin with, however, that archetype needs to be mediated by a complex. The ego complex is not helpful in this regard; in fact, it is an obstacle because its purpose is to maintain a unified field of consciousness and a conscious identity separate from the Self. If a union of the entire psyche is to be achieved, the ego complex must first allow itself to be displaced by the meditation complex and then actually dissolve itself within that complex. Here is a description of the process, using the koan *mu*, by Hakuun Ryoko Yasutani-roshi (1885–1973), a Japanese Zen master who was instrumental in bringing the practice of *zazen* to the United States:

> At first you will not be able to pour yourself wholeheartedly into Mu. It will escape you quickly because your mind will start to wander. You will have to concentrate harder—just "Mu! Mu! Mu!" Again it will elude you. Once more you attempt to focus on it and again you fail. This is the usual pattern in the early stages of practice. Even when Mu does not slip away, your concentration becomes disrupted because of various mind defilements. These defilements disappear in time, yet since you have not achieved oneness with Mu you are still far from ripe. Absolute unity with Mu, unthinking absorption in Mu—this is ripeness. Upon your attainment to this stage of purity, both inside and outside naturally fuse. "Inside and outside" has various shades of meaning. It may

——————— *Gathering the Light*

be understood as meaning subjectivity and objectivity or mind and body. When you fully absorb yourself in Mu, the external and internal merge into a single unity.[12]

This is *samadhi,* the union of the meditator with the object of meditation—in this case, with the *mu* complex and its archetypal nucleus, the personal Self. (See figure 4.) Here, a distinction is necessary between the personal Self and the transpersonal Self. The personal Self is composed of the sum total of the conscious and unconscious of an individual, while the transpersonal or universal Self is the sum total of all personal Selves—the Self of Selves. Both in Jungian psychology and in Zen there is a tendency to blur the distinction. Zen master Bassui (1327–1387), however, is very clear about the difference in terms of the meditation experience:

There are those who think that when one's mental functions have ceased, leaving one like a decayed tree or cold stone, one has attained no-mindedness; while still others maintain that in the practice of Zen a decisive point has been reached when one feels a deep void with awareness of neither inner nor outer, the entire body having become shining, transparent, and clear like a blue sky on a bright day.

This last appears when the True-nature begins to manifest itself, but it cannot be called genuine Self-realization. Zen masters of old would call it the "deep pit of pseudo-emancipation."[13]

The "deep pit of pseudo-emancipation," or the "cave of Satan," as it has been called, refers to a meditative state of mind characterized by a sublime sense of bliss, peace, and harmony. (See figure 3.) This is a manifestation of the archetype of paradise, which is a borderline archetype—a bridge between the personal and the transpersonal archetypes of the Self, containing elements of both. (Paradise myths bear out the liminal nature of this archetype.)

In Zen meditation, the union of the meditator with the

The Psychology of Zen ————

personal Self is not accepted as full Self-realization. The meditator is urged to continue until a union with the transpersonal Self is achieved. (See figure 5.) The union occurs because of an *enantiodromia* (the tendency of an extreme position to transform into its opposite). Jung describes the process:

> If consciousness is emptied as far as possible of its contents, they will fall into a state of unconsciousness, at least for the time being. In Zen, this displacement usually results from the energy being withdrawn from conscious contents and transferred either to the conception of "emptiness" or to the koan. As both of these must be static, the succession of images is abolished and with it the energy which maintains the kinetics of consciousness. The energy thus saved goes over to the unconscious and reinforces its natural charge to bursting point.[14]

Once the ego has been denuded of its personal contents and consciousness reduced to a single empty point, a reversal suddenly occurs in which the ego and consciousness are flooded by the contents of the Self. These contents are so overwhelmingly vast that they essentially defy expression and can be grasped only by intuitive insight. The extreme physical and psychic tension, meanwhile, gives way to a tremendous feeling of ecstatic release. The ego finds itself in a curious position. Through the perspective of the Self, the meditator experiences the ego as non-ego: its relative and illusory character are seen through. On the other hand, the ego experiences itself as the Self, as universal Ego.

Statements of those who have experienced this union attest to the paradoxical nature of this particular *coniunctio oppositorum*. "I saw and knew that I am the only One in the whole universe! Yes, I am that only One!" exclaims one man. A Japanese woman states: "*I am Buddha. I am I. I am* selfless *I.*" "For a fleeting eternity I was alone—I alone was," writes the

American Zen master Philip Kapleau.[15] "Yesterday the whole universe was suddenly born," an American woman declares. "How can it be that *I am the universe*. . . . Am I mad to think that I alone have created heaven and earth?"[16]

The danger of this experience, of course, is that it may produce a psychotic inflation. Zen teachers are insistent about the necessity of ridding oneself of these godlike feelings and the emotional attachment to the accompanying rapture of the experience, but they admit it is no easy matter. Daiun Sogaku Harada-roshi (1870–1961), Yasutani-roshi's teacher, writes: "An ancient Zen saying has it that to become attached to one's own enlightenment is as much a sickness as to exhibit a maddeningly active ego. Indeed, the profounder the enlightenment, the worse the illness."[17] He says that his own "sickness" lasted almost ten years.

SELF-REALIZATION AND WHOLENESS

Why do some individuals devote so much time and energy to the quest for a glimpse of the original state of being? First there is nostalgia, a longing to return to one's origins. Closely related to this is love of God as well as the urge to escape suffering. There is the desire for a religious experience of transformation: a dissatisfaction with the limitations of ego consciousness and with bondage to an incomplete way of being. Then there is the philosophic passion to know beyond the knower and the known. There is the mystical urge to become one with the universe. And finally, there is the desire to become whole. The last probably underlies all the other motivations.

Not every manifestation of the Self brings with it a sense of wholeness. Indeed, initial encounters with the Self in particular are often felt to be disruptive and unbalancing. Jung notes: "The self, in its efforts at self-realization, reaches out beyond the ego-personality on all sides; because of its all-encompassing nature it is brighter and darker than the ego. . . . For this reason *the experience of the self is always a defeat for the ego.*"[18] The dark side of the Self, when activated, can wreak havoc with the personal psyche. The alchemists were well aware of the fact that their work could lead in some instances to insanity and death. Serious meditation practice is not for everyone; nor is it a cure-all.

Jung felt that Eastern meditation practices that stress mastery over the mind, instincts, and emotions merely augment the ego-controlling, willful, and repressive capacities of consciousness. Yet this is just the opposite of what is required if one is to transform the volatile, disruptive, and undeveloped contents of the unconscious. *Zazen,* for example, moves directly over the personal unconscious to the archetypal Self. Consequently, one can have an enlightenment experience and yet harbor a personal psyche contaminated with infantile, violent, libidinous, and power-driven complexes. In a religious setting these problems are dealt with as part of preparatory training. Outside the religious context they can be addressed psychotherapeutically. Here, Western analytical psychology has an important contribution to make to the Eastern goal of Self-realization. Analytical psychology provides a technique for developing the personal psyche so that the entire individual is whole. Without such a development, the transcendent experience remains one-sided and disconnected from the personal realm.

Given the above reservations, *zazen* is effective in fostering equanimity, centeredness, and clarity of mind. An enlightenment experience of the Self usually brings with it contents from the unconscious that complement a person's conscious attitudes. For example, a woman who abhorred the mundane and the routine was surprised to learn that *everyday life* was the key to all her spiritual strivings. A philosophically minded man, who thought that Self-realization must be a most profound experience, was both disappointed and relieved to discover that "there is nothing to realize!"

The degrees of Self-realization that people may experience vary greatly. Initial enlightenment experiences are usually shallow. With persistence, however, it is possible to penetrate to the core of the Self. (See figure 6 on page 95.) Here, one leaves behind all religious and cultural beliefs and presuppositions. The medieval mystic Meister Eckhart (1250–1327) describes the final breakthrough in these words:

> In my breaking through I stand empty in the will of God, and empty also of God's will, and of all his works, even of God himself—then I am more than all creatures, then I am neither God nor creature: I am what I was, and that I shall remain, now and ever more! Then I receive a thrust which carries me above all angels. By this thrust I become so rich that God cannot suffice me, despite all that he is as God and all his godly works; for in this breakthrough I receive what God and I have in common. I am what I was, I neither increase nor diminish, for I am the unmoved mover that moves all things. Here God can find no more place in man, for man by his emptiness has won back that which he eternally was and ever shall remain.[19]

From a Christian and theistic standpoint, this is heresy if not blasphemy. (Not surprisingly, a number of Eckhart's propositions were declared heretical.) From an experience of the core of the Self, the traditional Christian and theistic conceptions of the ultimate Ground of Being appear far too narrow and anthropomorphic.

It remains to be seen what the world would be like if even a small number of men and women integrated this consciousness of humankind's universal nature as part of their personal psychology and social attitudes. Such an experience, when joined with analytical insight into one's personal shadow

The Psychology of Zen

"In form then of a pure white rose / the saintly host was shown to me"
(Dante, Divine Comedy: Paradiso, *canto 31). The mystical rose and the*
threefold Light that Dante describes in the concluding verses of The Divine
Comedy *represent the apex of the traditional Christian experience of the*
Self.

projections and motivations, would bring about a new consciousness of the world and humanity's place in it. This is a dire necessity if individuals and nations are to be spared a regressive union with the Self, via fundamentalisms of every kind.

Like the Nazi epidemic, the present-day reactionary movements are unconscious collective attempts at individuation and wholeness. They seek to heal the split between modern secular rational consciousness and the powerful archetypal forces rooted in our instinctive nature. Here, Jungian psychology, with its emphasis on integrating the conscious and the unconscious, and Zen enlightenment, with its experience of the paradoxical uniqueness and universality of every individual, have an important contribution to make to the sanity of individuals and the unity of humankind.

CHAPTER FOUR

CAN WEST MEET EAST?

One does not become enlightened by imagining figures of light,
but by making the darkness conscious.

—C. G. Jung

From his first encounter with Eastern religions, Jung had serious reservations about the use of Eastern meditative practices by Westerners. Western consciousness, he wrote in the conclusion of his commentary to *The Secret of the Golden Flower,* "is by no means the only kind of consciousness there is; it is historically conditioned and geographically limited, and representative of only one part of mankind. The widening of our consciousness ought not to proceed at the expense of other kinds of consciousness; it should come about through the development of those elements of our psyche which are analogous to those of the alien [Eastern] psyche."[1] He argued that in the West hardly a thousand years had passed since Christianity was imposed on what could be described as a semisavage group of animistic, polytheistic tribes. The philosophical and moral values of this sophisticated Mideastern religion made psychic demands on these people that went far beyond their instinctive capacities and spiritual development. In order for them to live up to the Christian ideals, their instincts had to be repressed. The result was a religious practice and morality that were often violent and reflected self-loathing. The problem is that repressed elements do not develop, but vegetate in the unconscious in their original form, or become unnaturally charged and distorted. "We would like to scale the heights of a philosophical religion," Jung writes, "but in fact are incapable of it. To grow up to it is the most we can hope for. The Amfortas wound and the Faustian split in the Germanic man are still not healed; his unconscious is still loaded with contents that must first be made conscious before he can be free of them."[2]

In contrast, the East has a culture that goes back thousands of years and that grew organically from the primitive instincts. The Chinese and the Indians, Jung argues, do not share our impulse toward a "violent repression of the instincts that poisons our spirituality and makes it hysterically exaggerated."[3] The idea of a heroic self-conquest is foreign to them. Not overcoming, but detachment is their way; and true detachment is possible only if one has more or less lived out one's desires. As a psychoanalyst, Jung was constantly confronted with the neurotic and sometimes psychotic consequences of a conscious or cultural attitude that led to a repression of instinctive drives. Consequently, he felt he could hardly encourage Europeans to adopt religious practices that dismissed the unconscious and ignored the instincts: "There could be no greater mistake than for a Westerner to take up the direct practice of Chinese yoga, for that would merely strengthen his will and consciousness against the unconscious and bring about the very effect to be avoided."[4] When *The Tibetan Book of the Dead* states that the gods and phantoms we fear and worship are nothing but the creation of our own minds, or when *The Hui Ming Ching* says that the "shapes formed by the spirit-fire are only empty colours and forms," the "enlightened" Westerner, Jung notes, couldn't agree more. He even flatters himself with thinking that he came to this conclusion long before he had heard of the wisdom of the East. But the truth is, Jung observes, that we have only outgrown the "words" and not the psychic facts that gave birth to the gods. The gods have simply become diseases: phobias, compulsions, and all sorts of neurotic symptoms. "Zeus no longer rules Olympus but rather the solar plexus, and produces curious specimens for the doctor's consulting room, or disorders the brains of politicians and journalists who unwittingly let loose psychic epidemics on the world."[5] When the East rejects all fantasy contents, it does so on a very different basis than we do. There, myth is still an integral part of everyday life. Yoga, for instance, takes the existence of the gods for granted, and its teachings are meant primarily for those who are already at the point of detaching themselves from the world. When the East rejects the fantasies of the unconscious, it does so because it has already extracted their essence and condensed it in profound teachings. We in the West have never experienced these fantasies in a conscious way, much less extracted their essence. Here we have a large portion of experience to catch up with. As a beginning, we need to acknowledge the inner psychic forces again and not wait for them to show up as moods, hallucinations, and painful neuroses. Jung continues:

> We can be sure that the essence we extract from our experience will be quite different from what the East offers us today. The East came to its knowledge of inner things in childlike ignorance of the external world. We, on the other hand, shall explore the psyche and its depths supported by an immense knowledge of history and science. At present our knowledge of the external world is the greatest obstacle to introspection, but the psychological need will overcome all obstructions. We are already building up a psychology, a science that gives us the key to the very things that the East

discovered—and discovered only through abnormal psychic states.[6]

These arguments, first voiced in the commentary to *The Secret of the Golden Flower,* are repeated and elaborated upon in almost every other essay Jung wrote on Eastern religions and meditation. For example, in his psychological commentary on *The Tibetan Book of the Great Liberation,* he takes up the moral issue of detachment. The One Mind, the Buddhist image of ultimate and total reality, is described in this book as "undefiled by evil" and "unallied to good." The description, Jung writes, is reminiscent of Nietzsche's "six thousand feet beyond good and evil" (i.e., beyond the conventional categories of morality). The practical consequences of such an otherworldly perspective are usually ignored by the devotees of Eastern wisdom. It is all very well and good to entertain such a transcendental perspective as an abstraction, but does the notion really agree with our feelings, our conscience, and our sense of justice? Can we truly be indifferent, Jung asks, not only as the doers of evil but, even more, as its victims? Writing in 1939, he mentions the "terrifying examples of the Superman's aloofness from moral principles" occurring at the time.[7] Also, he continues, every psychologist knows that moral conflicts are never settled by a mere declaration of superiority or transcendence, no matter how well intentioned or firmly believed. If someone is able to become completely detached from him- or herself and from the world, as some saints and yogis appear to have done, perhaps then we can speak of a liberation from vices as well as virtues. But given our almost obsessive involvement with the outer world, we are far from achieving such an all-encompassing detachment. To espouse detachment in the context of our present-day consciousness is highly suspect. One who does so is naive, avoiding moral responsibility, or escaping the as yet necessary conscious suffering we as Westerners have to undergo to bring our psyche to the point of true detachment and liberation.

Jung insists that we cannot simply take over and adopt Eastern spiritual insights and practices. These concepts and practices developed in the course of an uninterrupted tradition four or five thousand years old. In its cultural context, a system such as yoga is the appropriate method for uniting body and mind. The Indian mentality has no problem operating intelligently with a concept such as *prana;* the notion is part of the collective consciousness, so that every student of yoga has at least an intuitive grasp of what it means. When the term comes to us, we either have to suspend our judgment and believe that there is such a thing, or we subject it to a scientific or philosophic critique and reject it as "pure mysticism." Also, we tend to take over the Eastern teachings and apply them in an extraverted way, so that yoga becomes either a religious practice or a kind of scientific psychophysical training. In any case, not a trace of the unity and wholeness of nature characteristic of yoga is left. "I would not advise anyone," Jung cautions, "to touch yoga without a careful analysis of his unconscious reactions. What is the use of imitating yoga if your dark side remains as good a medieval Christian as ever?"[8] The aim of yoga is to gain control over one's mind and body. But for the typical Westerner, Jung insists, "it is sheer poison to suppress his nature, which is warped enough as it is, and to make of it a willing robot. . . . As a European, I cannot wish the European more 'control' and more power over the nature within and around us."[9]

In his foreword to D. T. Suzuki's *Introduction to Zen Buddhism,* Jung again cautions Westerners against adopting Zen practice for the purpose of religious transformation. The entire enterprise presupposes a Buddhist spiritual tradition and culture. However, he has less fear of Zen's becoming a popular Western preoccupation because in Zen there are "none of those marvellously incomprehensible words that we find in Indian cults. Neither does Zen play about with complicated *hatha*-yoga techniques, which delude the physiologically minded European into the false hope that the spirit can be obtained by just sitting and breathing."[10] In the West, only a few individuals have glimpsed the psychic reality, in which all opposites unite in a paradoxical whole, that is the basis of Buddhist teachings. And usually these individuals have had to remain silent, for there is almost nothing in our civilization to enable anyone to appreciate this insight. The entire Judeo-Christian tradition is inimical to such a radical, nondualistic conception of reality. Only the works of William Blake and the tragedies of Goethe's *Faust* and Nietzsche's *Thus Spake Zarathustra* give an intimation of this "breakthrough of total experience" in the West.

So far, only certain forms of psychotherapy provide a receptive milieu for this experience. Psychological knowledge in the Western context is the equivalent of the traditional spiritual atmosphere of Buddhism in Zen. But "the tasks of psychotherapy are much more varied, and the individual phases of the long process more contradictory, than is the case in Zen."[11] For example, Zen presupposes a cultivated ego on the part of the practitioner. In psychotherapy, one must often first help a person develop a conscious ego before he or she can even think of abolishing egohood. Similarly, Zen assumes a certain level of psychological understanding on the part of its adherents. In the West, people must frequently first be educated about the existence of the unconscious and about its autonomous, intelligent, and creative functioning. Finally, psychotherapy does not deal with men and women who, like Zen monks and nuns, are ready to make any sacrifice for the sake of truth and Self-realization. Instead, Westerners often want to use psychological knowledge for their egoistic needs and goals. Only in rare instances does psychotherapy become a dialectical relationship between doctor and patient where, Jung writes, "the goal is transformation—not one that is predetermined, but rather an indeterminable change, the only criterion of which is the disappearance of egohood. No effort on the part of the doctor can compel this experience. The most he can do is to smooth the path for the patient and help him to attain an attitude which offers the least resistance to the decisive experience."[12]

Meditation can actually exacerbate psychological problems, not only because it enhances receptivity and sensitivity, but also because it builds up psychic energy that then can activate the drives and complexes. The Rorschach study of meditators mentioned in chapter 1 concluded that there tended to be a "noticeable increase in drive-dominated responses in some subjects" in the beginners' group, and an intensification of aggressive, sexual, and other drive states in the advanced meditators.[13]

In the first chapter of *Transformations of Consciousness: Conventional and Contemplative Perspectives on Development,* Jack Engler addresses the issue of psychopathology and meditation. He also deals with other clinical features of meditation practice that are worth mentioning in view of Jung's arguments that Eastern meditation techniques cannot be torn out of their cultural context and successfully practiced by Westerners. Studies carried out by Engler and Daniel P. Brown, as well as informal reports from several Asian meditation centers, indicate that Westerners show relatively slow progress in the practice of *vipassana* (insight) meditation. "After three months of continuous intensive daily Vipassana practice, fully half of the N-group of 30 showed very little change on either post-test or on teacher ratings."[14] Asian practitioners, by contrast, had completed only one or two fourteen-day retreats before experiencing the first stage of enlightenment. Other studies indicate that Western meditators appear to "*become fixated* on what may be called a *psychodynamic level of experience.*"[15] Their meditation practice is dominated by "primary process thinking" and by an increase "in fantasy, daydreaming, reverie, imagery, spontaneous recall of past memories, derepression of conflictual material, incessant thinking and emotional lability, including dramatic swings in mood."[16] One could hardly ask for a better description of unconscious activity. This finding bears out Jung's contention that when Westerners begin to meditate, they immediately encounter their own subjective fantasies, rather than the transpersonal realms of form and formlessness. Eastern meditation presupposes a certain amount of authentic detachment from the shadow world of the personal unconscious. This is why Jung insisted that psychotherapy and active imagination are the appropriate methods for Westerners who are interested in psychological growth and spiritual development. (I assume psychotherapy is also appropriate for Easterners who are still engaged in a struggle with their personal unconscious.)

Engler acknowledges that part of the problem for Western meditators is that, when Eastern meditation is transplanted to the West, the practice is lifted out of a cultural context permeated by Buddhist perspectives and values and part of a total system of training and way of life. "When this therapeutic context is eliminated, meditation is *practiced as an isolated technique,* with disregard for many other important behavioral, motivational, intrapsychic and interpersonal factors."[17] Here Engler essentially reiterates and confirms Jung's argument stated during the 1930s.

Engler notes that there are two major groups who become interested in Buddhism and meditation: those in late adolescence and those entering or passing through a midlife transition. Individuals in these two groups, he writes, "often seem attracted to Buddhist practice as a short-cut solution to the developmental tasks appropriate and necessary to their stage of the life cycle":

The Buddhist teaching that I neither have nor am an enduring self is often misinterpreted to mean that I do not need to struggle with the tasks of identity formation or with finding out who I am, what my capabilities are, what my needs are, what my responsibilities are, how I am related to other selves, and what I should or could do with my life. The *anattā* (no-self) doctrine is taken to justify their premature abandonment of essential psychological tasks.[18]

In addition to the above two groups, Buddhism also seems to attract people with a marked narcissistic and borderline psychic organization. In part, Engler states, the attraction again is the *anattā*, or no-self, doctrine that helps such individuals rationalize, if not actually legitimize, their lack of self-integration, their feelings of inner emptiness and absence of a cohesive self. In these instances, meditation is exactly the opposite of what is needed. Buddhism, Engler goes on to say, has not much to offer in the treatment of these aspects of self-pathology. It has no theory of child development, no developmental psychology, and no developmental view of psychopathology. Buddhist psychology and meditation practice simply presuppose a more or less healthy psyche and a well-functioning, "normal" ego. This, again, was Jung's conclusion. He insisted that Eastern religious thought and meditation practice should not be used to escape the often humiliating and unpleasant task of dealing with one's own personal psychology, which is best done in a Western therapeutic setting.

Jung's reservations about Westerners taking over Eastern spiritual ideas and practices are based on his view of the very different evolution of Eastern and Western approaches to reality. Easterners, he argues, have pursued the subjective factors of existence for a much longer period than Westerners have. Over the centuries, they have developed a science of consciousness and defined certain basic laws and truths of psychic life. We, by contrast, have turned our attention to the external aspects of existence and developed a science that defines the laws and truths of nature. Easterners tend to view the external world as illusory forms of *maya*. Westerners tend to dismiss all manifestations of the inner world as illusions and fantasies. Eastern equivalents of natural science and modern technology are somewhat old-fashioned, if not primitive. This is also true of Eastern psychology as a science: it has still not separated itself out from philosophy and is in the early scientific stage of enumerating and classifying various psychological states and functions. On the other hand, what we have to show by way of spiritual insight and psychological technique, when compared with Zen or yoga, is just as undeveloped as native Eastern science and technology. If one compares, for instance, the Spiritual Exercises of Ignatius Loyola with yoga or with some of the Tibetan Buddhist meditation exercises, there is an enormous difference. To jump straight from that level into Eastern yoga and meditation is no more advisable, Jung suggests, than for Asians to suddenly turn themselves into imitation Europeans. Jung concludes: "I have serious doubts as to the blessings of Western civilization, and I have similar misgivings as to the adoption of Eastern spirituality by the West. Yet the two contradictory worlds have met."[19] His recommendation clearly is for each side to retain its own psychological and historical standpoint and to avoid an uncritical adoption or mindless imitation of the other.

Generally speaking, it is hard to disagree with Jung's advice. And yet, as he says, the two worlds have met. It is now impossible to go back. The question is how each can assimilate the knowledge of the other without losing its own ground. But this is something hardly amenable to control, for as Jung also observed, Western fascination with Eastern thought and spirituality is a development that "comes from the bottom up," while in the East, not only scientists but ordinary Asians are mesmerized by the achievements of Western science and technology. Each side is transforming the world of the other, for better or worse, and in my view,

Can West Meet East? ————

each has much to offer the other. Distortions and exaggerations in the adoption of new knowledge and techniques can hardly be avoided. But the ultimate outcome of this marriage between East and West may be beneficial for both. Western interest in Eastern thought, for example, has led Easterners to a greater appreciation of their own cultural heritage. The enthusiastic adoption of Western technology by Easterners, on the other hand, has made many a Westerner question the values of material and scientific progress when divorced from cultural and humanistic considerations.

On the whole, Jung's warnings about the uncritical adoption of Eastern spiritual thought and practices by Westerners appear reasonable and convincing. Yet, at times, they seem overstated. Did he really think that Westerners would embrace yoga or Buddhism en masse? There is hardly any chance of that. Or were his warnings meant for those individuals who were searching for personal self-knowledge and development? Here I think they are appropriate. But sometimes I think the warnings were meant more for himself than for anyone else, for he probably feared being intellectually and emotionally subsumed by the more evolved and sophisticated Eastern conceptions, which turned out to be so close to his own personal psychological experiences and discoveries.

My own feeling is that once the novelty and superficial allure of Eastern thought fade and its assimilation begins in earnest, many Westerners will lose interest. One cannot appreciate music unless one has a musical ear, and one cannot appreciate certain kinds of classical music unless one has a well-developed musical taste. The same is true of philosophical and religious concepts. There are probably as many Easterners as Westerners for whom the adoption of yoga or Buddhism is inappropriate and detrimental. On the other hand, Westerners no longer contained by the historically limited and image-bound aspects of Western religions find these more psychological teachings a godsend. I think Jung might have been surprised by the number of Westerners who have actually acculturated themselves to Hinduism and Buddhism and practice these religions not just in a superficial, imitative way.

Shortly before he died, D. T. Suzuki wrote an introduction to *A Flower Does Not Talk: Zen Essays* by Zenkei Shibayama. I believe he was responding directly to Jung when he wrote:

> There are some Western critics of Zen who contend that the Oriental approach to Zen does not necessarily apply to the Western way of thinking and that therefore the West must have or discover its own method whereby Zen can be readily made understandable for them. This is true in one way, but not at all in another way. To be sure the East, that is China and Japan, has had a long history of Zen, and "Zen" is a familiar word to them, and "satori" is not a strange and inaccessible experience. It is imagined that the East is, therefore, naturally at an advantage in this respect. For the Western people, however, this is not the case, and it is thought that their approach must be different.
>
> Superficially, this may sound reasonable. But the fact is, Zen is as remote for the Easterner as it is for the Westerner when Zen tells us to change or reverse our usual way of understanding. This is to say, Zen teaches that in order to understand a mountain to be a mountain in the Zen way, this experience is to be negated first—a mountain is not a mountain—and it is only when this negation is understood that the affirmation "a mountain is a mountain" becomes Reality. This identity of contradiction is at the basis of all Zen thought however bizarre and irrational they may appear to a Westerner as well as an Easterner.[20]

Suzuki's protest notwithstanding, Jung would still argue that Westerners need to arrive at the same insights, but on the basis of a natural evolution of the contents of their own psychology. A psychological or spiritual development that ignores or represses the instincts and the unconscious simply perpetuates the split between these two aspects of the Western psyche introduced by Christianity and perpetuated by modern-day rationalism.

A perusal of Western traditions analogous to those of the East points out the psychological differences between the two cultures. Western mysticism, with very few exceptions, is highly personal, emotional, and religious. Eastern mysticism, again with some exceptions, is primarily impersonal, intuitive, and philosophical. Western alchemy, on the whole, is externally oriented: the alchemists worked with matter in order to produce the miraculous philosophers' stone that they believed would embody the essence of all being and bestow immortality on its possessor. Eastern alchemy, in its most evolved form, is internally oriented, seeking through the practice of meditation to extract the germ of immortality from the body of the practitioner and then to bring about a union of this personal germ with the universal Mind or Tao. Western religious and alchemical traditions take into account sexuality and gender differences in a much more personal way than the Eastern religions, with the exception, perhaps, of Hinduism. In fact, this emphasis on the personal, sexual, and romantic seems to be a unique characteristic of the Western path of psychological development. The Christian mystics, for example, are often moved by an erotic-like desire for a union with their "beloved," their "bride" or "bridegroom," and they experience the mystical union in ecstatic states analogous to romantic and sexual love. The Western alchemists worked with their *soror mystica*, whether a real woman or a soul sister, and the alchemical imagery makes use of the anthropomorphic figures of the King and the Queen as symbols of the opposite principles and depicts the final *coniunctio* in sexual terms. When sexuality and the sexual union appear in Eastern religions, for example in tantric yoga, the connection is seldom personal or romantic.

——— *Gathering the Light*

On the contrary, such feelings are to be eschewed. The goal is to use the psychological and physiological energies aroused by sexual feelings for the purpose of an impersonal and nonromantic experience of oneness. Similarly, Eastern alchemists speak of sublimating the "generative force" that develops in the genitals and of "copulation" between the positive and negative energies, but the entire process takes place within the body of the adept and is without reference to any personal feelings of sexuality and love.

Given the Western emphasis on personal feelings and love, it is not surprising that Western psychotherapy has developed a treatment for furthering conscious and mutually affirming relationships between men and women. Eastern spirituality, in spite of its humanism and compassion, tends to treat relations between men and women primarily in terms of social roles, in other words, impersonally. There is a portrait of Bodhidharma, by an unknown seventeenth-century Japanese artist, in which the legendary founder of Zen Buddhism is depicted with a common prostitute. She is straddling his shoulders and calmly resting her hands on the top of his head. He is trying to look up at her and is deeply perturbed. I think the painting illustrates the fact that in spite of its commitment to wisdom, through the experience of ultimate reality, Zen has failed to come to terms with the personal embodiment of wisdom—the anima. She is a common prostitute, not even a geisha, because no personal relationship has been established with her. (See illustration on page 118.)

In Jung's opinion, psychotherapy is the appropriate Western method for the expansion of consciousness: it takes into account both our personal and cultural characteristics and is based on an empirical and scientific study of human psychology. The psychology he has in mind is not the behavioral, cognitive, or Freudian model that dismisses the spiritual aspects of human experience. In this regard, Jung has a particular quarrel with Freudians. The Freudian school, he

Can West Meet East?

Bodhidharma and a Prostitute *by an unknown seventeenth-century Japanese artist. By focusing on the archetype of the Self, Zen leaves unresolved the relationship of the meditator to the archetypes of the personal unconscious, among them the anima and the animus and the corresponding personal relationships between men and women.*

———— *Gathering the Light*

argues, got stuck at the Oedipus motif, that is, the archetype of incest. It failed to see that the Oedipus complex is an exclusively masculine affair, that sexuality and aggression are not the sole determinants of psychic life, and that incest is closely connected to and sometimes a symbolic expression of the religious instinct. In his autobiography Jung writes:

> In retrospect I can say that I alone logically pursued the two problems which most interested Freud: the problem of "archaic vestiges" and that of sexuality. It is a widespread error to imagine that I do not see the value of sexuality. On the contrary, it plays a large part in my psychology as an essential—though not the sole—expression of psychic wholeness. But my main concern has been to investigate, over and above its personal significance and biological function, its spiritual aspect and its numinous meaning, and thus to explain what Freud was so fascinated by but was unable to grasp.[21]

For Jungians, who for over sixty years have been labeled mystical and unscientific by the more established schools of psychology, it is odd to observe the current "discovery" of the role of religion in therapy and in psychological development. However, an impressive effort in this vein is *Transformations of Consciousness,* by Ken Wilber, Jack Engler, and Daniel P. Brown, mentioned earlier. This book, which contains the Rorschach study of meditators referred to previously, purports to present the first "full-spectrum model" of human growth and development, a model that includes the psychodynamic, object-relational, and cognitive lines studied by conventional psychology and psychiatry, but also takes into serious account the "higher" or "subtler" lines and stages embodied in the world's great contemplative and meditative disciplines.[22] The fact is that Jungian psychology, from its inception, has had a "full-spectrum" model of human development. It always took into account the psychology of spiritual development in the religious traditions of both the East and the West, and it always was and still is receptive to new data on the stages of development investigated by conventional psychology.

ACTIVE IMAGINATION

In addition to psychotherapy, Jung introduced the practice of active imagination as another potent method for exploring the unconscious and nurturing psychological growth. He discovered the technique after his break with Freud when he went through a long period of disorientation and introspection. The rupture with Freud was only the precipitating cause of what was probably an inevitable coming to terms with his own personal psychology and a necessary review of his goals at midlife. During this period Jung wrote very little, and, having given up his Freudian perspective, he simply listened to his patients with no preconceived notions and no attempts at interpretation. Personally, he felt lost, deeply disturbed, and under intense psychological pressure. Twice he reviewed all the details of his life, paying particular attention to childhood memories, but nothing helped. Finally he decided that since he knew nothing, he would just submit himself to the impulses of the unconscious. The first thing that then came to him was a childhood memory from his tenth or eleventh year when he had had a passionate spell of playing with building blocks and stones. The memory was accompanied by a good deal of emotion. He realized that that small boy was still alive in him and possessed a creative life that he now lacked. But how to get back to that? For as a grown man he could not imagine himself playing with stones and building blocks. Yet he felt he had no choice if he was going to bridge the gap and reconnect with that creative energy. "This moment was a turning point in my fate," he writes, "but I gave in only after endless resistances and with a sense of resignation. For it was a painfully humiliating

―――― *Gathering the Light*

experience to realize that there was nothing to be done except play childish games."[23]

This is a fairly typical experience for people who are faced with the prospect of doing active imagination. Usually one must reach a point of despair and give up all egoistic and conscious aims. My own breakthrough came when I was working with an analyst who was my opposite in typology. I was then an intuitive thinking type, he a sensation feeling type. After several months of mutual frustration, he finally said to me, with a tone of exasperation, "If you can't get any feeling into this, we just can't continue." I felt despondent: I had come all the way to Zurich and was deeply committed to inner work. But the next time, I came with a tiny clay figure I had made. His face lit up—here was something he could relate to. He picked up the figurine and touched it gingerly. At last, we had found a point of contact. And I had learned how to let go of all conscious intentions and control and allow the unconscious to take the lead.

Having overcome his resistance, Jung played with the blocks for days, building an entire village, with cottages, church, and castle. As he played, he noticed that he had regained his emotional and mental equilibrium. He thought about what he was doing: " 'Now, really, what are you about? You are building a small town, and doing it as if it were a rite.' " He had no answer to the question, only the inner certainty that he was on the way to discovering his own myth. The building game was only the beginning. It led to the release of a stream of fantasies that he later carefully wrote down. But to grasp these fantasies, stirring in him below the surface, he felt that he had to let himself drop into them. Here again he was resistant, and more than that, he was afraid that should he be overcome by the fantasies, he would lose his sanity. But once again, he saw no way out. As a way of maintaining some conscious control, he decided to undertake the encounter as a scientific experiment.

Can West Meet East? ————

It was during Advent of the year 1913—December 12, to be exact—that I resolved upon the decisive step. I was sitting at my desk once more, thinking over my fears. Then I let myself drop. Suddenly it was as though the ground literally gave way beneath my feet, and I plunged down into dark depths. I could not fend off a feeling of panic. But then, abruptly, at not too great a depth, I landed on my feet in a soft, sticky mass. I felt great relief, although I was apparently in complete darkness. After a while my eyes grew accustomed to the gloom, which was rather like a deep twilight. Before me was the entrance to a dark cave, in which stood a dwarf with a leathery skin, as if he were mummified. I squeezed past him through the narrow entrance and waded knee deep through icy water to the other end of the cave where, on a projecting rock, I saw a glowing red crystal. I grasped the stone, lifted it, and discovered a hollow underneath. At first I could make out nothing, but then I saw that there was running water. In it a corpse floated by, a youth with blond hair and a wound in the head. He was followed by a gigantic black scarab and then by a red, newborn sun, rising up out of the depths of the water. Dazzled by the light, I wanted to replace the stone upon the opening, but then a fluid welled out. It was blood. A thick jet of it leaped up, and I felt nauseated. It seemed to me that the blood continued to spurt for an unendurably long time. At last it ceased, and the vision came to an end.[24]

He was stunned by the vision. He realized it was a hero and solar myth, a drama of death and rebirth, but, at the end, instead of a new dawn, there came that outpouring of blood. He did not understand that. Only when World War I broke out less than a year later was he able to make sense of it.

He continued to explore the inner images and fantasies. In the course of the work he would get so emotionally wrought up that he resorted to yoga breathing exercises to calm himself. Then he would plunge in again and let the images and inner voices speak. Actually, he was doing just the

───── *Gathering the Light*

opposite of what yoga and certain forms of meditation strive to achieve. Instead of seeking to let go of and eventually abolish all psychic contents and images, he concentrated on the images and let them affect him emotionally. He found that when he was able to translate the emotions into images—that is, to find the images that were concealed within the emotions—he was calmed and reassured. He realized that it was highly therapeutic to uncover the images buried within the emotions, and he incorporated this discovery in the practice of active imagination.

In order to seize hold of the fantasies, I frequently imagined a steep descent. I even made several attempts to get to the very bottom. The first time I reached, as it were, a depth of about a thousand feet; the next time I found myself at the edge of a cosmic abyss. It was like a voyage to the moon, or a descent into empty space. First came the image of a crater, and I had the feeling that I was in the land of the dead. The atmosphere was that of the other world. Near the steep slope of a rock I caught sight of two figures, an old man with a white beard and a beautiful young girl. I summoned up my courage and approached them as though they were real people, and listened attentively to what they told me. The old man explained that he was Elijah, and that gave me a shock. But the girl staggered me even more, for she called herself Salome! She was blind. What a strange couple: Salome and Elijah. But Elijah assured me that he and Salome had belonged together from all eternity, which completely astounded me. . . . They had a black serpent living with them which displayed an unmistakable fondness for me. I stuck close to Elijah because he seemed to be the most reasonable of the three, and to have a clear intelligence. Of Salome I was distinctly suspicious. Elijah and I had a long conversation which, however, I did not understand.[25]

I will not pursue Jung's interpretation of these figures, which can be found in *Memories, Dreams, Reflections*. My aim is to describe how Jung came upon and developed the method of encountering the unconscious in a direct, active way. He felt that this method, which he later called active imagination, was the appropriate Western technique, analogous to certain forms of Eastern meditation that aim to depotentiate the images of the unconscious and lead to greater consciousness. Active imagination, unlike many Eastern techniques, however, stays grounded in the personal psychology of the practitioner and confronts the unconscious forces operating in that individual. Without such an *Auseinandersetzung*— having it out or coming to terms—with the unconscious, all psychological or spiritual development rests on a shaky foundation at best, or is incompatible or even in conflict with the underlying psychic contents.

Jung's commentary to *The Secret of the Golden Flower* has one of the earliest formulations of active imagination. "Each time the fantasy material is to be produced," he writes, "the activity of consciousness must be switched off." Actually, one must enter into a semitrance or trancelike condition.

> In most cases the results of these efforts are not very encouraging at first. Usually they consist of tenuous webs of fantasy that give no clear indication of their origin or their goal. Also, the way of getting at the fantasies varies with individuals. For many people, it is easiest to write them down; others visualize them, and others again draw or paint them with or without visualization. If there is a high degree of conscious cramp, often only the hands are capable of fantasy; they model or draw figures that are sometimes quite foreign to the conscious mind.
>
> These exercises must be continued until the cramp in the conscious mind is relaxed, in other words, until one can let things happen, which is the next goal of the exercise. In this way a new attitude is created, an attitude that accepts the irrational and the incomprehensible simply because it is happening. This attitude would be poison for a person who is

—————— *Gathering the Light*

already overwhelmed by the things that happen to him, but it is of the greatest value for one who selects, from among the things that happen, only those that are acceptable to his conscious judgment, and is gradually drawn out of the stream of life into a stagnant backwater.[26]

A more detailed outline of the technique can be found in Jung's last major work, *Mysterium Coniunctionis: An Inquiry into the Separation and Synthesis of Psychic Opposites in Alchemy:*

You choose a dream, or some other fantasy-image, and concentrate on it by simply catching hold of it and looking at it. You can also use a bad mood as a starting-point, and then try to find out what sort of fantasy-image it will produce, or what image expresses this mood. You then fix this image in the mind by concentrating your attention. Usually it will alter, as the mere fact of contemplating it animates it. The alterations must be carefully noted down all the time, for they reflect the psychic processes in the unconscious background, which appear in the form of images consisting of conscious memory material. In this way conscious and unconscious are united, just as a waterfall connects above and below. A chain of fantasy ideas develops and gradually takes on a dramatic character: the passive process becomes an action. At first it consists of projected figures, and these images are observed like scenes in the theatre. In other words, you dream with open eyes. As a rule there is a marked tendency simply to enjoy this interior entertainment and to leave it at that. Then, of course, there is no real progress but only endless variations on the same theme, which is not the point of the exercise at all. What is enacted on the stage still remains a background process; it does not move the observer in any way, and the less it moves him the smaller will be the cathartic effect of this private theatre. The piece that is being played does not want merely to be watched impartially, it wants to compel his participation. If the observer understands that his own drama is being performed on this inner stage, he cannot remain indifferent to the plot and its dénouement. He will notice, as the actors appear one by one and the plot thickens, that they all have some purposeful relationship to his conscious situation, that he is being addressed by the unconscious and that *it* causes these fantasy-images to appear before him. He therefore feels compelled, or is encouraged by his analyst, to take part in the play and, instead of just sitting in a theatre, really have it out with his alter ego. For nothing in us ever remains quite uncontradicted, and consciousness can take up no position which will not call up, somewhere in the dark corners of the psyche, a negation or a compensatory effect, approval or resentment. This process of coming to terms with the Other in us is well worth while, because in this way we get to know aspects of our nature which we ourselves would never have admitted. It is very important to fix this whole procedure in writing at the time of its occurrence, for you then have ocular evidence that will effectively counteract the ever-ready tendency to self-deception. A running commentary is absolutely necessary in dealing with the shadow, because otherwise its actuality cannot be fixed. Only in this painful way is it possible to gain a positive insight into the complex nature of one's own personality.[27]

There are other ways of getting at the unconscious than those mentioned in the above paragraphs, including music, dance, filmmaking, poetry, and story writing. Some people even manage to maintain an ongoing daily dialogue or relationship with a dream figure or some other personified content of the unconscious, such as the anima or the shadow. Lucid dreaming, for those who have the talent or are able to acquire the skill, is another way of doing active imagination.

Today there are many techniques (and drugs) for releasing unconscious fantasies and repressed or long-forgotten memories and emotions. On the whole, these exercises have a salutary effect on the psyche. The danger remains the same that concerned Jung—the possibility that the released fantasies and emotions will overpower the conscious mind and lead to severe psychotic episodes or unleash a full-blown psychosis. Because of this danger, Jung tended to recommend the practice of active imagination only after some analysis and preferably toward the end of it, when it became a way for the patient to maintain a relationship with the unconscious and continue the work of psychic integration. Jung would regard many of the current techniques for bringing up unconscious material as passive imagination. Usually, their aim is the release of unconscious fantasies for the sake of emotional catharsis or the cultivation of a peaceful state of mind for the sake of a spiritual uplift. The hallmark of active imagination, by contrast, is that it seeks to further the attainment of psychological wholeness, that is, the integration of one's personal unconscious and the establishment of an ongoing relationship between the ego and the Self. Indeed, Marie-Louise von Franz, one of Jung's closest collaborators, feels that active imagination is *"the* most powerful tool in Jungian psychology for achieving wholeness—far more efficient than dream interpretation alone."[28]

The Jungian analyst James A. Hall proposes that a distinction be made between "pure" active imagination, done intrapsychically and relying only on the imagination, and "enactments," expressing the imagination by means of a medium such as writing, movement, or painting. The distinction rests on the notion that pure active imagination allows the fullest play of imagination without the "restraints caused by resistances in the medium of expression."[29] I am not certain the distinction is valid, for the simple reason that the imagination often seeks out and even demands the medium through which it wants to be expressed, for example, the stones and building blocks that Jung used. The medium, whether paint, words, music, or dance, becomes part and parcel of the imaginative activity, so that no real separation can be made between the "intrapsychic" fantasy and the external enactment.

In the end, it is a combination of the inherent psychological endowments—not everyone's psyche is as fertile or as ener-getically charged as Jung's—and the conscious attitude of the practitioner that makes for the successful use of active imag-ination, and not the medium in which it is done. A person's psychological makeup provides the impetus and the raw material. The conscious attitude determines how this impetus and raw material will be used.

GUIDELINES FOR ACTIVE IMAGINATION

In this regard, there are certain guidelines for the practice of active imagination. First of all, it should be done alone. This requirement in itself is a source of resistance for many people. But the aim of active imagination is to have a personal encounter with the unconscious. The presence of other peo-ple, no matter how inconspicuous or well intentioned, has an effect on the unconscious and on one's reactions to it.

Active imagination should not be done with figures of living people. There are two reasons for the prohibition. Intense concentration on another can affect that person's psyche: this possibility is the basis of certain types of prayer, of white and black magic, and of voodoo. Also, it is almost impossible to do active imagination with a living person without one's personal desires entering into the process. Using the technique for personal ends subverts its purpose, which is the objective exploration of the unconscious for the sake of attaining wholeness.

Another rule is that the inner world must be accorded the same reality as the outer world. For example, if in a visuali-zation someone is run over by a car, one can't say: "Oh, it's just a fantasy. Let me do it again, and this time the car will miss." If someone is run over by a car in an active imagina-tion, that is a real psychic event, and the fantasy must be pursued from that point onward.

——— *Gathering the Light*

Once one has learned to let the unconscious images, fantasies, or voices (not everyone has a talent for visualization) come to consciousness, it is important to hold on to them. This is especially true when doing active imagination without some sort of medium that can fix the process in outer reality. One must overcome the natural tendency of the psyche to pursue its kaleidoscopic play with shapes and images. Like Menelaus in the *Odyssey,* one has to hold on to Proteus, the Old Man of the Sea, until he takes his true form and reveals what he knows. The first image or fantasy that appears has to be held and interacted with. In the beginning, stopping the flow of the conscious mind, keeping it in a suspended state of attention, and then holding on to the first unconscious images that arise entail a tremendous effort of concentration. Active imagination of this kind, which works with the imagination alone, hardly lasts more than five or ten minutes before exhaustion sets in; sometimes one or two minutes is all that one can manage. When the process seems to flow freely and effortlessly, chances are that one is engaged in a passive form of imagination. It is also important to fix the encounter in writing, either while it is happening or immediately after, otherwise it will sink back into the unconscious. Anyone who has had any dealings with the unconscious knows how easily even the most vivid dreams, images, and insights are lost in the conscious light of day.

The use of a medium through which the unconscious can express itself is in some ways an easier form of active imagination than the one that relies on imagination alone. The process of writing, drawing, and so on, helps to anchor the attention so that less purely mental effort is required. In either case, as the images and fantasies unfold, it is important to suspend all reality-based, critical, or aesthetic judgments; otherwise the unconscious becomes cramped, its spontaneity destroyed. On the other hand, one cannot take a neutral stand either. One must react to the events taking place in the same way that one would in everyday life. In this way, the same conflicts, emotions, and complexes that are experienced in daily life come up in active imagination and have to be dealt with.

There are many levels at which the unconscious can be engaged. On the whole, the more easily active imagination flows and the less intense one's reactions, the more superficial the level of engagement. The level and intensity of engagement determine whether the experience will have a lasting and transformative effect on one's psychic structure and personality.

Different forms of active imagination activate different aspects of the psyche. Also, a person's psychology should be taken into account when selecting the form or medium to work with. For example, people who are facile with words should probably avoid the dialogue form. Artists should avoid drawing or painting unless they can really not care about the content and the aesthetics of what comes out. Intuitive types seem to do well with clay. Some people need to get their bodies into the process and work best with dance or movement. A degree of experimentation is usually required before one hits upon the technique that allows the unconscious to surface with the least amount of conscious intervention, engaging it at a level deep enough for the process to have a significant psychological effect. Sometimes two techniques—say, dialogue and painting—can be used at different times. In such cases, each technique seems to work on a different aspect or level of the psyche, so that a parallel development is taking place. When people stop active imagination, or one form of it, and then return to it, they usually find that they pick up exactly where they left off. This simple fact actually provides dramatic evidence that work done on the unconscious has a lasting effect, and conversely, that when no such work is being done, no development takes place on its own.

———— *Gathering the Light*

When doing active imagination it is important to enter into the process fully, with one's entire being, retaining one's common sense, one's sense of humor, and the full range of one's emotional and ethical reactions. Actually, Marie-Louise von Franz writes, "one must be potentially 'whole' already in order to enter the drama; if one is not, one will learn to become so by painful experience."[30] The potential wholeness the practitioner brings to active imagination is important because the images and figures of the unconscious have positive and negative, good and evil sides, often changing from one to the other, and one must not just cling to the positive and minimize the negative. In this connection, Jung writes that even though we cannot avoid making moral judgments, "we must beware of thinking of good and evil as absolute opposites. The criterion of ethical action can no longer consist in the simple view that good has the force of a categorical imperative, while so-called evil can resolutely be shunned. Recognition of the reality of evil necessarily relativizes the good, and the evil likewise, converting both into halves of a paradoxical whole."[31] The relativization of both good and evil does not, however, mean that these categories are invalid or no longer exist; it is just that one can't simply be dogmatic or simple-minded about them. The integration of the personal unconscious and a coming to terms with the archetypes of the collective unconscious are not possible without this attitude. In Tibetan Buddhism the encounter with the positive and negative archetypal forces is described as experiencing the mandalas of the peaceful and wrathful deities. Normally this experience occurs after death, but one can prepare for it by evoking these deities in meditation and establishing a connection with them.

As can be gathered from the above description, active imagination is really a form of meditation. Jung feels that for Westerners it is the most appropriate form of meditation and that if it is pursued for some time, it leads to the same

Can West Meet East? ————

psychological development and spiritual realization as the Eastern methods. To begin with, one need not have—and usually it is best not to have—any spiritual or religious expectations. As the work progresses and the archetypes are encountered, the religious aspects become apparent of their own accord. Active imagination has the advantage that it starts with the personal concerns and psychological problems of the practitioner and provides a gradual, easily ascertained process of development. In these respects, it is a method and an orientation that can be used with benefit by Eastern practitioners of meditation as well. Another advantage of active imagination is that the process remains rooted in a person's individual and cultural symbolism. For Westerners, practicing meditation with images from Eastern cultures and religious traditions is akin to speaking in a foreign language. The words, images, and tones do not resonate with one's being in the same way as one's mother tongue. Radmila Moacanin, who has a thorough personal grounding in both Jungian psychology and Tibetan Buddhism, writes: "Tibetan Buddhists urge Westerners not to abandon the values of their own culture. In fact a proper understanding of one's own culture and being deeply rooted in it—they would say—is a prerequisite for venturing into and benefiting from practices of a foreign tradition. There is also always the danger of grasping the literal rather than the intrinsic meaning of symbols and rituals, and thereby going astray and getting lost in one's practice."[32]

The practice of active imagination, too, is fraught with all kinds of dangers, mistakes, and possibilities of misuse and self-deception. It should not be undertaken without the guidance of someone who has had extensive experience with the method and who is not caught up in shamanistic or power-oriented showmanship.

CHAPTER FIVE

MEDITATION AND ALCHEMY

Images of the Goal in East and West

If a man understands the Tao in the morning, it is well with him
even when he dies in the evening.

—*Confucius*

Jung's decision to undertake a thorough study of Western alchemy was inspired by his reading of *The Secret of the Golden Flower,* a ninth-century Chinese Taoist text describing the process of meditation in alchemical terms. When he first read the book in German translation in 1928 and wrote a commentary for it, he completely ignored its alchemical aspects. He simply tried to make the text comprehensible to Western readers by explaining its basic psychological concepts and assumptions.

In the foreword to the second German edition of the book, Jung acknowledged the oversight: "At that time it seemed unimportant to me that *The Secret of the Golden Flower* is not only a Taoist text of Chinese yoga but also an alchemical tract. However, a subsequent, deeper study of Latin tracts has corrected my outlook and shown me that the alchemical nature of the text is of prime significance."[1]

In this chapter I would like to demonstrate that the meditation aspect of the book is of equal importance and that the alchemical imagery refers to psychological and spiritual processes that take place during meditation. However, the experiences that the *Golden Flower* describes do not take place in every form of meditation. They are characteristic of meditation practices that aim at a direct experience of the Self in its most fundamental and universal form—as Pure Consciousness or Formless Form. In Jungian terms, this is the uroboric aspect of the Self, the potential world of being, outside of time, in which the Self contains in a latent state all the archetypes that eventually separate out and take on manifest form.

Jung's last book, *Mysterium Coniunctionis,* gives a final account of his researches in alchemy. The concluding chapter deals with the symbolism of the "greater" *coniunctio*—the union of opposites through which the *lapis philosophorum,* the "philosophers' stone," was to be produced. In what follows, I will summarize this chapter of Jung's, emphasizing his psychological interpretation of the *coniunctio* and its development. Then I will outline the Eastern conception of the stages leading up to the final *coniunctio* and the goal of psychological-spiritual transformation in meditation. Finally, I will compare the two systems and further discuss the meditation complex that I introduced in chapter 3 as an important process in psychological-spiritual development.

JUNG'S INTERPRETATION
OF THE *CONIUNCTIO*

The *coniunctio,* or alchemical "marriage," was the last procedure through which the alchemists hoped to produce the philosophers' stone. The task of the *coniunctio* was to unite previously "purified" substances that existed in a complementary but opposed position in relation to each other. That complementary opposition was depicted in different ways: heaven/earth, sun/moon, spirit/matter, masculine/feminine, fire/water, mercury/lead, and so on. The terms on each side of the opposition were interchangeable: *heaven* was synonymous with *sun, spirit, masculine, fire,* and *mercury,* while *earth* was synonymous with *moon, matter, feminine, water,* and *lead.* The work of alchemy consisted of separating out these opposites, which were thought to exist in various metals and other physical substances, and then purifying the differentiated elements until only the essence of each remained. By means of *coniunctio*—the reunion of the essence of the two opposites—the alchemists hoped to produce a substance that would have miraculous, utopian qualities: cure all ills, ensure immortality, bestow wisdom, reconcile all conflicts, establish peace and harmony.

In psychological terms, the opposites that need to be differentiated, purified, and then reunited are the conscious and unconscious aspects of the psyche. The final goal is a reconstitution of the Self. The alchemical *mysterium coniunctionis,* Jung writes, "is nothing less than a restoration of the original state of the cosmos and the divine unconsciousness of the world. . . . It is the Western equivalent of the fundamental principle of classical Chinese philosophy, namely the union of *yang* and *yin* in *tao.*"[2]

In his discussion of this final union, Jung makes use of the three stages proposed by the alchemist Gerard Dorn:

1. overcoming the body by a *unio mentalis* of soul and spirit;
2. reuniting the separated-out soul and spirit with the body; and
3. uniting soul, spirit, and body with the original *unus mundus*—the world in which all is one.

Like later alchemists, Dorn began to realize that the alchemical opus was not merely an external enterprise but also involved the *psyche* of the alchemist. Jung notes that Dorn was possibly the first Western alchemist to recognize that the philosophers' stone was hidden in the *individual* and that the goal was reached by reading and meditating. Dorn therefore insisted that students of alchemy have a good physical and moral constitution and approach the work with a religious attitude.

Dorn was also unique among the alchemists in his definition of the final goal of the opus as the union of the "integrated" or whole individual with the *unus mundus*. The usual alchemical goal stopped with the second stage, the production of the *lapis*. With his addition of the third stage, Dorn pushed the Western opus a step closer to the Eastern alchemical-meditative goal. Not surprisingly, Dorn's three stages parallel the typical medieval descriptions of the process of meditation: first turning away from the world of sense, then turning toward the inner world of mind, and finally uniting with God.

Like many alchemists, Dorn distinguished between *soul* and *spirit*. Soul lies caught in the embrace of *physis* (matter); it animates and favors the body and everything sensuous and emotional. Yet the soul also burdens the body; its desires extend "beyond physical necessity." Its wish-fantasies, as Jung writes, impel the body to deeds, both good and ill, to which it would not rouse itself, "for the inertia of matter is inborn in it and probably forms its only interest except for the satisfaction of physiological instincts."[3]

According to Dorn, soul can be recalled from its entrapment in the world of fantasy and matter by the "counsel of the spirit." Spirit has a connection with the eternal world outside time and therefore is able to convey to the soul "a certain 'divine influx' and the knowledge of higher things."[4] Jung elaborates by saying that spirit is more independent of the body and its affects than the soul and consists of such higher faculties as reason, insight, and moral discrimination.

The Western alchemical distinction between soul and spirit is also found in Chinese alchemy. Soul is *p'o*, written with the combined characters for "white" and "demon." Spirit is *hun*, written with the combined characters for "clouds" and "demon." During life they cohabit in human nature: *p'o* clings to the heart and creates desires, moods, and impulses to anger; *hun*, by contrast, lives in the eyes during the day and in the liver at night. At death the two separate. *P'o* sinks downward and becomes *kuei* (demon), a ghost. *Hun* rises upward and becomes *shen* (spirit). Both return to their origins—*p'o* to its elemental connection with matter and earth, *hun* to "the primal beginning," "the great emptiness," with which it is identical in form. *P'o* wanders toward the west while *hun* wanders toward the east, but eventually they reunite in sacred marriage at the "Yellow Springs"—the land of the dead and the place of resurrection.[5]

The *unio mentalis*, the first stage of the *coniunctio*, consists of the separation of the soul from the body and its union with the spirit. In *Mysterium Coniunctionis*, Jung interprets the separation of the soul from the body as the withdrawal of projections "from the bodily sphere and from all environmental conditions relating to the body."[6] It means "a turning away from sensuous reality, a withdrawal of the fantasy-projections that give 'the ten thousand things' their attractive and deceptive glamour. In other words, it means introversion, introspection, meditation, and the careful investigation of desires and their motives."[7] Jung interprets the union of the soul with spirit as the establishment of "a spiritual-psychic counterposition—conscious and rational insight—which would prove immune to the influences of the body."[8] In psychological terms, the *unio mentalis* implies the possibility of governing natural bodily impulses and the blind desires of the soul by the conscious insights of the spirit.

As everyone knows, this method of self-governing is no easy or permanent accomplishment. Stripping away illusions about ourselves and about the world can be experienced as painful and distressing, for we are brought face to face with the dark, unconscious shadow side of our personality. Depression and a certain dissociation of the conscious personality inevitably follow this intrapsychic confrontation. In the language of alchemy, the withdrawal of the soul from the body places the body in a moribund condition, described as the grave, death, *nigredo*, melancholia, an affliction of the soul, confusion.

Having united the soul with the spirit while placing the body in a deathlike state, the alchemists were next faced with the difficult task of reuniting the now conjoined soul and spirit with the "inanimate" body. If things were left to take their natural course, the soul, being more attached to the body, would simply leave the spirit and return to its former union with the body. Psychologically this "would mean that the insight gained by the withdrawal of projections could not stand the clash with reality and, consequently, that its truth could not be realized in fact."[9] Hence the *unio mentalis*—the essence of the united soul and spirit—had to be carefully sealed in the hermetic vessel so that it would not escape and revert to its separated and contaminated condition. Only by maintaining the tension of opposites caused by a feeling awareness of the shadow can one proceed to the next task— the embodiment of the impulses of the spirit in one's daily life.

As the reference to the hermetic vessel, or *vas*, indicates, Dorn suddenly shifts the procedure from body, soul, and spirit, and attempts to effect the second stage of the *coniunctio* through work on physical substances. In Dorn's case, these substances were honey, chelidonia (celandine, an herb of the poppy family), rosemary flowers, the herb mercurialis (dog's mercury), red lily, and human blood. The entire concoction was then mixed with "the heaven of the red or white wine."[10] This last "substance," called *caelum* (heaven) or the "philosophic wine," was prepared from grain, grape pips, or other seeds. The essence of these wine-producing seeds was "reduced to its 'greatest simplicity' by 'assiduous rotary movements,' whereby the pure is separated from the impure."[11] Then, according to Dorn:

> You will see the pureness floating to the top, transparent, shining, and of the colour of purest air. . . . You will see the heretofore spagyric [secret] heaven, which you can bedeck with the lower stars. . . . The lower stars are all individuals produced by nature in this lower world by their conjunction with heaven, like [the conjunction] of the higher with the lower elements.
>
> The caelum therefore is a heavenly substance and a universal form, containing in itself all forms, distinct from one another, but proceeding from one single universal form. Wherefore, he who knows how individuals can be led on to the most general genus by the spagyric art . . . will easily find the universal medicine.[12]

The *caelum* was the universal medicine that could unite all opposites, including that of the *unio mentalis* with the body. (Incidentally, *medicine*, "to heal, to make whole" has the same etymological root, as *meditation*.) But which body? The human body? Or the "phlegm" (the "dead" matter) that remained in the retort after the *caelum* was extracted? The answer for the alchemists was both. The consciousness of the alchemists was still characterized by a quality of *participation mystique;* they believed that a change effected on the physical plane automatically had a corresponding effect on the spiritual or psychological plane. Similarly, the *caelum* was considered to be both the spiritual essence hidden in the human body *and* the quintessence sublimated from the materials in the retort.

Jung wryly observed that it never occurred to the alchemists "to cast any doubt whatsoever on this intellectual monstrosity."[13] Moreover, the entire procedure was nonsense from a literal perspective, for no universal medicine, philosophers' stone, or gold was ever produced by this or any other alchemical method. But if one realizes that the alchemical endeavor was motivated by the *psyche's search for wholeness,* then it begins to make sense as a means of conducting careful work on unconscious fantasies and symbols. The later alchemists (such as Dorn and his teacher Paracelsus) had an inkling of this fact, for they insisted that the right theoretical or spiritual approach to the opus was as important for its success as practical work in the laboratory.

After outlining his recipe for the production of the *caelum,* Dorn writes: "It is true that these things are scarcely to be understood . . . unless one has full knowledge of the terms used in the art, and these we . . . have defined in . . . treating of meditative knowledge. . . . No man can truly know himself unless first he see and know by zealous meditation . . . *what* rather than *who* he is."[14] Dorn then describes the production of the universal medicine in spiritual and cosmic terms—still, however, making no distinction between the spiritual and physical realms. As the individual begins to turn away from his or her physical nature, freeing the mind from worldly cares and distractions, "little by little and from day to day . . . [he or she will perceive] with . . . mental eyes and with the greatest joy some sparks of divine illumination."[15] The soul, being moved by this, will unite with the spirit:

> At length the body is compelled to resign itself to, and obey, the union of the two. . . . That is the wondrous transformation of the Philosophers, of body into spirit, and of the latter into body. . . . Seek the incorruptible medicine which not only transmutes bodies from corruption to their true disposition . . . but preserves those so disposed . . . for any length of time. Such medicine you can find nowhere but in heaven. For heaven, by virtue of invisible rays coming together from

all sides in the centre of the earth, penetrates, generates, and nourishes all elements, and all things that arise from the elements. This child of the two parents, of the elements and heaven, has in itself such a nature that the potentiality and actuality . . . of both parents can be found in it. [And what remains or is generated in the center of the earth is the stone—the center and the stone being one and the same.] . . . Learn from within thyself to know all that is in heaven and on earth. . . . Knowest thou not that heaven and the elements were formerly one, and were separated from one another by divine artifice, that they might bring forth thee and all things? If thou knowest this, the rest cannot escape thee. . . . Thou wilt never make from others the One which thou seekest, except first there be made one thing of thyself.[16]

In *Mysterium Coniunctionis* Jung has explained that what the alchemists called *meditation* he called "coming to terms with the unconscious."[17] He interpreted the second stage of the *coniunctio* as "the union of consciousness (spirit), differentiated by self-knowledge, with a spirit abstracted from previously unconscious contents."[18] The production of the *caelum*, therefore, is a "representation of the individuation process by means of chemical substances and procedures."[19] The *caelum* and its various synonyms (the center, the stone, the child of heaven and earth) is the *imago Dei* (God-image) imprinted in man—in Jung's terms, the archetype of the Self. He does not interpret the meaning of the "lower stars" that bedeck the secret invisible heaven, but I think it is clear that they refer to individuals who have attained wholeness: the "immortals" who become centers of conscious energy in the collective unconscious—Christ or the buddhas. The psychic preparation of the *magisterium* as described by Dorn, Jung observes,

is therefore an attempt, uninfluenced by the East, to bring about a union of opposites in accordance with the great Eastern philosophies, and to establish for this purpose a

Meditation and Alchemy ———

principle freed from the opposites and similar to the *atman* or *tao*. Dorn called this the *substantia coelestis,* which today we would describe as a transcendental principle. This "unum" is *nirdvandva* (free from the opposites), like the *atman* (self).[20]

The production of the *caelum* or the *lapis* was the final goal in most of Western alchemy. Dorn was exceptional in this regard, because for him this was only the second stage of the *coniunctio.* For Jung, Dorn's notion was in accord with the nature of psychic reality: "Just as a lapis Philosophorum, with its miraculous powers, was never produced, so psychic wholeness will never be attained empirically, as consciousness is too narrow and too one-sided to comprehend the full inventory of the psyche."[21] Moreover, the sense of inner security realized by an experience of the Self is never permanent. More than once it is shattered under the impact of reality. Unlike the alchemists, we cannot dispose of the residue of the "wine"-producing materials. No matter how much soul and spirit we extract or sublimate from the body, the unconscious, and the outer world, we remain psychically and organically bound to them. (Perhaps at death some individuals are finally free.)

The third and final stage of the *coniunctio* for Dorn was the union of the whole human being with the *unus mundus.* By the *unus mundus* he meant, Jung writes, "the potential world of the first day of creation. . . . the eternal Ground of all empirical being."[22] In more secular terms, one can speak of it as the "transcendental psychophysical" background of all empirical phenomena. Jung speculated that as physics reaches deeper into the mystery of matter, and psychology penetrates the unknown nature of the psyche, the two fields may discover that their subject matters converge.[23] The hypothesis of an underlying unity of all being would help explain synchronistic and parapsychological phenomena. And while mandala symbolism is the psychological expression of the *unus mundus*, synchronicity, Jung contended, is its parapsychological equivalent.[24]

Dorn offered no procedure for the attainment of this union; he simply hoped and expected that once the second stage was achieved, the third would naturally follow. The third conjunction, Jung explained, is "the relation or identity of the personal with the suprapersonal atman, and of the individual tao with the universal tao."[25] The distinction between the personal Self and the transpersonal or universal Self is important yet rarely encountered in Jungian literature. Most writers seem to combine the two, although it is obvious that there are as many expressions of the Self as there are layers of the unconscious—personal, familial, tribal, racial, universal. In wording the distinction in the above manner, Jung was building a bridge between the psychologies of the East and the West. The experience of wholeness, perfection, and universality described by Dorn, he writes, can be compared to the "ineffable mystery of the *unio mystica*, or *tao*, or the content of *samadhi*, or the experience of *satori* in Zen."[26] That experience is also universally defined by mandala symbolism.

Too often, people assume that the experience of the Self is always numinous, fascinating, and inspiring. Actually, "all degrees of emotional evaluation are found, from abstract, colourless, indifferent drawings of circles to an extremely intense experience of illumination."[27] Similarly, people assume that an experience of the Self will make one whole and integrated, solving all problems: the old expectation of the alchemical *lapis*. This is only potentially so. One may have an experience of enlightenment or Self-realization that is not succeeded by a transformation of the personality, because the experience did not become the *spiritus rector* (guiding spirit) of the person's daily life. Also, because the Self is both brighter and darker than the ego, problems arise that may go beyond the ego's capacities: "either one's moral courage fails, or one's insight, or both, until in the end fate decides."[28]

THE *CONIUNCTIO* IN
EASTERN ALCHEMY

The Western alchemical goal and procedures are paralleled by Eastern alchemy. As in the West, in recent centuries the tendency has been to view the alchemical procedure as more of an internal than an external enterprise: the elixir of immortality was to be produced *within* the alchemist. In this later version of Chinese alchemy, the body is the matter into which spirit has fallen and from which it must be extracted through meditation. In the East, alchemy was amalgamated into the already existing religious beliefs and yogic practices. In China, the final product (of which The Secret of the Golden Flower is a good example) is an intriguing mixture of alchemy, *kundalini* and tantric yoga, Taoist and Confucian philosophy, and Buddhist meditation.

The Chinese view is that every individual possesses a central core that is an aspect of the universal Tao (Jung's *imago Dei*). In the Tao, the principles of opposites, *yin* and *yang*, are united. In human beings, the yang principle is expressed as *hsing* (the essence of human nature) and the yin as *ming* (life). *Hsing* is the spirit that is the basis of all consciousness, while *ming* is the life force inherent in physical existence and in destiny or *karma*. Jung translated *hsing* as *logos spermaticos* and *ming* as *eros*. Before birth, *hsing* and *ming* "are intermingled and form a unity, inseparably mixed like the sparks in the refining furnace, a combination of primordial harmony and divine law."[29] At birth the two separate: *hsing*, which is responsible for the formation of the human body, withdraws into a passive, potential state of being, while the conscious or perceiving spirit (*hun*) takes its place. The conscious spirit dwells in the heart, which is the seat of consciousness for the ancient Chinese (like the head for us). *Ming,* which is responsible for the course of one's life, sinks to the lower abdomen and becomes the personal soul (*p'o*).

Spirit and soul together make up the personality, but they are in constant conflict with each other, attracted and repelled, each striving for supremacy. Spirit loves movement and is very adaptable; but it is also bound to the soul, to feelings and desires. Thus, "day and night it wastes the primal seed till the energy of the primal spirit is entirely used up. Then the conscious spirit leaves the shell and goes away."[30] If the person has led a moral life, the conscious spirit floats upward and reunites with the primal spirit. If one's life has been motivated by base or selfish feelings and desires, the conscious spirit crystallizes downward and sinks into hell, the realm of instincts and desires.

The goal of Chinese alchemy was to free the spirit from its entanglement with instinctive drives and emotions by providing a place in the human body where the primal spirit (*hsing*) could crystallize. For that to occur, the personal spirit (*hun*) and soul (*p'o*) have to be joined to the transpersonal spirit (*hsing*) and soul (*ming*), and then *hsing* and *ming* have to be reunited. The individual's prenatal condition is thus reestablished, but now it is situated in a conscious adult and in the human body. The product of this union is a spiritual-psychic structure called the "golden flower" or the "elixir of life" (*chin-tan,* literally golden ball, golden pill), which ensures the conscious survival of the individual after the death of the body.

In *The Secret of the Golden Flower,* the way to achieve this union was through the introversion and concentration of psychic energy: "If one wants to maintain the primal spirit one must . . . first subjugate the perceiving spirit. The way to subjugate it is through the circulation of the light . . . and the maintaining of the centre. . . . The work on the circulation of the light depends entirely on the backward-flowing movement, so that the thoughts . . . are gathered together."[31] The "circulation of the light" refers to a number of psychological processes. It entails the fixing of attention and the focusing of concentration inward. In this way, an enclosure or *temenos* is created. This is identical to what I have termed the meditation complex. Once concentration is focused, the "light" or energy of consciousness begins to accumulate and "the sun wheel" begins to turn—that is, the Tao or the Self takes over the work of concentration. The meditator must now bring down the concentrated energy to the lower abdomen; this is the "center" that is to be maintained. If the concentration is kept only in the head or between the eyes, the spirit energy (*hsing*) does not unite with the soul energy (*ming*), the spirit cannot be "crystallized," and no embryo or fruit of the golden flower develops. Therefore, the "circulation of the light" also refers to this repetitive cyclical mixing of spirit (psychic) and soul (physical) energies, of the positive (yang) and negative (yin) principles.

"If one practices the circulation of the light," the text continues, "one must forget both body and heart [mind]. The heart must die, the spirit live."[32] And if one is able to contain the primal energy of the spirit, one can "prolong the span of life, and can then apply the method of creating an immortal body by 'melting and mixing.' "[33] The text assumes a knowledge of the internal alchemical tradition without which most of the procedures and terms make no sense. An example of the earlier internal alchemical techniques is provided by Charles Luk in his *Taoist Yoga: Alchemy and Immortality*. In this earlier method influenced by *kundalini* and tantric yoga, the goal is achieved by sublimating the "generative force" (*ching*, sperm), which develops in the genitals; it becomes semen if allowed to flow outward and *ch'i* (vitality or vital energy) if held back and sublimated. One is tempted to translate the "generative force" of this earlier alchemy as the Freudian libido. However, a full description of the generative force brings the concept closer to Jung's translation of *hsing* and *ming* as *logos spermaticos* and *eros* than to Freud's *libido*. For it turns out that the generative force corresponds to the "primal spirit" of the *Golden Flower* and is identical with the spirit Mercurius in Western alchemy. Like Mercurius or the *lapis*, the generative force has many names and refers to the beginning of the work as well as to the goal:

> The real generative force is the true seed in the human body. Since it is indistinct, it is called t'ai chi (the supreme ultimate) [i.e., the golden elixir or the final union of opposites] and since it is the beginning of creativity, it is called prenatal (hsien t'ien). Since it is the undivided yin-yang (the union of the negative and the positive) it is called the One vitality. It is also called the yellow bud (huang ya), the mysterious pearl (hsuan chu), and positive generative force (yang ching). If this generative force is frozen between heaven (the head) and earth (the lower abdomen) it becomes the light of immortal seed.[34]

The generative force can be extracted from the genital fluids and, after a certain point in the process, also from saliva. Instructions are given about the proper method of swallowing saliva so that it is not discharged as waste but changes into the generative force. There is also discussion about how the generative force is to be gathered, through breathing techniques, when the penis is erect. Older men are advised to masturbate to arouse the genital organs and then to gather the generative force, while younger men are taught breathing techniques to check a stubborn erection. (The text does not address how the process is done by women, although we may assume it entails a similar arousal of the genital organs.) The process of sublimation is accomplished by a combination of mental concentration and regulated breathing:

By regulated breathing is meant deep breathing that reaches the lower abdomen to arouse the inner fire and then bring pressure on the generative force already held there, forcing both fire and generative force to rise in the channel of control in the spine to the head. This is followed by an out breathing which relaxes the lower abdomen so that the fire and generative force that have risen to the head sink in the channel of function in the front of the body to form a full rotation in the microcosmic orbit. These continued ascents and descents cleanse and purify the generative force which is then held in the lower tan t'ien under the navel so that it can be transmuted into vitality [ch'i].[35]

There are three *tan-t'ien* ("field of the drug," or the psychic center where the alchemical agent is produced). The lower *tan-t'ien* is about one and a half inches below the navel where the generative force is stored; it is also called the "ocean of lead" or the "cavity of the dragon." The middle *tan-t'ien* is at the solar plexus, where the generative force is transmuted into vitality (*ch'i*). The upper *tan-t'ien* is between and behind the eyes, where the vitality is transmuted into mercury (spirit or *shen*). (In *kundalini* yoga these three centers correspond to the *svadhishthana, manipura,* and *ajna* chakras.) As work progresses, the lower *tan-t'ien* plays the role of a burning stove supporting a cauldron that contains the generative force. With further work, the cauldron rises to the solar plexus and then to the brain, where it is called the "precious cauldron," the "original cavity of the spirit," or the "ancestral cavity."[36]

As the generative force is gathered and circulated, positive and negative energies are brought to bear on it. For example, the adept is instructed to roll the eyes (which are considered to hold positive energy) from left to right, as the generative force passes various cardinal points in its "microcosmic orbit" through the body, which holds negative energy. (See figures 7–9.) After a time, when the generative force has been purified and matured by this "inner copulation" of the

---

Gathering the Light

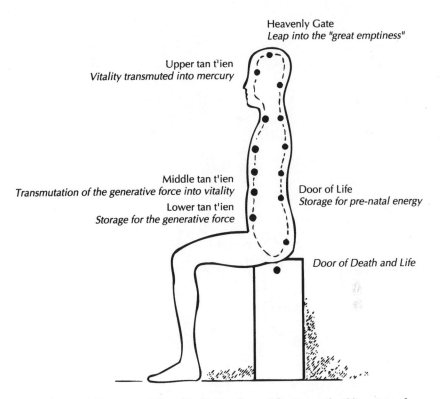

Heavenly Gate
Leap into the "great emptiness"

Upper tan t'ien
Vitality transmuted into mercury

Middle tan t'ien
Transmutation of the generative force into vitality

Lower tan t'ien
Storage for the generative force

Door of Life
Storage for pre-natal energy

Door of Death and Life

Figure 7. The microcosmic orbit depicts the purification and sublimation of instinctive and emotional psychic energy through sustained concentration of the circulation, storage, and transformation of energy in the three tan-t'ien, or psychic centers of the subtle body. If such a transformation does not take place during a person's lifetime, there is no leap into the "great emptiness," i.e., no Self-realization, and the cycle of death and birth continues.

negative and positive principles, a "crystallization" occurs. The first manifestation of this crystallization is the appearance of an inner light, which is white like moonlight, and "its fullness is equivalent to one half of a whole."[37] This white light indicates the position of the "precious cauldron" in the head and should not be confused with the luminous inner fire (produced in the lower *tan-t'ien*) that rises to the head with the microcosmic orbiting of the generative force.

The next step requires a descent of the crystallized positive

Meditation and Alchemy ————

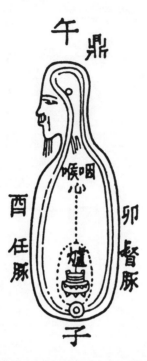

Figure 8. The microcosmic cauldron and stove. Unlike Western alchemists, who sought to produce the philosophers' stone with external elements, Eastern alchemists used the instinctive and psychic energy of the body to give birth to the immortal fetus or diamond body.

generative force (*hsing*) to the lower *tan-t'ien*, where it unites with the negative generative force (*ming*), which emits a golden light. The light is reddish yellow and "its fullness is equivalent to the other half of the whole."[38] The union of the crystallized positive and negative generative forces is the immortal seed. Further concentration on the immortal seed in the lower abdomen will cause a golden light to appear in the white light between the eyebrows. At the appearance of this positive light, which is the union of the two lights, the

<hr />

Gathering the Light

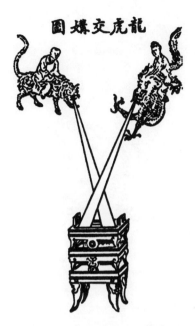

Figure 9. The dragon (negative vitality) and the tiger (positive vitality) "copulating" in the alchemical cauldron in the brain to realize the oneness of heaven and earth. After a sustained period of meditation, enough psychic energy is sublimated so that the central focus moves from the abdomen to the head and the former instinctive and emotional energy is experienced as a vision of light— the first manifestation of the archetype of the Self. This archetype is constellated by the repeated bringing together of instinctive and spiritual energies, here depicted by the dragon and the tiger.

practitioner should move the concentration to the head so as to unite the energies of *hsing* and *ming* and help the primal spirit form the immortal fetus and the elixir of immortality.

The final stages require the practitioner to help the primal spirit emerge from the fetus and leap into the "great emptiness" through the heavenly gate at the top of the head (the *sahasrara* chakra). (See figs. 10 and 11.) Then the primal spirit leaves the human body to appear "in countless transformation bodies," or to appear in the world to perform the work

Meditation and Alchemy

道 胎 圖

Figure 10. *The initial expression of the archetype of the Self is joined with the remaining instinctive and emotional energy of the body. The result is a more concrete expression and experience of the Personal Self, here represented by the immortal fetus.*

出 胎 圖

Figure 11. *This illustration depicts the leap into the "great emptiness" or the attainment of full Self-realization and buddhahood. In Western terms, this is a breakthrough into the* unus mundus *and an experience of the archetype of the transpersonal Self.*

—————   *Gathering the Light*

of salvation, alleviating human suffering, curing the sick, and so on. In time, even these activities, as well as others, such "as walking on the sun and playing with the moon" and the "thousands of transmutations," should be stopped.[39] One should gather the primal spirit in its original cavity again and enter a state of profound stillness. "This is called the condition of a hibernating dragon."[40] It leads to a further sublimation of the primal spirit and to the extinction of all phenomena:

> As time passes while dwelling in utter serenity, the true fire of positive spirit will develop fully and radiate inside and outside its cavity to become all-embracing, shining on heaven, earth and myraid things which will appear within its light.
>
> The training should continue no matter how long it takes until the four elements (that make the body) [body, breath, corporeal and incorporeal souls, symbolized by water, fire, wood, and metal] scatter, and space pulverises leaving no traces behind; this is the golden immortal stage of the indestructible diamond-body. This is the ultimate achievement of the training which now comes to an end.[41]

THE *CONIUNCTIO* IN MEDITATION

With the above exposition as background, it is now possible to understand the abbreviated four-stage summary of the *coniunctio* in *The Secret of the Golden Flower*. First, the spirit must be brought down to have "intercourse" with the energy of the lower abdomen:

> In time, the primal spirit transforms itself in the dwelling of life into the true energy. At that time, the method of turning of the millwheel [the microcosmic orbit] must be applied so that it becomes the Elixir of Life. That is the method of concentrated work.
>
> When the Life Elixir pearl is finished the holy embryo can be formed; then the work must be directed to the warming

and nourishing of the spiritual embryo. That is the method of finishing.

When the energy body of the child is fully formed, the work must be so directed that the embryo is born and returns to emptiness. That is the method of ending the work.[42]

Following the procedures of this alchemical opus requires intense inward focusing and concentration. The procedures play the same role as mantras, koans, and visualizations in other meditation practices. Since the goal of Self-realization can be achieved by various methods, it must be the *concentration itself*, rather than the content of concentration, that is responsible for this development.

Even though the *Golden Flower* and its companion text, *The Book of Consciousness and Life,* make use of alchemical imagery, they actually define the entire process and its goal in psychological terms. The latter text states: "This embryo is nothing corporeally visible . . . but is in reality the spiritual breath-energy of the ego. . . . When spirit and breath-energy [soul] are firmly united and thoughts quiet and immobile, this is described as the embryo."[43]

In the earlier alchemical texts the tendency toward concretization is stronger. The opus is done with a combination of "chemical" (physiological) and psychological energies and, as in the West, the two are not clearly differentiated. And although in the later texts there is no mention of "generative energy," there are still references to the creative spirit that can "flow outward" with the semen, and to the necessity of sublimating the "seed" into energy if one is to attain longevity.

Jung's often quoted statement from *The Secret of the Golden Flower*—"When the right man . . . makes use of wrong means, the wrong means work in the right way. . . . But if the wrong man uses the right means, the right means work in the wrong way"[44]—refers to this issue. The right man using the wrong means is the adept withholding and sublimating the genital energy. The wrong man using the right means is "the bodily union of man and woman from which spring sons and daughters."[45] The text continues: "The fool wastes the most precious jewel of his body in uncontrolled lust, and does not know how to conserve his seed-energy. When it is finished, the body perishes. The holy and wise men have no other way of cultivating their lives except by destroying lusts and safeguarding the seed."[46]

This is a leftover notion of physiological alchemy and entails a projection of the creative spirit and energy onto genital functioning. Like all projections, it has a kernel of truth. In this case, that truth is that the sexual and religious drives are closely related: both seek union and wholeness, and both are associated with feelings of ecstasy that accompany the release of tension and the union of the ego with a psychic content greater or other than itself. The gratification of sexual desires, therefore, may satisfy or lessen the drive for psychic or spiritual wholeness. The same applies to creative energy: it can find satisfaction in the parenting of children, which may reduce the need for cultural achievement. Hence comes the emphasis on celibacy—or, in concrete terms, on the retention of genital fluids—in many religious practices.

Generally speaking, it appears that the later stages of the *coniunctio* are more elaborated in Eastern than in Western alchemy. Western alchemy, on the other hand, seems more differentiated in the preliminary and secondary stages. Western alchemy, Jung writes, ends with the production of the *lapis*, which corresponds to the crystallization of the elixir of life into the pearl or the golden flower. If Jung is correct, then the evolution of the *lapis* into the spiritual embryo and child is a development that is missing in Western alchemy. But there are Western alchemical images of the *foetus spagyricus*, the *filius macrocosmi*, and the *filius philosophorum*. Jung considers these simply synonyms for the *lapis* when, in fact, they might refer to a further differentiation of the *lapis*.

The emergence of the embryo through the top of the head and its leap into the "great emptiness" corresponds to Dorn's third stage—the union of the "whole" man with the *unus mundus*. In Western alchemy, no procedure is offered for that development. There also does not seem to be a Western equivalent of the countless transmutations in space where "every separate thought takes shape and becomes visible in colour and form" and where "all separate shapes appear as bodies."[47] Perhaps these notions are foreshadowed in the Western depiction of the miraculous and transformative capacities of the *lapis* and of its ubiquity and multiplicity. Even the Eastern goal of further sublimating the spiritual embryo and its dissolution into nothingness so that "space pulverizes, leaving no traces behind" has a parallel in the West. A fourteenth-century text, quoted by Jung, states:

> It was through their knowledge of the art that the old philosophers knew of the coming of the end of the world and the resurrection of the dead. Then the soul will be united with its original body for ever and ever. The body will become wholly transfigured [*glorificatum*], incorruptible, and almost unbelievably subtilized, and it will penetrate all solids. Its nature will be as much spiritual as corporeal. When the stone decomposes to a powder like a man in his grave, God restores to it soul and spirit, and takes away all imperfection; then is that substance [*illa res*] strengthened and improved, as after the resurrection a man becomes stronger and younger than he was before.[48]

This pulverized and reconstituted "resurrection body" is identical with the "indestructible diamond body" of Chinese alchemy. Perhaps Jung's conclusion that Western alchemy ends with the production of the *lapis* has to do with the fact that Western alchemy does concern itself more with the

---

Gathering the Light

earlier stages of the opus and provides only sporadic references to the further evolution of the *lapis*.

Even though Jung compares Dorn's third stage, union with the *unus mundus*, to the *unio mystica*, the Tao, *samadhi*, or *satori*, his interpretation of the first two stages does not take into account the possibility that some of the imagery may refer to psychological events that occur during the process of meditation. Instead, he interprets the separation of soul from body as the withdrawal of projections. He defines the resulting deathlike state of the body (the *nigredo*) as a depression caused by a confrontation with the shadow and the loss of illusions about ourselves and the world. He sees the union of soul with spirit as the establishment of conscious and rational insight relatively immune from the influences of the body and the emotions. He views the difficulty of maintaining the *unio mentalis* intact or the containment of the spirit Mercurius in the *vas* as analogous to the difficulty of holding on to the insights gained by the withdrawal of projections. The reunion of the *unio mentalis* with the moribund body and the production of the *lapis* is equated with the union of consciousness with the "spirit" abstracted from previously unconscious contents and with the attempt to realize this spirit in practice. And just as the *lapis* was never produced, Jung concludes that psychic wholeness will never be attained empirically because consciousness is too narrow to comprehend the entire psyche.

Acquaintance with Eastern alchemy and with accounts of meditation experiences raises the possibility of another interpretation of the *coniunctio* stages. As his comparison of Dorn's third stage with the *unio mystica* indicates, Jung was aware of this possibility. Moreover, he considered all of alchemy a form of active imagination. If the *prima materia* and the spirit Mercurius embedded in matter are seen as synonyms for the unconscious, he writes, then the alchemical opus can be translated as follows:

Take the unconscious in one of its handiest forms, say a spontaneous fantasy, a dream, an irrational mood, an affect, or something of the kind, and operate with it. Give it your special attention, concentrate on it, and observe its alterations objectively. Spare no effort to devote yourself to this task, follow the subsequent transformations of the spontaneous fantasy attentively and carefully. Above all, don't let anything from outside, that does not belong, get into it, for the fantasy-image has "everything it needs." ("*Omne quo indiget*" is frequently said of the lapis.) In this way one is certain of not interfering by conscious caprice and of giving the unconscious a free hand. In short, *the alchemical operation seems to us the equivalent of the psychological process of active imagination.*[49]

In spite of this connection between alchemy and meditation noted by Jung, when it came to an interpretation of Dorn's first two stages—which were derived from medieval meditation instructions—Jung chose to discuss the *coniunctio* imagery only in an analytical psychological manner. Perhaps his concern about being labeled a "mystic" made him shy away from the conclusion that the *coniunctio* imagery was also a depiction of psychological processes that occur during meditation. The other possibility is that he considered the experiences that take place during meditation similar to the visionary experiences of the alchemists and felt that both consisted of projections that had to be interpreted and understood in psychological terms. Or he may have thought that the experiences of the alchemists and the mystics express elements of the objective or collective psyche and do not belong to the psyche of any particular individual. But the latter conclusion does not seem warranted, for Jung quotes numerous alchemists, saints, and others who were personally transformed by their encounter with the objective psyche. There is a problem here, because as I will try to indicate briefly below, it is possible to see the *coniunctio* stages and goal as descriptions of actual psychological experiences that take place during meditation. These experiences do need to be discussed in psychological terms, but not only in the terms in which Jung dealt with them. Perhaps his interpretation applies to the practice of active imagination and to other forms of meditation, but it is incomplete or inapplicable when applied to practices, such as Zen meditation, that from the beginning aims exclusively at the experience of the archetype of the Self in its primorial form.

THE MEDITATION COMPLEX
IN ALCHEMY

A meditation-centered view of *coniunctio* imagery would maintain that the separation of the soul from the body refers to the meditation practice of withdrawing psychic energy from physical sensations, emotions, and thoughts. The separation of the soul from the body is not just a withdrawal of projections, as Jung believed, but a refusal to be psychologically moved by any sensations, feelings, thoughts, or images. The resulting deathlike condition of the body is an actual experience and not just a metaphor or a symbol of depression; Saint Augustine describes it as a state midway between sleep and death. The union of the soul with spirit has to do with the union of the psychic energy that was withdrawn from the body, emotions, and thoughts with the energy of empty or suspended consciousness. This union of the two energies does not establish conscious and rational insight immune from the influences of the body, but *creates a new psychological energetic field, the meditation complex.*

The difficulty of maintaining the *unio mentalis* does not have to do with the problem of holding on to the insights gained by the withdrawal of projections; rather, it arises from the difficulty of maintaining concentration, for the psychic energy gathered in the meditation complex seeks to return to its natural dispersal among the physical, emotional, and

CONIUNCTIO *imagery as interpreted from alchemical,*
psychological, and meditational points of view

ALCHEMY	PSYCHOLOGY	MEDITATION
Separation of soul from body	Withdrawal of psychological projections	Withdrawal of psychic energy from body, emotions, thoughts
Deathlike condition of the body; *nigredo*	Depression as inner psychological incubation	Loss of awareness of the body
Union of soul with spirit: *unio mentalis*	Insight free from compulsion of complexes and instincts	Union of withdrawn psychic energy with "empty" consciousness
Difficulty of maintaining *unio mentalis* due to mobile nature of spirit	Problem of retaining insights gained from withdrawal of projections	Difficulty of maintaining concentration
Reunion of *unio mentalis* with inanimate body	Embodiment of insights gained in daily life	Holding concentration in the lower abdomen
Hermetic *vas* or alchemical furnace	Maintaining a spiritual-psychic counterposition to the instincts	The meditation complex
"Assiduous rotary movements" applied to substances in the *vas*	Circumambulation of the Self: winding path of individuation	"Circulation of the Light": rhythmic pattern of concentration
Distillation, bathing, washing	Conscious work on complexes and unconscious attitudes	Transforming psychic energy withdrawn from somatic and psychic functions
Whitening: *albedo*	Conscious illumination, emotional equilibrium	Vision of moonlike luminescence; feeling of deep stillness
Caelum: universal medicine that unites all opposites	Symbolic image of the Self	Vision of transparent shining sky; sense of unity and oneness.
Production of the *caelum*	Working on one's individuation process	First experience of the transpersonal Self; *samadhi, kensho*
Production of *lapis*	Solidifying psychological wholeness in real life	Crystallization of united energy of opposites: "Golden Flower"
Union of *caelum* with *unus mundus*	Self-Actualization	Union of personal *atman* with suprapersonal *Atman;* Self-realization, Enlightenment

Gathering the Light

mental functions. Furthermore, the reunion of the *unio mentalis* with the inanimate body is not about applying the insights gained to daily life and realizing them in the real world; rather, it is about focusing and holding the meditation complex in the area of the lower abdomen.

The purpose of this abdominal focus is twofold. First, placing the attention in the lower abdomen centers and anchors the meditation complex in an area of the body that can maintain tension for long periods of time. If the meditation complex is held in the head or chest, the head begins to throb or the chest feels constricted. Second, the focus of attention in the lower abdomen stimulates sensations and feelings connected with that area of the body, and the psychic energy so stimulated is now used to build up and sustain the meditation complex. In addition, the lower abdomen is associated with the *manipura* chakra, the fire center: in psychological terms, the center of emotional life. The meditation complex is actually the alchemical furnace or the hermetic *vas* that is placed over the "fire" of one's emotional being. This is where raw psychic energy is transformed or sublimated.

The alchemical application of "assiduous rotary movements" to the chemical substances in the *vas* that represent the *unio mentalis* is identical with the Eastern notion of the "circulation of the light" and the rotation of positive and negative energies. This parallel use of rotary movements (1) reflects the fact that circumambulation of the Self is a basic principle of psychological development; (2) is an expression of the circular, mandala-like quality of the Self composed of both positive and negative forces; and (3) refers to the meditation practice of maintaining a steady focus of attention or "con-centration," in the etymological meaning of the word. In the beginning concentration is connected with the rhythm of breathing, but later there is a rhythm to concentration that may reflect the wavelike energetic patterns of the brain and the nervous system.

The alchemical procedure of *distillatio* and the related images of "bathing" and "washing" are not only references to conscious work on one's complexes and unconscious attitudes; they also refer to the transformation of psychic energy that takes place when the energy is withdrawn from somatic and psychic functions and held in suspension in the meditation complex. To the extent that alchemical imagery is a depiction of events taking place within the psyche, it appears that that energy is gradually cleansed or decontaminated of its former associations. Just as angry or sexual energies are charged with given feelings, for example, this decontaminated energy has a feeling associated with it; the usual comparison is with clear mountain air or a fresh mountain spring.

Both Western and Eastern alchemy posit a new stage, the *albedo* or whitening, that results after a certain amount of "washing" and "distilling" have taken place. Psychologically, the *albedo* is interpreted as conscious "illumination" and emotional equilibrium—seeing things in an objective light—after the complexes and unconscious affects have been subjected to analysis. In meditation, the whitening pertains to the vision of a subtle moonlike luminescence that suffuses one's entire being. This takes place after a certain level of proficiency in concentration has been attained, and it heralds the onset of a new form of consciousness characterized by emotional stability and equanimity.

Jung interprets the production of the *caelum* described by Dorn as a representation of the individuation process; the *caelum* itself is interpreted as an image of the Self. For the practicing meditator, the *caelum*—or the appearance of a transparent, shining sky—is often described as an actual experience. Far more than an alchemical metaphor, the phenomenon appears after a certain amount of psychic energy has been cleansed and consciousness held empty. For example, Saint Nilus, one of the Desert Fathers, writes: "He who wishes to see what his mind really is must free himself of all thoughts; then he will see it like a sapphire or the hue of heaven."[50] A contemporary meditator exclaims: "I felt as though I were looking at the vast, utterly transparent sky."[51] Jung is right: the *caelum* is an image of the Self, but it is *also* a phenomenological experience.

Jung interprets the production of the *lapis* as an attempt to establish psychic wholeness in empirical reality. He is skeptical about the permanence and extent of this union of the conscious with the unconscious; yet the existence of the Self as a more or less permanent and distinct psychological entity is a fact attested to by many, Jung included. In meditation, the production of the *lapis* (the crystallization of the purified and united psychic energy of the opposites into the golden flower) has to do with the establishment of a psychic structure that specifically embodies and functions with the energy of the Self. Prior to the existence of this structure, the Self must function through the various instincts and complexes and is affected by their characteristics.

When it comes to Dorn's third stage—the union of the *caelum* with the *unus mundus*—Jung suddenly changes his orientation and interprets this union as an actual mystical experience. To be consistent, Jung should argue that Dorn's notion is an imaginative grasp of the common transcendental ground of the psychophysical universe. Instead, Jung claims that this union of the personal *atman* or individual Tao with the suprapersonal *atman* or universal Tao concerns a "mystical" experience that is, nevertheless, "an empirical one in so far as there are unanimous testimonies from the East and West alike, both from the present and from the distant past, which confirm its unsurpassable subjective significance."[52]

Jung's reading of the final stage of the *coniunctio* as the *unio mystica* lends support to my view that the first two stages can also be interpreted as meditation experiences. According to Jung, the production of the *lapis*—psychologically, the establishment of the archetype of the personal Self as the unifying center of the personality—is the final goal of Western alchemy. Western spirituality and Eastern alchemy, on the other hand, posit a further goal—the union of the personal Self with the transpersonal Self. Even though these two archetypes of the Self are related, they represent vastly different forms of consciousness. (Perhaps the closest analogy of these differences is that of the relationship between the ego and the personal Self.) The personal Self is an aspect of the *imago Dei* and potentially possesses the attributes of the universal *imago Dei*. However, only a union of the two gives the person a complete experience of the power and extent of the universal Self.

With the help of Eastern alchemy it is possible to identify three phases of this union. The first phase, represented by the emergence of the embryo through the top of the head, is the initial breakthrough into the realm of the *unus mundus*. The second phase entails an increased knowledge of the characteristics of this realm. *The Book of Consciousness and Life* describes this phase as one in which "every separate thought takes shape and becomes visible in colour and form." (See illustration.) These phenomena refer to the ability of the psyche to become dissociated and experience various forms of consciousness and being.

The third phase, symbolized by the diamond body, is the crystallization of the archetype of the universal Self as a permanent part of the individual's psyche. The diamond body is the immortal *dharma* body (*dharmakaya*)—the resurrection body of Christian theology and Western alchemy.[54] In her book *On Dreams and Death*, Marie-Louise von Franz has made a heroic attempt to provide some hints about how this postphenomenal, postmortal state of being can be envisioned. The mystics who have had a glimpse of this ultimate

This illustration depicts a further evolution of the experience of the archetype of the transpersonal Self. At this stage every thought and feeling can be imbued with actual form. The adept can now freely function in the psychospiritual realm and have an influence on events and people through "thought" alone. The Western alchemical analogy to this phenomenon is the miraculous ability of the philosophers' stone to "project" and "multiply" itself indefinitely.

Meditation and Alchemy

coniunctio either are reduced to silence, say it is indescribable, or proclaim: "Eye hath not seen, nor ear heard, neither have entered into the heart of man, the things which God hath prepared for them that love him" (I Cor. 2:9).

The union of the personal Self with the transpersonal Self and the creation of a psychic energy field that makes this union a permanent part of an individual's personality are the ultimate goal of meditation, both in the East and West. This achievement expresses the highest psychological and spiritual development of which human beings are capable. Such a development is a rare and unique event, because it is not wholly dependent upon the good will, skill, and effort of the practitioner. The ego can lay the groundwork, but the Self determines the rest. The alchemists, therefore, often prefaced their work with the prayer *Deo concedente,* "God willing."

In this chapter, and throughout the book, I have sought to demonstrate, and where necessary to apply and extend, Jung's contribution to an understanding of the psychology of meditation. His pioneering exploration of complexes, archetypes, psychic energy, projection, the collective unconscious, and the archetype of the Self provide the concepts that make a psychological description of the processes and goals of meditation possible. In his commentaries on a number of significant Eastern texts, such as *The Secret of the Golden Flower* and *The Tibetan Book of the Dead,* Jung attempted to make Eastern religious ideas and meditation techniques and goals comprehensible to Westerners. His wide-ranging exploration of religious, mythological, and alchemical symbolism enabled him to place contemporary expressions of individual psychology within the context of a general psychological and spiritual evolution of humanity. For example, because of his descriptions of the archetypes of the anima and animus, or soul and spirit, it is now possible to define and work with these aspects of an individual's psyche in a specific and concrete way. The same is true of the archetype of the Self—in religious terms, the *imago Dei,* the God-image present in every person. Jung provided an outline of the phenomenological structure and historical evolution of this archetype in the West in his book *Aion,* while in the concluding chapter of *Mysterium Coniunctionis,* discussed above, he made an attempt to bridge the Western and Eastern experience of this archetype. In these instances and many others, Jung was able to translate religious symbols into psychological language, without, in my opinion, distorting or destroying their basic principles and intrinsic validity. Consequently, he has given many contemporary men and women a renewed appreciation of religious symbolism and has helped heal the centuries-old split between science and religion, faith and reason.

If I were to define the leitmotif that weaves through Jung's entire life and work, I think it would consist of two basic ideas: the overriding importance of individual consciousness and the necessity of a realistic appraisal of one's personal psychology. In his youth, Jung had a dream in which he was moving slowly and painfully against a mighty wind. Dense fog was flying everywhere. His hands were cupped around a tiny light that threatened to go out at any moment. Everything depended on his keeping this little light alive. When he awoke, he realized that the light was his consciousness. Though infinitely small and fragile in comparison with the powers of darkness, it is, Jung writes, a light, our only light, and the sole treasure that each and every one of us possesses. The individual, Jung always insisted, is the carrier of consciousness; every significant discovery, every personal, moral, and social advance, is introduced and sustained by the individual. Jung's emphasis on the individual is a needed counterbalance to the ever-present danger of ego consciousness being swallowed up by unconscious, family, religious, political, and commercial forces.

His second theme, the necessity of a realistic appraisal of one's personal psychology, requires first and foremost an honest examination of our personal unconscious, of our unacknowledged strengths and weaknesses, our fears and hatreds, our egoistic passions and instinctive drives, and our all-too-human tendency to project everything we don't like about ourselves onto others. Many people are aware of this form of scapegoating, at least as a theoretical construct. But it is not often recognized that the projection of the positive aspects of our personality is also a prevalent practice and just as pernicious. The archetype of the Self and the potential for wholeness and spiritual development, for example, are regularly projected onto religious and political figures and ideas or onto the institutions of church and state. In every case, such projection and the resulting self-sacrificing devotion to external figures, beliefs, and institutions result in a loss of individual consciousness and represent an abdication of responsibility for one's personal reality. The human cost of this practice is horrendous. One need only recall the past and present persecutions, murders, wars, and atrocities committed in the name of political or religious purity or for the sake of the establishment of a religious or political paradise on the earth.

In the last two decades, many Westerners have been ensnared by the projection of the archetype of the Self onto Eastern religious figures and beliefs. In chapter 4 I discussed Jung's objections to such unconscious adoption and imitation of Eastern religions. As someone who is familiar with Western psychology and who has been at least partially exposed to Hinduism, yoga, Zen, vipassana meditation, and Tibetan Buddhism, I do not view the issue in as uncompromising a light as did Jung. I cannot speak about Europe and Europeans, but in the United States, new cultural and religious developments are not inimical to the spirit of the country. This is a culture still in formation, and its native population, whose influence is subtly felt, had Asiatic roots. Nevertheless, I do agree with Jung that a blanket adoption of spiritual beliefs and practices whose origins and evolution took place in another time and culture does violence to who we are.

It seems to me that there are a number of alternatives for Westerners who are serious about exploring Eastern spiritual concepts and meditation techniques. Some, thanks to circumstance or temperament, can wholly immerse themselves for an extended period of time in a specific Eastern religious culture and eventually come to embody it in a personal way. For most people, however, this is not a realistic option. The other choice, therefore, is some sort of partial adoption of Eastern spirituality in a contemporary Western context. That might entail, for example, devotional or meditation practice at home with periodic weekend or yearly retreats. Others find that they cannot or do not want to divest themselves of their Christian or Jewish heritage but seek to enrich their religious practice through the incorporation of yoga or vipassana or Zen meditation. Indeed, there are a good number of ministers, rabbis, priests, monks, and nuns who have contributed significantly, through scholarly or other writings and through community activities, in fostering this unique merging of Western religious beliefs and Eastern spiritual practices. And finally, there are those, like myself, who pursue personal development through psychoanalysis or psychotherapy combined with Eastern meditation. I sometimes think of this method as hatching an egg, to borrow a metaphor from *The Secret of the Golden Flower*: psychotherapy chips away at the protective ego structure from the outside while meditation supplies the necessary psychic energy for the archetype of the Self to form and eventually break through from the inside.

For a psychoanalyst who spends a good deal of time dissuading people from their illusions, projections, and unrealistic hopes and expectations about themselves, the world, and others, and whose main aim is to foster consciousness as a means of alleviating suffering, it is highly gratifying to discover that the major Eastern religions have exactly the same aims. Moreover, their basic approach and technique, even though embedded in a religious context, are essentially psychological.

Here, finally, is the place where East and West can meet and begin a mutually enriching dialogue. We know a good deal about ego psychology and the personal unconscious. The Eastern religious practitioners know a good deal about Self psychology and the collective unconscious. And both sides can readily attest, in Jung's terms, to the *self-liberating power of the introverted mind*.

APPENDIXES

WILBER ON JUNG:
A CRITIQUE

ARCHETYPES

Ken Wilber, a prolific exponent of transpersonal psychology, offers an evolutionary theory of consciousness that incorporates Western developmental and Eastern transpersonal psychology. Although openly indebted to and appreciative of Jung, he is highly critical of Jung's use of the term *archetype*. He acknowledges that Jung used the word in different ways, but argues that Jung's "classic definition" of an archetype is "a mythic-archaic image or form collectively inherited" and, as such, an exact psychic counterpart of physical instincts.[1] Far from being the classic definition, this is actually Jung's first formulation of the concept. Jung's later writings—for example, his essays "On the Nature of the Psyche" and "Synchronicity: An Acausal Connecting Principle"—describe archetypes in terms that parallel the energetic-material phenomena observed in the realm of nuclear physics.[2] In these more considered formulations, Jung no longer ties the origin of archetypes to inheritance but leaves the question open. He also adds a distinction between "archetypes" and "archetypal images." He now speaks of archetypes as innate structural *predispositions* that can be defined only in terms of form or patterns, never in terms of specific content. He also speculates that, in the end, the archetypes might be partly nonpsychic and are the ordering principles behind all material, biological, and psychological phenomena. In terms of their ordering function in the psychic field, the archetypes are mediated by the unconscious and appear in the psyche as images and ideas. These images and ideas, then, in the form of mythological symbols are common to entire cultures and epochs. For example, the various religious, philosophical, or political images and concepts that dominated certain cultures and historical periods are archetypally determined.

As for the archetype's relation to instincts, Jung concluded that in the same way that psychic contents seem to "flow over" into the physiological process, instinctual structures appear in the psyche as abstract arrangements or patterns, i.e., as archetypes. The archetypes, therefore, provide a certain "self-image" of the instincts or of their structure. Also, like the instincts, the archetypes can be described as "elementary behavior patterns," for once an archetype is energetically charged, it can take possession of the entire personality and "drive" it in a certain direction. If the same archetype becomes activated in a group of individuals, then a collective possession takes place.

It seems to me that Wilber, who is usually precise in his outline of various psychological theories, should have taken Jung's mature formulations of the concept of archetype as a basis for discussion. This is especially important in Jung's case because he was a pioneer and constantly revised and refined his original ideas. With this caveat in mind, what follows is an outline of Wilber's critique, found in *The Spectrum of Consciousness, The Atman Project, Eye to Eye,* and other writings.

Wilber argues, on the basis of Jung's initial definition, that since archetypes are inherited structures of human evolutionary development, they belong to the early stages of evolution. In contrast to Jung, Wilber wants to locate the archetypes at the teleological end of the evolutionary spectrum. He conceives the evolution of consciousness in three major hierarchical stages: the prepersonal or pre-egoic stage; the personal or egoic stage; and the transpersonal or trans-egoic stage. The line of development, then, is from an archaic collective unconscious experience of unity or wholeness, through the development of ego consciousness and the separation of subject and object, and ending in the highly evolved consciousness of transpersonal unity or ecstatic oneness experienced as a spiritual reality. He feels that both Freud and Jung confuse the prepersonal fusion of "infantile cosmic consciousness" with the transpersonal unity of the ultimate realm of being; the infantile oceanic state, he argues, is based on a pre–subject/object differentiation.

Given Wilber's erroneous view that Jung relegates the archetypes to the prepersonal collective stage of consciousness, it is understandable why he is critical of Jung's statement that "mysticism is experience of the archetypes."[3] Wilber goes on to say that "there are collective prepersonal, collective personal, and collective transpersonal elements; and Jung does not differentiate these with anything near the clarity that they demand, and this skews his entire understanding of the spiritual process."[4] Archetypes may be collective but not transpersonal, and there is nothing mystical about the collectively inherited forms. Furthermore, even if Jung defines the archetypes as "basic mythic *forms* devoid of content; mysticism is *formless* awareness. There's no point of contact."[5] Wilber speaks of "lesser" mystical states that are the direct experience of archetypes—as he defines them—which entail "finding the light beyond form," and "true" mysticism that is beyond even the archetypes, namely, "finding the formless beyond the light."[6]

Finally, Wilber argues that even though Jung borrowed the term *archetype* from the great mystics such as Plato and Augustine, he does not use the term in the way they use it. For the mystics the world over, Wilber states, "archetypes are the first subtle forms that appear as the world manifests out of formless and unmanifest Spirit. They are the patterns upon which all other patterns of manifestation are based. . . . And in most forms of mysticism, these archetypes are nothing but radiant patterns or points of light, audible illuminations, brilliantly colored shapes and luminosities, rainbows of light and sound and vibration—out of which, in manifestation, the material world condenses, so to speak."[7]

The power of the "real archetypes," the transpersonal archetypes, Wilber states, comes from their being the first form of timeless Spirit; the power of the Jungian archetype comes from its being the oldest form of temporal evolution. The only Jungian archetype that is genuinely transpersonal is the Self, he continues, but even that archetype is weakened by Jung's failure to sufficiently emphasize its ultimately nondual character. Individuation, for Jung, involves a process of differentiating oneself from the archetypes. That is true, Wilber writes, "but one must *move toward* the real archetypes, the transpersonal archetypes."[8] Had Jung not placed the archetypes toward the beginning of evolution, he "could have seen that the *ascent* of consciousness was drawn *toward* the archetypes *by* the archetypes themselves."[9]

ARCHETYPES AS SCINTILLAE

First, Jung was aware of the meaning and historical use of the term *archetype*. Strictly speaking, Plato and Augustine did not use the term. *Archetype,* Jung notes, is often used as an explanatory paraphrase of the Platonic *eidos*—idea or form.[10] Saint Augustine speaks of *"ideae principales,* which are themselves not formed . . . but are contained in the divine understanding."[11] The term occurs in the writings of the Jewish philosopher and theologian Philo Judaeus (13 B.C.–ca. A.D. 45–50), with reference to the *imago Dei* (God-image) in man. In the alchemical *Corpus Hermaticum* God is called "the archetypal light." The term is also used by the early Church Father Ireneus (ca. 140–ca. 202): "the creator of the world did not fashion these things directly from himself but copied them from archetypes outside himself."[12] A number of alchemists made use of the term when they spoke of God containing "all the treasures of his godhead . . . hidden in himself as in an archetype," and in writing that "the world is made after the likeness of an archetype."[13] Dionysius the Areopagite (Pseudo-Dionysius, sixth century) speaks of the "immaterial Archetypes" and of the "Archetypal stone."[14]

Second, Jung devotes an entire section of his essay "On the Nature of the Psyche" to the image of the archetypes as "points of light." He had probably first encountered this image in his studies of Gnostic texts that speak of the Seeds of Light that had been dispersed throughout the universe in the course of creation. For the Gnostics, salvation entailed the gathering or re-collecting of these Seeds of Light: "from wherever thou willst thou gatherest me; but

---

Appendix A

in gathering me thou gatherest thyself."[15] This self-gathering went hand in hand with an increase of self-knowledge: "He who attains to this gnosis and gathers himself from the cosmos . . . is no longer detained here but rises above the Archons."[16] (In Gnostic cosmology the Archons are the creators and rulers of the universe; God and the divine realm of light are absolutely transmundane.) The Manichaeans even had a form of Eucharist in which melons were ritually eaten because melons, with their many seeds, were thought to be a particularly rich source of the Seeds of Light.

In his studies of alchemy, Jung came across identical imagery. A sixteenth-century alchemist, Khunrath, for example, writes: "There be . . . *Scintillae Animae Mundi igneae, Luminis nimirum Naturae,* fiery sparks of the world soul, i.e., of the light of nature . . . dispersed or sprinkled in and throughout the structure of the great world into all fruits of the elements everywhere."[17] He also refers to the fiery sparks of the soul as pure *formae rerum essentiales.* Jung comments: "These *formae* correspond to the Platonic Ideas, from which one could equate the scintillae with the archetypes on the assumption that the Forms 'stored up in a supracelestial place' are a philosophical version of the latter. One would have to conclude from these alchemical visions that the archetypes have about them a certain effulgence or quasi-consciousness, and that numinosity entails luminosity."[18] Like that of the Gnostics, the task the alchemists set themselves was to free the soul particles imprisoned in matter; in their case, to distill them into the form of the philosophers' gold or stone; and, in the course of this work of redemption, to gain immortality. For example, the fourteenth-century alchemist Petrus Bonus of Ferrara writes:

> This art is partly natural and partly divine or supernatural. At the end of the sublimation there germinates through the meditation of the spirit, a shining white soul which flies up to heaven with the spirit. This is clearly and manifestly the stone. So far the procedure is indeed somewhat marvellous, yet still within the framework of nature. But as regards the fixation and permanence of the soul and spirit at the end of the sublimation, this takes place when the secret stone is added, which cannot be grasped by the senses, but only by

the intellect, through inspiration or divine revelation, or through the teaching of an initiate. . . . This secret stone is a gift of God. There could be no alchemy without this stone. It is the heart and tincture of the gold, regarding which Hermes says: "It is needful that at the end of the world heaven and earth be united: which is the philosophic Word." . . . Therefore [at this stage of the opus] God alone is the operator, while nature remains passive. It was through this knowledge of the art that the old philosophers knew of the coming of the end of the world and the resurrection of the dead. Then the soul will be united with its original body for ever and ever. The body will become wholly transfigured, incorruptible, and almost unbelievably subtilized, and it will penetrate all solids. Its nature will be as much spiritual as corporeal. When the stone decomposes to a powder like a man in his grave, God restores to it soul and spirit, and takes away all imperfection; then is that substance strengthened and improved, as after the resurrection a man becomes stronger and younger than he was before. The old philosophers discerned the Last Judgment in this art, namely in the germination and birth of this stone, for in it the soul to be beatified united with its original body, to eternal glory.[19]

The Gnostic idea of gathering the Seeds of Light and the alchemical notion of fixating the "shining white soul" are direct analogies, in projected form, of the process of meditation. The Seeds of Light and the "fiery sparks" of the World Soul that need to be gathered together or fixated in the philosophers' stone or gold refer to the naturally dispersed flow of psychic energy that must be gathered together into a concentrated point of consciousness. (The Seeds of Light would be the archetypes in their original, purely energetic manifestation, while the World Soul refers to the collective unconscious.) Such psychic unification is the goal of meditation. And enlightenment is the experience of the original unified Collective Unconscious or the Self before its dispersal among the "ten thousand things."[20]

In his essay on the nature of the psyche Jung was interested in the analogy between the *scintillae* visualized by the alchemists and his hypothesis that the unconscious is a psychic field composed of separate points of consciousness. (Von Franz compares the unconscious to an electromagnetic field with the archetypes, when activated, appearing as "excited points" in the field.)[21] He came to this conclusion because of his experience with the fragmentation of the psyche in schizophrenia, in the dissociability of the psyche in somnambulism and other trance states, in multiple personality disorders, in various compulsions and automatisms, and in auditory, visual, and dream images and fantasies. In all these instances, the unconscious operates as though at least a partial consciousness were present: there is perception, thinking, feeling, volition, and intention, and in multiple personality disorders even other egos appear.

Thus Jung interpreted the Gnostic and alchemical notions about the dispersal of the Seeds of Light or fiery sparks throughout the universe as self-descriptions on the part of the unconscious. Beginning with the Renaissance, some of the alchemists became aware of the psychological meaning of the "fiery sparks." The earlier *participation mystique* with matter began to give way, and the projection of the unconscious onto material substances and processes was gradually withdrawn. For example, Gerard Dorn describes the progress of the opus in the following way: "Little by little . . . [the alchemist] will come to see with his mental eyes a number of sparks shining day by day and more and more and growing into such a great light that thereafter all things needful to him will be made known."[22] This psychological perspective was already evident in Dorn's teacher, Paracelsus, who conceived of the *lumen naturae*, the light of nature, as something inherent to the "inner man" or the inner body (*corpus subtile*, breath body). The *lumen naturae*, according to Paracelsus, is invisible and comes from the "star" in man, and one learns about it, among other ways, through dreams: "as the light of nature cannot speak, it buildeth shapes in sleep from the power of the word" (i.e., of God).[23] Given his idea of the "stars" embodied in human beings, Paracelsus came to the conclusion that *Astronomia* was the "mother of all the other arts" and the "cornerstone" of all truth: "after her beginneth the divine wisdom, after her beginneth the light of nature," even the "most excellent

Religiones" rest on her.[24] The Apostles, for example, are "Astrologi," and every person is in essence an "Astrum," a star. Paracelsus explains, in a manner not easily comprehensible to us unless his explanation is translated into psychological terms: "Now as in the star lieth the whole natural light, and from it ["it" probably refers to the "natural light" found in the matter of the earth, the *lumen naturae*] man taketh the same like food from the earth into which he is born, so too must he be born into the star."[25] Jung comments:

> It strikes me as significant, particularly in regard to our hypothesis of a multiple consciousness and its phenomena, that the characteristic alchemical vision of sparks scintillating in the blackness of the arcane substance should, for Paracelsus, change into the spectacle of the "interior firmament" and its stars. He beholds the darksome psyche as a star-strewn night sky, whole planets and fixed constellations represent the archetypes in all their luminosity and numinosity. The starry vault of heaven is in truth the open book of cosmic projection, in which are reflected the mythologems, i.e., the archetypes. In this vision astrology and alchemy, the two classical functionaries of the psychology of the collective unconscious, join hands.[26]

In alchemical literature the fish's eye motif is even more common than the spark motif but has the same significance. Thus the *prima materia*, for instance, is to be worked until it has "the lustre of fish's eyes," or until a substance appears that "glitters like a fish's eye."[27] The allusions, Jung feels, are to the sun (God's eye) and stand for the final product, the philosophers' gold. Astrology comes into the picture again with an alchemical reference to the words of Zechariah 4:10: "And . . . they shall see the tin plummet in the hand of Zorobabel. These are the seven eyes of the Lord that run to and fro through the whole earth."[28] The seven eyes are probably the seven planets, which together with the sun and moon are the eyes of God. The constellation of the Dragon is also described as one who never sleeps and "who from the height of the Pole looks down upon all things and sees all things, so that nothing that happens shall be hidden from him."[29] This astrological Dragon is sometimes represented as carrying six signs of the zodiac upon his back, and because of this, some writers erroneously thought the symbol represented the sun's serpentine passage through the sky. In this connection, Ignatius Loyola is said to have had visions of a bright light that seemed to have the form of a serpent full of what appeared to be shining eyes. At first he was pleased by the beauty of the vision, but eventually, no doubt under the influence of Christian symbolism, he concluded that it was an evil spirit. Nevertheless, his vision, Jung writes, "sums up all the aspects of our optic theme and presents a most impressive picture of the unconscious with its disseminated luminosities."[30] Jung finds a parallel to Ignatius's vision in the multiple eyes of Purusha, the Cosmic Man in Hinduism who is thousand-headed, thousand-footed, and thousand-eyed. All the above images and visions of the scintillae, the fish's eyes, and the multiple eyes, Jung concluded, "must be understood as introspective intuitions that somehow capture the state of the unconscious."[31] The motif has the same meaning in modern dreams and fantasies, where it may appear as the starry heavens, stars reflected in dark water, nuggets of gold or golden sand scattered in black earth, as a regatta at night with lanterns reflected on the dark surface of the sea, as a solitary eye in the depths of the sea or earth, as a parapsychic vision of luminous globes or circles:

> Since consciousness has always been described in terms derived from the behaviour of light, it is in my view not too much to assume that these multiple luminosities correspond to tiny conscious phenomena. If the luminosity appears in monadic form as a single star, sun, or eye, it readily assumes the shape of a mandala and must then be interpreted as the self. It has nothing whatever to do with "double consciousness," because there is no indication of a dissociated personality. On the contrary, the symbols of the self have a "uniting" character.[32]

In Paracelsus the symbol of the Self is the "star" in a person, but it is a potential that has to be fully realized, when the individual who is born on the earth is born again "into the star." Dorn expresses the same idea: "For the life, the light of man, shineth in us, albeit dimly, and as though in darkness. . . . In this wise we are made like unto Him, that he has given us a spark of his light."[33] And again, our task is to bring the originally given and perfect light out of the darkness into which it has fallen and to reunite it with the light from which it came. Similarly, Khunrath writes that the "sparks" come from the *ruach elohim*, the Spirit of God. Among the many scintillae he distinguishes a *scintilla perfecta unici potentis ac fortis*, a perfect scintilla unique in power and strength.[34] He also refers to this scintilla as the Monad and the Sun. Monoimos the Arabian, a Gnostic mentioned by Hippolytus of Rome (ca. 170–ca. 235), taught that the First Man (Anthropos) "was a single Monad, not composed, indivisible, and at the same time composed and divisible."[35] This Monad, as the tiniest of units, which corresponds to Khunrath's One scintilla, has "many faces" and "many eyes."[36] In other words, again paradoxically, it is both one and many.

PARADOXICAL NATURE OF THE SELF

Thus for the alchemists, even though the soul or spirit substance, described variously in the above ways, is originally present in human beings and in nature, the matter in which it is embedded must be subjected to the various alchemical operations (e.g., *mortificatio, coagulatio, sublimatio, coniunctio*) in order to extract it and fix it in a stable and purified form as the philosophers' stone or gold. Jung pursues all the above references, and many others, because he feels that they are the best empirical evidence we have about the nature of the unconscious and its central archetype, the Self. The paradoxical character of the Self stems from its being both the center and the totality of the unconscious. Saint Augustine's definition of God as a circle "whose centre is everywhere and the circumference nowhere,"[37] is another attempt to describe the same paradox. As the totality of the unconscious, the archetype of the Self also encompasses both the beginning and the end of all things—it is both Alpha and Omega. This particular paradoxical aspect of the archetype is evident, for instance, in the *lapis*, which in all of alchemical literature is a symbol for the beginning and the goal of the opus. Similarly, the image of the child stands for both the *prima materia* and the philosophers' gold. The oldest pictoral symbol in alchemy of which there is documentary evidence (*Codex Marcianus*, eleventh century) is the uroboros, the tail-eater, described as "the One, the All."[38] This symbol and accompanying legend express the alchemical idea that "the *opus* proceeds from the one and leads back to the one, that it is a sort of circle like a dragon biting its own tail."[39] And one of the most pervasive figures in all of alchemy is Mercurius, who also stands for the beginning and the end of the work:

> He is the *prima materia*, the *caput corvi*, the *nigredo* [the original matter, the head of the raven, the state of blackness—all referring to the beginning of the opus]; as dragon he devours himself and as dragon he dies, to rise again as the *lapis*. He is the play of colours in the *cauda pavonis* [the peacock's tail with its combination of all colors and hence a symbol of integrated wholeness] and the division into four elements. He is the hermaphrodite that was in the beginning, that splits into the classical brother-sister duality and is reunited in the *coniunctio*, to appear once again at the end in the radiant form of the *lumen novum*, the stone. He is metallic yet liquid, matter yet spirit, cold yet fiery, poison and yet healing draught—a symbol uniting all opposites.[40]

Thus the *lapis* at the end has the same multiplicity in unity as it had in the form of the *prima materia*. Both are described as uncreated, eternal, ubiquitous, the source of all being, the Alpha and Omega, round, simple, and perfect, i.e., all-encompassing. All these descriptions and symbols are attempts on the part of the unconscious to convey to us the complex, yet simple, paradoxical nature of the Self.

A RESPONSE TO WILBER

I think that Wilber's criticism of Jung's notion of archetypes is misinformed. Contrary to what Wilber states, Jung *does* refer to the archetypes as "the patterns upon which all other manifestations are based."[41] Jung does speak of the archetypes as "radiant patterns or points of light . . . luminosities, rainbows of light." And he does speak of them as being the first forms of timeless Spirit. Their power does come from that fact and not from their being the oldest forms of temporal evolution. When Jung, therefore, said that "mystical experience is experience of the archetypes," he was referring to the archetypes as emanations of the spirit and not as inherited prepersonal collective images. Moreover, I should point out that Wilber's notion that mysticism is "formless awareness" and that "true" mysticism is beyond even the archetypes and entails "finding the formless beyond the light" fails to take into account that "formless awareness"—Nothingness—is itself an archetype. Moreover, archetypes are not "the light beyond form." The "light" itself is a conceptual or parapsychic visual manifestation of archetypes. The archetypes in themselves are in the end unknowable and irrepresentable in any manner, including such notions as "formlessness" or "empty awareness."

Again, contrary to what Wilber claims, Jung does not locate the archetypes only at the beginning of the evolutionary spectrum—they are present both at the beginning and at the end. This does not mean, however, that Jung confuses the wholeness of infantile cosmic consciousness with the transpersonal unity of the ultimate realm of being. The first is defined in alchemy as the *prima materia,* the second as the philosophers' gold. And the entire alchemical opus is devoted to the task of transforming the *prima materia* into the philosophers' gold. The alchemists recognized the similarities, even the essential identity, between the two, but they also worked to restore the original whole and unified state of the *prima materia* into the wholeness and oneness on a new level in the philosophers' gold.

The spirit Mercurius is the archetype that expresses the notion, stated much too generally by Wilber, that "the ascent of consciousness was drawn *toward* the archetypes *by* the archetypes themselves." Far from being a criticism of Jung, this was Jung's discovery and not Wilber's.

According to Wilber, Jung's archetypes are collective but not transpersonal. What is the difference? The terms are synonymous. It is Wilber who is confusing here, not Jung. What Wilber means by *transpersonal,* as he makes clear elsewhere, is really "transcendent" or "spiritual." And Jung would agree: there are indeed collective or transpersonal spiritual images, motifs, and aspirations in the psyche, and at their core lie the archetypes. And again, it is Jung and not Wilber who first proposed clear distinctions among "collective prepersonal, collective personal, and collective transpersonal" elements of the psyche. Much of Jung's writing, in fact, is an exposition of the various manifestations of these three separate psychological realms, their archetypal core, and their interactions with one another.

Jung would also object to Wilber's use of the term *transcendent* as a synonym for *spiritual,* or in such references as "transcendent consciousness." *Transcendent* means "beyond experience." It is a contradiction in terms to speak of "transcendent consciousness." Jung uses the terms "transcendent" or "transcendental" to characterize the ultimately unknowable nature of matter and spirit. For both matter and the archetypes are "beyond experience and irrepresentable," because the psyche and its contents are the only reality that is given to us *without a medium;* that is, material and archetypal reality are known to us only through the medium of the psyche.[42] Finally, even though Jung did define the archetypes as the "first form of timeless Spirit," this in no way contradicts their also being manifestations of "the oldest forms of temporal evolution." Also, the fact that the archetypes are present at the evolutionary beginning of consciousness does not exclude their being operative today in the ongoing creation and further evolution of consciousness. Each creation of consciousness, indeed every conscious or creative act, requires a new infusion of archetypal energy. Even the sustaining of consciousness and the continuity of one's personal identity depend on an ongoing connection with archetypal energy. In an analogous way, the same holds true for the physical universe:

> The exploration of the subatomic world in the twentieth century has revealed the intrinsically dynamic nature of matter. It has shown that the constituents of atoms, the subatomic particles, are dynamic patterns which do not exist as isolated entities, but as integral parts of an inseparable network of interactions. These interactions involve a ceaseless flow of energy manifesting itself as the exchange of particles; a dy-

namic interplay in which particles are created and destroyed without end in a continual variation of energy patterns. The particle interactions give rise to the stable structures which build up the material world, which again do not remain static, but oscillate in rhythmic movements. The whole universe is thus engaged in endless motion and activity; in a continual cosmic dance of energy.[43]

In Hindu mythology this cosmic dance is depicted by the image of the dancing god Shiva. Shiva is a personification of Brahman, who in turn is a symbol of ultimate reality, of the essence of all being. Shiva's dance portrays Brahman's myriad and ongoing manifestation in the world, the daily and continuous creation-preservation-destruction of the universe.

Instead of arguing erroneously that Jung places the archetypes at the beginning of the evolutionary process and thereby loses their dynamic and spiritual meaning, Wilbur might have more profitably addressed the following issue: what happens to archetypes once they become manifest in history, in space, time, and matter? For once the archetypes take on material or psychic form, they appear as energetic structures that can be defined, described, and studied; that is, they behave according to certain "natural laws." The subatomic particles, for example, behave according to the laws of quantum theory. Thus in the psychic realm, for instance, one can examine the various historical and cultural manifestations of the mother archetype or of the God-image, and draw certain conclusions about their evolution on the basis of their earliest and current form. One of Jung's coworkers, Erich Neumann, made such an attempt in his book *The Great Mother*, while Jung himself subjected the Western God-image to a historical and phenomenological examination in *Aion* and *Answer to Job*. In principle, however, there is no reason why the archetypal energy that maintains a certain phenomenal structure or symbolic form in existence cannot be withdrawn so that these physical or psychic entities become empty forms that eventually wither and die. Similarly, there is no reason why the archetypal energy cannot create entirely new phenomenal structures or symbols and imbue them with energy and life. (Perhaps the unexplained appearance and disappearance of certain species, cultures, and astronomical structures may be accounted for in this manner.) In astrology, there is even an attempt to define and anticipate the changes in fundamental energy patterns that influence life on the earth with the concept of the Platonic year. The Platonic year is a two-thousand-year cycle during which the earth moves through one of the twelve signs of the zodiac and is marked by the characteristics of that sign. Definite psychological—and, some people would say, even physical—changes accompany the end of one Platonic month and the beginning of another. These are changes, Jung writes, "in the constellation of psychic dominants, of the archetypes or 'gods' as they used to be called, which bring about, or accompany, long-lasting transformations of the collective psyche."[44] We are now, for example, passing from the aeon of Pisces into that of Aquarius and experiencing the change of archetypal dominants. (Another attempt to define the archetypal constellations that determine each moment in time is the ancient Chinese book of divination, the *I Ching*.)

In spite of Wilber's avowed aim to integrate Western and Eastern thought, his theoretical assumptions and even the style of his thinking are imbued with a strong Western bias. The presentation of his theories, whether in *The Atman Project, The Spectrum of Consciousness,* or his other writings, is highly abstract, structured, and characterized by linear, hierarchical thought. The Western bias is equally evident in the fundamental assumption of his theoretical outlook. In the prologue to *The Atman Project,* he begins with the philosopher Jan Smuts's view that nature consists of hierarchical wholes: "each whole is a part of a larger whole which is itself a part of a larger whole."[45] The universe is constantly producing "higher- and higher-level wholes, ever more inclusive and organized. This overall cosmic process, as it unfolds in time, is nothing other than evolution. And the drive to ever-higher unities, Smuts called *holism*."[46]

Wilber applies this theory to the evolution of human consciousness, which, he finds, is divided into three distinct "levels and stages." The lower levels and stages of the psyche are prepersonal, "instinctive, impulsive, libidinous, id-ish, animal, ape-like."[47] The middle stages are personal, "socially adapted, mentally adjusted, egoically integrated, syntaxically organized, conceptually advanced."[48] And the highest stages, represented by the great mystics and sages, are ones in which consciousness is transcendent, transpersonal, and transtemporal.

This hierarchic schema, with its Hegelian overtones (thesis, antithesis, and higher-level synthesis), provides the theoretical skeleton that Wilber then fleshes out in elaborate detail. In the process he tries to incorporate and classify every major Western and Eastern psychological system of thought. Western psychology, of course, deals with the prepersonal and personal spheres, while Eastern psychology deals primarily with the transpersonal realm.

Far from being a synthesis, this entire project is ruled by the core values of Western civilization—monotheism, dualism, progress. The belief in monotheism and progress is evident in the notion that the universe is constantly evolving into an all-encompassing integrated whole. The dualism is present in the stark opposition between the prepersonal and transpersonal realms—instinct versus spirit, the unconscious infantile experience of cosmic wholeness versus the transcendent experience of oneness by the mystics.

His sympathetic approach to Eastern thought notwithstanding, Wilber is not able to extricate himself from his Western unconscious and archetypal background. Also, he has gotten caught by the archetype of oneness, which organizes and embraces psychic totality. Since he is a thinking type, that archetype operates through his theoretical notions. The archetype of oneness is especially active in our day because it compensates the tremendous social, political, intellectual, and religious disruptions of the twentieth century. In his book *Flying Saucers,* Jung interprets the visions and rumors of UFOs as projections of the archetype of wholeness:

> They are impressive manifestations of totality whose simple, round form portrays the archetype of the self, which as we know from experience plays the chief role in uniting apparently irreconcilable opposites and is therefore best suited to compensate the split-mindedness of our age. It has a particularly important role to play among the other archetypes in that it is primarily the regulator and orderer of chaotic states, giving the personality [and the transpersonal or collective psyche] the greatest possible unity and wholeness.[49]

———— *Appendix A*

Because of the influence of this archetype today, Jung writes, it is "dawning on us that humanity is *one*, with *one* psyche."[50] Wilber's attempt to unify Eastern and Western thought is actually an expression of this currently active archetype.

The theoretical manner, however, in which he envisions this union is off the mark. To begin with, his notion, borrowed from Jan Smuts, that the universe is steadily evolving toward "higher- and higher-level wholes, ever more inclusive and organized," is more a pious wish or belief, motivated by the archetype of wholeness, rather than a hypothesis based on empirical data. There is no scientific evidence that evolution, whether physical, biological, or psychological, proceeds in this efficient and orderly manner. On the contrary, there is evidence that there are many false starts, dead ends, degenerations, and disappearances of once-thriving physical structures, biological organisms, and human cultures. Evolution or progress is hardly lineal or hierarchical; more often it is haphazard or spiral, with regressions or no further evolution to a larger whole growing out of a smaller whole. When it comes to psychological development, we know that it is possible to point out a person, or a culture, with highly evolved intelligence and consciousness while his, or its, instinctive, emotional, and ethical development lags far behind. In fact, the development of the higher psychic faculties may take place at the expense of progress in the instinctive and emotional realms. In other words, it is possible to have a higher consciousness that is "transcendent, transpersonal, and transtemporal" and a personal unconscious that is "instinctive, impulsive, libidinous, id-ish, animal, ape-like." I know that for Wilber this is not possible by definition, but definition is theory. The reality is that such cases occur, as evidenced by many recent accounts of unethical behavior by both Eastern and Western religious leaders.

Finally, Wilber's insistence that the Self is ultimately nondual in character is another example of his Western bias—a variation on the All-Good Deity and the basic irreconcilability of good and evil. Again, the empirical facts are that almost every major symbol of the Self, especially in the East, is dual or paradoxical in nature: the Tao is composed of *yin* and *yang*: Brahman is both being and nonbeing; the philosophers' stone is a *complexio oppositorum*. The

Heart Sutra states: form here is only emptiness, emptiness only form. In Zen, a *kensho* experience of emptiness is considered incomplete; the experience must also contain form. What is true of all these basic opposites is also true of good and evil. In the archetype of the Self, all the opposites are and are not reconciled. That is the paradox! The tension remains.

It is tempting to speculate that the core of the archetype of the Self is of a nondual nature and that there all the opposites are reconciled. But in all probability, no category, including nonduality and reconcilability, applies to this mysterious core. As soon as one attempts to characterize it in any manner whatsoever, one has already fallen into a condition of consciousness in which separations and dualities appear.

APPENDIX B

CLEARY, JUNG, AND

THE SECRET OF THE

GOLDEN FLOWER

WILHELM'S AND CLEARY'S
TRANSLATIONS COMPARED

Thomas Cleary, who has translated many classic Chinese and Japanese texts, published in 1991 a new translation of *The Secret of the Golden Flower*.[1] Cleary states that Richard Wilhelm's 1929 German translation is "a truncated version of a corrupted recension of the original work."[2] Wilhelm, according to Cleary, was not familiar with Taoist alchemical language nor with the "several types of Buddhist Chinese" in which the text is written, and therefore his "readings of grammar, terminology, and conceptual structures" are so seriously flawed as to make his translation "practically dysfunctional."[3] Before embarking on his own translation, Cleary had read and translated a number of Buddhist and Taoist classics closely related to the tradition of *The Secret of the Golden Flower* and became familiar with its terminology and concepts. He also claims to have found an original Chinese text of the book along with a Taoist commentary on its practical application. In addition, Cleary has practiced several forms of Eastern meditation and brings that knowledge to the work as well. The result is a book that is eminently more readable, but not always more comprehensible and in some instances, it seems to me, not necessarily better than the Wilhelm–Baynes edition.

For example, Cleary's opening sentences read:

> Naturalness is called the Way. The Way has no name or form; it is just the essence, just the primal spirit. Essence and life are invisible, so they are associated with sky and light. Sky and light are invisible, so they are associated with the two eyes.[4]

The passage is certainly readable, but what does it mean? Cleary's notes hardly explain the Taoist meaning of "the essence," "the primal spirit," or "the two eyes." "Essence," Cleary writes, "is open and spacious like the sky; life is a quantity of energy, like light. When the text talks about the two eyes guiding attention [which the text does not do here], it means that both spacelike awareness and specific perception are operative at the same time."[5]

Wilhelm's translation of the same text reads:

> That which exists through itself is called the Way (Tao). Tao has neither name nor shape. It is the one essence, the one primal spirit. Essence and life cannot be seen. They are contained in the light of heaven. The light of heaven cannot be seen. It is contained in the two eyes.[6]

I cannot comment on the Chinese terminology that is the source of these two different translations, but having some notion of the basic concepts of Taoism, it seems to me that "that which exists through itself" is a better definition of Tao than "naturalness." "Essence" and "life," Wilhelm notes, are translations of *hsing* and *ming*.[7] They appear to be the first formative principles of yang and yin as these apply to human nature. *Hsing* is made up of the character for heart or mind (*hsin*) and the character for origin, being born. The character *ming* signifies a royal command and then destiny, the fate alloted to man, the life span, and the measure of vital energy at one's disposal. The closest Western equivalents might be *logos* or spirit for *hsing* and *eros* or matter for *ming*. Like spirit and matter, *hsing* and *ming* are the two essential archetypal principles that form human nature and human existence. "The light of heaven" that first contains *hsing* and *ming* must refer to the creative spirit—the Spirit of God moving upon the face of the waters, for example, in Genesis. And the light of heaven being contained in "the two eyes" refers to the *yin* and *yang* aspects of the creative spirit—Malkhuth and Tifereth, for instance, the feminine and masculine principles within the Godhead in the kabbalistic tradition. For "the two eyes," Wilhelm states, refer to the sun and moon, and in both Eastern and Western alchemy they symbolize masculine and feminine energy. In a broader sense, the eyes also symbolize consciousness, and the implication is that yang and yin, sun and moon and what they stand for, are two different aspects of the human psyche. Jung sometimes translates these as conscious and unconscious, and sometimes as anima and animus. Erich Neumann speaks of patriarchal and matriarchal consciousness, the one more focused, the other more diffuse. Neumann's notion is similar to Cleary's "spacelike awareness and specific perception," except that in Neumann's view, one form of consciousness tends to be dominant, either habitually or culturally, while Cleary speaks of both being operative at the same time. Cleary here is referring to a meditative state of mind and not to the normal operation of consciousness.

Now, it may be valid to describe "essence" as "open and spacious like the sky," and "life" as "a quantity of energy, like light," but this does not define essence as *hsing* and life as *ming,* nor does it tell us what these terms mean. Similarly, "the two eyes" may represent "spacelike awareness and specific perception," but this does not tell us that the two eyes symbolize the sun and the moon and, therefore, the yang and yin aspects of human consciousness. Wilhelm's and Jung's notes in these respects are more helpful in conveying the meaning of these important initial passages of the book.

Even though Wilhelm, because of his medical training, may have had a predilection for a physiological and yogic reading of the text, as far as I know he had no particular motive that guided his translation. Cleary, on the other hand, wants to make the text a practical meditation guide for Westerners, and that intention influences his interpretation and explanations, and probably accounts, for example, for his interpretation of "the two eyes" in terms of meditation practice.

Cleary and Jung ————

Cleary also tends to underplay the alchemical aspects of the book, and in spite of his claims of familiarity with Taoist alchemy, when alchemical motifs appear he does not fully understand them. For instance, the text states that "the golden flower is the same thing as the gold pill."[8] The "gold pill" is the goal of the alchemical opus and identical with the "philosopers' gold" of Western alchemy. As an explanation of the gold pill, Cleary simply quotes a Taoist master, Liu-i: "The pill is the original, primal, real unified energy. This energy, when passed through fire to refine it, becomes permanently indestructible, so it is called the gold pill."[9] Cleary does not explain, or perhaps does not realize, that the unrefined, original, primal energy, the *prima materia* of Western alchemy, is usually subjected to a number of operations, among them a passage through fire, called *calcinatio*. Jung interprets this entire alchemical procedure as the gradual differentiation of the archetype of the Self from its contamination with instinctive and unconscious contents.

When the book speaks of "the lead in the homeland of water," or "metal in the middle primary water," or "lead in the region of water,"[10] Cleary again interprets the image in primarily Taoist terms and does not explain its alchemical meaning: "Lead symbolizes the true sense of real knowledge. Water stands for a symbol from the ancient *I Ching* representing the true sense of the knowledge of reality enclosed within conscious knowledge."[11] In alchemy "lead" is the same as the "pill," that is, the *prima materia* before it has been subjected to the various alchemical operations. Translated psychologically, lead is the spirit or psychic energy embodied in the instincts and in the unconscious. In Taoist alchemy, the lower abdomen is called the "house of water," and the body as a whole is identified with the element of water.

Again, when the book refers to "dragon and tiger," "water and fire," and the cycle of their interaction, and that this interaction is the "revolving of Heaven" and "the method of 'bathing' spoken of in alchemical classics,"[12] Cleary is unable to make any sense of this. "Dragon and tiger, water and fire," he writes, "are metaphors for yin and yang. The meaning of this passage is not entirely clear, but it seems to refer to dilettantism."[13] In Eastern alchemy "dragon" stands for negative energy and "tiger" for positive energy, and in both Eastern and Western alchemy water is feminine, yin and fire masculine, yang. The cycle of their interaction and the "revolving of Heaven" refer to the Eastern alchemical "microcosmic orbit," also called "the turning of the water-wheel."[14] Eastern alchemy, at least in some of its later phases, and in contrast to the externally oriented Western alchemy, sought to produce the Golden Flower or the Elixir of Immortality within the body of the practitioner through specific forms of concentration and meditation. Thus, as in yoga, and particularly in *kundalini* yoga, consciously regulating the flow and the mixture of physical and psychic energies was the method of producing the Golden Flower. The practice entailed focusing the attention on a rising and descending stream of energy through the body, coordinated with inhalation and exhalation. This turning of the water-wheel, or microcosmic orbit, begins "at the base of the spine, called the first gate . . . rising in the backbone to the second gate between the kidneys . . . and then to the back of the head, called the third gate . . . before reaching the brain, to descend down the face, chest and abdomen to return to where it rose and so completes a full circuit."[15] (See the illustration on page 149).

In this connection, I believe Cleary is right that the Wilhelm-Baynes translation of a central concept of the book as the "circulation of the light" was influenced by this meditative-alchemical exercise. Cleary translates the same phrase as "turning the light around" and states that it refers to the Zen Buddhist exercise of "mentally looking inward toward the source of consciousness."[16] Given the alchemical and Buddhist mixture of the text, one could probably translate the phrase either way. But, on the whole, in spite of the frequent references to alchemical imagery, I think the text emphasizes the Buddhist mode of meditation, and Cleary's translation, therefore, is closer to the spirit of the book.

In Western alchemy the cycle of interaction of the opposites and "the method of bathing" are accomplished through the operations of *circulatio* and *distilatio* (circular distillation), which purify the opposites to their essence and then bring them together in the operation of *coniunctio,* the alchemical wedding. (See chapter 5 for

Cleary and Jung ———

a more detailed discussion of *coniunctio* and its relation to the goals of alchemy and meditation.) The product of this union is the philosophers' gold or the elixir of immortality. (Alchemy has numerous designations for both the beginning [e.g., *prima materia*, lead, pill] and the goal of the opus [e.g., philosophers' stone, *lapis*, golden flower, elixir of life].

Jung interprets *circulatio* as the repeated circuit of all aspects of one's being, the activation of "the light and dark forces of human nature, and together with them all psychological opposites of whatever kind they may be."[17] The goal of this exercise is first of all self-knowledge and then the integration of these activated light and dark forces and of all essential opposite and conflicting forces in a transpersonal center, the archetype of the Self. In *Mysterium Coniunctionis* Jung describes *circulatio* as follows:

> Ascent and descent, above and below, up and down, represent an emotional realization of opposites, and this realization gradually leads, or should lead, to their equilibrium. This motif occurs very frequently in dreams, in the form of going up- and downhill, climbing stairs, going up or down in a lift, balloon, aeroplane, etc. It corresponds to the struggle between the winged and the wingless dragon, i.e., the uroboros. . . . This vacillating between the opposites and being tossed back and forth means being contained *in* the opposites. They become a vessel in which what was previously now one thing and now another floats vibrating, so that the painful suspension between opposites gradually changes into the bilateral activity of the point in the centre. This is the 'liberation from opposites,' the *nirdvandva* of Hindu philosophy, though it is not really a philosophical but rather a psychological development.[18]

The "microcosmic orbit," or "turning the water-wheel," is only one of the meditation techniques alluded to in the *Golden Flower*. In fact, one of the problems of translating and presenting the *Golden Flower* is that the book is an amalgam of Taoism, Theravada Buddhism, Confucianism, Zen Buddhism and alchemy. On the whole, it seems to be a syncretistic Taoist work, yet Cleary presents

---
Appendix B

it as a coherent Taoist teaching. I think the author and commentators sought to make a coherent whole out of the culturally different religious notions and meditation practices that appeared in China over the centuries. The result is confusing, and the book is neither a Taoist, Buddhist, Confucian, nor alchemical tract exclusively. For example, when the text speaks of the "creative," the "receptive," and the "open center," these are Confucian notions. When it speaks of yin, yang, and finding the "potential" and its "opening" or the "primal opening," these are Taoist terms. The text also refers to mindfulness and looking "back again and again into the source of mind," which is similar to the Theravadin Buddhist practice of *vipassana* meditation. The influence of Zen is present in references to "undivided concentration" and the "teaching of the special transmission outside the doctrine." But references to alchemy are the most numerous: the golden flower; the gold pill; the water of vitality; the fire of spirit; the earth of attention; the eyes as the sun and moon, combining their vitalities, crystallizing their energy; congealing the spirit in the lair of energy; the major medicinal ingredient present from beginning to end in the metal in the middle of primary water; the lead in the region of water; heaven entering earth; bathing; the union of fire and water; true intercourse when the opposites are united; the channels stilled and the energy stopped; turning the light around for a hundred days until intercourse is achieved, the embryo found, and the child develops. Because Cleary lacks knowledge of alchemy, all these expressions make little sense to him, and this unfamiliarity with alchemy is, in the end, the major liability of his translation of *The Secret of the Golden Flower*. This is the same problem that the Wilhelm translation faced, and to date, therefore, this situation has not been remedied.

CLEARY'S CRITIQUE OF JUNG

Throughout his notes to the translation, Cleary conducts a running dialogue with Jung, not as a translator but as a proponent of the spiritual perspective and meditation techniques described in *The Secret of the Golden Flower*. Cleary states that Jung's knowledge of Taoism, Buddhism, and Eastern meditation was limited and that

Cleary and Jung ———

like many Westerners of his day, Jung thought that Eastern meditation and yoga produce "abnormal psychic states" and aim at a total detachment from the external world.[19] Jung applied these assumptions to the Taoist and Buddhist teachings of the *Golden Flower* where they are simply not warranted. Cleary's point is well taken. *The Secret of the Golden Flower* was Jung's first serious encounter with Eastern thought, and his knowledge was indeed limited at the time. Cleary is also right in pointing out that Jung tried to make sense of the book in his own terms and used its concepts as confirmations or illustrations of his psychological discoveries and ideas—the concept of the Self, for example, or the notions of animus and anima. Cleary argues that because of Wilhelm's theistic bias in translating certain terms, Jung did not fully realize the extent to which the text was a discussion of psychological phenomena. "He then," writes Cleary, "tried to repsychologize the terminology, but since he did not quite understand it to begin with he could not but wind up with a distortion in the end."[20] This is putting matters too strongly. *The Secret of the Golden Flower* is not pure psychology; it relies heavily on symbols to convey its meaning, and these symbols do need to be translated into psychological terms, as Cleary does himself in his notes. But Jung did realize that the philosophers of the East were "symbolic psychologists," and he therefore felt justified in his psychological treatment of what appear to be metaphysical statements in the book.[21]

The most serious limitation, which Jung acknowledged in his foreword to the second German edition, was his lack of knowledge of alchemy. Because he did not know alchemy, he thought he was dealing with a Chinese variant of yoga. But Cleary, too, is not fully conversant with alchemy. Without knowledge of alchemy, Jung focused on the religious and psychological features of the text, while Cleary concentrates on its spiritual contents and meditation instructions. But alchemy is central to the *Golden Flower*, for the book relies heavily on alchemical imagery to convey its meaning. Jung's reading of the book eventually led him to a comprehensive study of Western alchemical literature. That study culminated in what might be called his magnum opus, *Mysterium Coniunctionis: An Inquiry into the Separation and Synthesis of Psychic Opposites in*

Alchemy. In this book, in his discussion of the alchemical operation of *coniunctio,* Jung was able to complete the task he had set himself in the commentary to the *Golden Flower,* namely, building a bridge between the aims of Western psychological development and those of Eastern meditation practice.

Cleary ignores Jung's work on alchemy and treats the alchemical images in the *Golden Flower* as metaphors for different states or forms of consciousness. This is a serious undervaluation of alchemical symbolism, for that symbolism is an objective description of the psychodynamic processes that take place during the course of a psychological-spiritual development. Just as we have no internal knowledge of the structures and functions of our body and have to rely on anatomical studies, analyses of blood and urine, and so forth, similarly we are unconscious of the structures and operations of the psyche and must rely on external observation and analysis. Alchemy provides the broad outlines of an objective "anatomy" and "physiology" of the psyche. For in the fantasies and projections of the alchemists, the archetypal psyche provides a mirror image of its internal operations. And just as it takes training in anatomy, organic chemistry, and the like, to understand the structures and functions of the body, so also does it take training in alchemy, mythology, cultural anthropology, and so on, to understand the operations of the collective unconscious.

Cleary seems personally committed to the Buddhist perception of reality, and many of his arguments with Jung stem from this bias. As a contemporary Western Buddhist, Cleary is actually more psychological in his reading of the *Golden Flower* than Jung was. For Jung accorded a much greater degree of reality to the imaginal life of the psyche than Buddhism does, particularly Buddhism in the hands of a psychologically sophisticated twentieth-century Westerner. For example, Cleary completely dismisses the symbolic import of the "lower" (*p'o*) and "higher" (*hun*) souls that Wilhelm translated as "anima" and "animus." C. F. Baynes, the English translator and editor of Wilhelm's text, writes that "earthly-soul" and "spirit-soul" are probably better translations than "animus" and "anima."[22] Baynes's terminology also avoids the confusion with Jung's gender-specific "anima" and "animus," which, Cleary rightly points out, was an illegitimate extension of Wilhelm's use of the terms by Jung in his commentary.

Wilhelm writes that *p'o* is composed of the characters for "demon" and "white," while *hun* is made up of the characters for "demon" and "cloud."[23] (Here *daimon* is probably a better term for demon because for the Chinese, *demon* does not necessarily carry an evil connotation.) *P'o*, the "earthly-soul," is dark and earthbound; it is located in the abdomen and connected to the physical, instinctive, and emotional life. *Hun*, the "spirit-soul," is bright and active; it "lives" in the eyes and is connected to mental, intellectual, and conscious functioning. At death the two souls separate: *p'o* sinks to the earth and decays; *hun* rises in the air, where it is active for some time, and then flows back to the common reservoirs of life. In ancient China the dead were buried on the north side of the house where the seed grain was stored for the next sowing in spring. The Chinese thought that the dead go on living in the groundwater under the house, and that this underground water was connected to the Yellow Springs, which was the land of the dead. Here *p'o* and *hun* were reunited, their energies restored and made ready for a new life.

Cleary has no interest in any of this, since he has no appreciation of the psychic reality that this symbolism conveys. For him the " 'lower soul' simply means the feeling of being a solid body physically present in a solid world."[24] He takes the matter even further and distorts the meaning of the two terms by arguing that "there is no real lower soul that is in substance different from the higher soul. Both are aspects of one spirit, artificially alienated by confusion. When energy is freed from obsessive clinging to the body or lower soul, it can be used to restore the original spirit to completeness."[25] He goes on to say that several passages in the *Golden Flower* indicate that the division of the lower and higher souls is not a metaphysical reality but a temporal phenomenon. The implication is that temporal phenomena and distinctions can be readily dismissed. This is tantamount to saying that since matter is a manifestation of energy and psyche a manifestation of spirit, all material and psychological manifestations and distinctions can be ignored. Perhaps one can entertain such a notion theoretically by identifying with a transcendental perspective, but experientially this makes no sense.

In any case, having reduced the "lower soul" to the feeling of being a solid body, Cleary proceeds to reduce the "higher soul" to an "equanimous spacelike awareness."[26] The "light, clear energy characteristic of the higher soul" that is "obtained from cosmic space" simply refers, he states, to a spacelike awareness that "contains everything while resting on nothing."[27] The goal is to live "in the midst of the things of the world yet free from bondage to them. This contrasts with the limitations of awareness represented by the lower soul, mixed up in the objects of its perception."[28]

Cleary's reduction of the richly evocative, culturally indigenous symbolism of the "earthly soul" and the "spirit soul" to states of consciousness is an example of the type of treatment that Jung felt Eastern religious traditions would suffer at the hands of Westerners. This is Zen without Buddhism, Tao without Taoism.

Cleary acknowledges that what attracted him to Zen Buddhism was his interest in transcending "religious and cultural forms to get at the heart of reality in itself by direct experience and direct perception."[29] That heart of reality in Taoism and Zen Buddhism is "formless consciousness," so that both in the means and the goal Cleary feels that he is able to transcend specific religious and cultural forms. Indeed, he is critical of "ritualized Zen cults with highly cloistered and involuted attitudes" and of all "cultism, scholasticism, and cultural traditionalism."[30] He takes the phrase in the *Golden Flower,* "you need not give up your normal occupation," as an indication that the essential teachings of Taoism and Buddhism are best pursued outside an ecclesiastical or monastic setting.[31] He thinks that Jung and most Westerners labor under the misconception that monasticism represents the mainstream of Eastern spiritual practice. In part, he argues, that notion comes from the Western tradition of spirituality, but primarily the idea is propagated by "some professional Japanese Zennists . . . and many Western Zennists following latter-day Japanese schools."[32]

One could perhaps understand Cleary's attitude as an expression of an introverted bias on his part. But he carries this bias too far in failing to recognize that the experience of "formless consciousness," or more precisely, the valuation and understanding of that experience, takes place in a specific cultural setting and, indeed, is a spiritual attainment of a particular cultural milieu. The experience of "formless consciousness" by a Christian, Muslim, or Jew will be viewed in quite a different light than it is viewed in the East. And when that experience comes to a Westerner, sometimes spontaneously and outside any religious context, it tends to alienate the person from his or her social and cultural surroundings, for there is nothing in our culture to enable us to appreciate and make sense of it.

An example of such a personal encounter with "formless consciousness" by a Westerner is that of Flora Courtois, as recounted in her booklet, *An Experience of Enlightenment*.[33] She did not even have the words to describe this form of consciousness and referred to it as "Open Vision." She tried to explain her new perspective on reality to her college professors and the college psychiatrist but was met with indifference and misunderstanding. "I came to feel," she writes, "that to talk about this personal experience was to expose to shallow interpretation and disrespect what was most worthy of respect. I decided then never to speak of it again until I was confident it would be appreciated."[34] Twenty-five years passed before she was fortunate enough to meet the Japanese Zen master Yasutani-roshi in 1968. She finally told him of her encounter, and without testing her, he verified that she had had a *kensho* or *satori* experience and instructed her on how to broaden and deepen her insight through the practice of *shikantaza*.

Cleary's dismissive attitude toward the traditional cultural forms that contain and embody the consciousness of ultimate reality reminds me of a story about an American who came to a Japanese monastery to practice Zen. Having read about the radical, iconoclastic approach of Zen, he was surprised to find the Zen master making prostrations before a gaudily painted statue of the eighteenth-century Zen master Hakuin. "Why are you bowing to that statue?" the American exclaimed. "Zen is supposed to be concerned only with ultimate reality. I would spit on that piece of wood!" The Zen Master looked at him somewhat startled, and then said: "You spit. I'll bow."

Appendix B

Cleary seems to think that if Jung had had a better knowledge of Buddhism, and a better translation of the *Golden Flower,* he would have avoided getting bogged down in the realms of form, fantasy, and desire. For example, Wilhelm translated the Buddhist concept of the "three realms" as "heaven, earth, and hell," rather than as the realms of desire, form, and formlessness. "Jung's work on archetypes and dreams," Cleary feels, "would have benefited immensely from an accurate understanding of the real Buddhist concept of three realms or worlds. As it was, Jung does not seem to have been able to distinguish these realms of experience clearly; most of his work appears to hover on the border of the realms of form and desire; the realm of formless consciousness seems to have been unfamiliar to him."[35] Wilhelm translated "the realms of form and desire" as "the world of illusory desires." This was unfortunate for Jung, Cleary continues, because he "showed a marked inability to distinguish between the realm of form and the realm of desire. This tended to skew his interpretations of fantasies and led him to imagine that golden flower meditation is culture-bound in spite of his belief in universal archetypes."[36] As it was, Jung became "fascinated by the images that came to mind when he tried to meditate according to his own method, which he apparently believed to be similar to that of the golden flower," when, in fact, the instructions are not to stick to "any image of person or self at all."[37] Jung's collective unconscious, Cleary goes on, still has form, and "must therefore be classified with the lower soul and ordinary mind; his hope was to make this conscious in order to transcend it, but Jung himself appears to have become so involved in the discovery and discussion of the unconscious that he became attached to it and as a consequence was never able to experience the higher soul and open the golden flower. His commentary on Wilhelm's translation bears witness to this, as do his other writings on Eastern mysticism."[38] Because Jung did not, as he himself admits, follow the directions of the *Golden Flower* and pursued his own meditation practices, he became "deluded by unusual psychic experiences" and then "projected his imaginings on Taoism and thus believed that the teachings of the golden flower came from 'abnormal psychic states.'"[39]

Such, in summary, is Cleary's scathing criticism of Jung. I will not discuss in detail Cleary's mistaken notions about Jung's hypothesis of the archetypes and the collective unconscious. (Appendix A, "Wilber on Jung," provides an outline of Jung's definition and description of archetypes.) Suffice it to say that Jung made a distinction between archetypes per se, which in their essence are unknowable, purely hypothetical potential fields of energy or consciousness, and archetypal images, which take on specific form in time and space. Only the archetypes per se are truly universal in the sense that Cleary means. Archetypal images, although similar in form, which includes a specific emotional charge, conceptual or symbolic meaning, and behavioral impulse, are always culturally defined in content. One need only think of the various cultural expressions of the Great Mother or the Father God, or, for that matter, of the archetypes of the personal mother or father. In fact, when the archetype per se is activated and not mediated culturally or personally, serious social or psychological disturbances follow. This is one of the most important reasons why meditation practice should not be undertaken outside a religious or therapeutic context. Some intensely self-contained individuals, like Cleary perhaps, may be able to pursue meditation on their own, but I would not recommend it, as he does, for everyone, nor would I say that individual practice is superior to practice in a religious setting.

Cleary accuses Jung of "careless arrogance" in his treatment of the *Golden Flower* and states that that arrogant attitude hindered him from a "more serious and sober investigation of Taoism."[40] I am tempted to apply the same observation to Cleary and his attitude toward Jung's work in alchemy and the psychology of religion. But in Cleary's case, that arrogant stance seems to extend to all culturally elaborated spiritual forms and traditions. A similar attitude is evident in his dismissal of the realms of form and desire. Only the realm of formless consciousness appears to be worthy of his respect. And yet one of the earliest Chinese Zen documents, *Affirming Faith in Mind*, states: "If you would walk the highest Way, do not reject the sense domain. For as it is, whole and complete,

---

Appendix B

this sense world is enlightenment."[41] Also, the *Heart of Perfect Wisdom Sutra* states: "Form here is only emptiness, emptiness no other than form; form is no other than emptiness, emptiness no other than form."[42] I realize that these declarations are made from the vantage point of enlightened consciousness; nevertheless, if one examines the realms of form and desire in a conscious way, as Jung did, one comes to the realization that they are, in the end, interchangeable with the formless realm. In other words, one can approach the realm of formless consciousness directly as Zen does, or through the realms of form and desire, which is the way of most Western and many Eastern mystical traditions.

In the Buddhist vision of the universe, the three realms of desire, form, and formlessness make up the entire world of conditioned existence (*samsara*). The realm of desire, in which the senses rule, is the lowest or coarsest of the three and consists of hell beings, hungry ghosts, animals, human beings, fighting demons, and heavenly beings. None of these states or conditions are eternal or permanent; even the heavenly beings and the hell beings are in time reborn in other realms. Only the unconditional suprasamsaric *nirvana* state of the buddhas is eternal or transcendent over time. Beyond the realm of desire is the realm of form with sixteen levels of gods, also called the sixteen worlds of Brahma. Here sensual attachment is absent but form is still present. The highest Brahma heavens consist of four levels of gods in the formless realm where neither sense attachment nor form is present. This realm of enlightened existence is made up of *shravakas*, those who attain enlightenment by hearing the teachings of Buddha and deeply assimilating them; *pratyekabuddhas* ("private buddhas"), those who practice alone and attain enlightenment without a teacher; *bodhisattvas*, enlightened beings who defer their own full buddhahood in order to help others attain liberation; and buddhas, fully enlightened beings who have become *whole*, complete in themselves, no longer identified with the limitations of an individual personality, character, or existence, and whose consciousness encompasses the infinity of the universe.[43] From an introverted point of view, the three realms and their subdivisions can be seen as descriptions of various forms or states of consciousness, which is how they are sometimes spoken of by Buddhists. Jung would interpret this cosmology as a depiction of the collective unconscious, from its instinctive to its spiritual manifestations, with each of the realms representing a different archetypal level.

Cleary does not elaborate on the psychological or archetypal meaning of the three realms, except to interpret the realm of formlessness in purely personal psychological terms as "equanimous spacelike awareness." He also ignores or seems to be unaware of the need to repeatedly return to the realms of form and desire as preparatory states for each advance in meditation:

> The meditator who graduates from the first form-realm *dhyana* [meditation] to the second enters it too through appropriate *dhyana* of the realm of desire. (Likewise, first entry into the third and fourth *dhyana* stages of the realm of form is achieved through desire-realm *dhyana*.) The meditator does not pass directly from the first *dhyana* of the form realm into the second but moves back to the desire realm and practices preliminary *dhyana* on that level.[44]

In essence, this method is similar to Jung's technique of active imagination, which begins with an emotion or complex and pursues it until its archetypal meaning or form is revealed. One can then take the archetypal meaning or form and concentrate on that, until it dissolves into a formless energy field or formless consciousness. And one needs to apply this procedure repeatedly, each time an emotion, complex, or archetype appears that requires attention because of its disruptive influence on one's conscious functioning. One can also pursue the process voluntarily as a way to self-knowledge and psychological integration.

Jung was familiar with the realm where personal attachments disappear and one exists, as he put it, in an "objective form." He had a series of near-death dreams and visions, after a leg fracture and a heart attack in 1944, in which he experienced himself and others in this objective way. These experiences, he writes, depict a state of consciousness that is detached from emotional ties. "In general," he states, "emotional ties are very important to human beings. But they still contain projections, and it is essential to withdraw these projections in order to attain to oneself and to objectivity. Emotional relationships are relationships of desire, tainted by coercion and constraint; something is expected from the other person, and that makes him and ourselves unfree. Objective cognition lies hidden behind the attraction of the emotional relationship; it seems to be the central secret. Only through objective cognition is the real *coniunctio* possible."[45]

Jung was also familiar with the realm of formlessness and defined it as "the original, non-differentiated unity of the world or of Being," or as the "potential world of the first day of creation, when nothing was yet 'in actu,' i.e., divided into two and many, but was still one."[46] This potential world is the *mundus archetypus* of the medieval Scholastics and is defined by Gerard Dorn as the *unus mundus*. Dorn argued that "on the basis of a self known by meditation and produced by alchemical means," it is possible for an individual to become one with the *unus mundus*.[47] This union, Jung argues, is the same as the "relation or identity of the personal with the suprapersonal *atman,* and of the individual *tao* with the universal *tao*."[48] To the Westerner, Jung continues,

> this view appears not at all realistic and all too mystic; above all he cannot see why a self should become a reality when it enters into relationship with the world of the first day of creation. He has no knowledge of any world other than the empirical one. Strictly speaking, his puzzlement does not begin here; it began already with the production of the *caelum,* the inner unity. Such thoughts are unpopular and distressingly nebulous. He does not know where they belong or on what they could be based. They might be true or again they might not—in short, his experience stops here and with it as a rule his understanding, and, unfortunately, only too often his willingness to learn more. I would therefore counsel the critical reader to put aside his prejudices and for once try to experience on himself the effects of the process I have described, or else to suspend judgment and admit that he understands nothing. For thirty years I have studied these psychic processes under all possible conditions and have assured myself that the alchemists as well as the great philoso-

Cleary and Jung ————

phies of the East are referring to just such experiences, and that it is chiefly our ignorance of the psyche if these experiences appear "mystic."[49]

MEDITATION AND PSYCHOPATHOLOGY

Jung, therefore, had both personal and clinical experience with the realms of objective form and formlessness, but he deliberately chose to pursue the realms of attachment and desire in order to extract from them their energy and meaning. As a psychiatrist and a psychoanalyst he was faced with the task of alleviating the unconsciously driven and often senseless suffering of his patients. He knew he could not achieve his end by counseling his psychologically disturbed patients to detach themselves from the desires and objects of the "lower soul" and work toward the establishment of an "equanimous spacelike awareness." Even if some individuals, through sheer force of will, had been able to acquire such detachment and equanimity, this would have been simply sweeping the problems under the rug. The disturbance, if not permitted psychic expression, would continue to function in the unconscious and eventually appear in the form of physiological symptoms, somatic outbreaks, and actual physical illnesses. After all, Freud was initially a neurologist and was led to the discovery of the powers of repressed psychological desires through the treatment of neurological symptoms that had no physical basis for their manifestation.

Obviously with no practical experience with psychological problems and illnesses, and in spite of the current knowledge of the disastrous effects of repression and schizoid splitting, Cleary, in the afterword to his translation, actually proposes the "practice of golden flower meditation" as a cure for neurotic compulsions and even for psychoses:

Rightly understood and correctly practiced, it does not have the dangers Jung attributed to it because it does not submit to the fascination of what he referred to as unconscious contents of mind.

The exercise of turning the light around is in fact so penetrating an avenue to insight and transcendence that it is

―――――― *Appendix B*

tempting to consider applying its theory and practice to the search for direction in treatment of some of the more serious disorders currently being addressed by the psychiatric community, crippling conditions such as those now known as acute manic depression, schizophrenia, psychosis, and multiple personality disorder.[50]

Fortunately, toward the end of his afterword, Cleary retracts the proposal and reiterates the opening statement of the *Golden Flower* that people should first of all have a firm foothold on ordinary reality before they begin to practice meditation. "This means that they should be able to function adequately in their own culture and society, whatever that may be. The golden flower practice is not primarily a therapeutic method for severely unbalanced people; it is a way of higher development for ordinary people."[51] And he acknowledges that the method does have its dangers and "is not particularly recommended for severely neurotic people, or for people with schizoid or psychotic tendencies," because "the enhanced receptivity and sensitivity fostered by the practice might exacerbate feelings of illness and fear."[52]

INTROVERSION AND EXTRACTION OF LIBIDO

Jack Engler's experience with Western practitioners of Eastern meditation (recounted in chapter 4) demonstrates why Jung pursued what Buddhists call the realms of form and desire. Like the alchemists who labored to extract the spirit embedded in matter, Jung sought to free up the libido and potential consciousness embedded in the instincts, drives, and complexes. In close analogy to Buddhism and Taoism, the Western alchemists, too, sought a universal cure that would end all human suffering and grant immortality. In other words, the alchemical opus, if interpreted as the psyche's own prescription for its liberation from ceaseless suffering, provides another method for attaining the same ends as Buddhism. That method consists of taking the unconscious seriously, subjecting its blind drives and passions to close scrutiny and analysis (the alchemical *separatio*, "bathing," and "washing"), paying close attention to emotions, dreams, and fantasies (*meditatio*), extracting their meaning and assimilating or rejecting their message (*distillatio*), raising to consciousness the conflicting drives that make up our being (*sublimatio*), and bringing them together in a paradoxical union in the Self (*coniunctio*).

Unlike religious methods of alleviating suffering, Jung's therapeutic method has the advantage of not requiring any religious beliefs or motivations; it simply uses the material at hand—the person's own psychological concerns and suffering. Moreover, Jung's method also works to integrate the entire person and does not reject and then split off the unconscious, the instincts, and the emotions, which is exactly what can happen if one pursues the meditation practices espoused by Cleary.

Because Cleary is unfamiliar with alchemy, he does not realize the importance the body and the emotions play in the meditation technique described by the *Golden Flower*. For example, when the text speaks of "congealing the spirit in the lair of energy" or of the "union of fire and water," it calls for an integration of the conscious with the unconscious, of instinctive and psychic energy, into an integrated whole. This is just the opposite of what Cleary thinks is the primary message of the text, namely, splitting off consciousness from the instinctive drives and cultivating an "equanimous spacelike awareness." Cleary's misunderstanding in this instance is another example of what Jung felt was the problem with Westerners adopting Eastern teachings and practicing meditation techniques outside the cultural context from which they sprang and in which they were usually surrounded by generally known but often unspoken assumptions.

Wilhelm's phrase "circulation of the light" for the process of integrating the instinctive and psychic energies is descriptively closer to the actual practice of the meditation technique of the *Golden Flower* than Cleary's "turning the light around." Cleary sees the entire practice as that of "mentally looking inward toward the source of consciousness." But the practice entails much more than just a mental exercise or discipline. Cleary's phrase is useful only in stressing the fact that this form of meditation rests on the reversal of the normal flow of libido, which is usually directed toward the

---

Appendix B

satisfaction of instinctive, emotional, and conscious drives and goals. This is why the practice is also referred to as the "method of reversal" or of "interrupting consciousness."[53] But that is only the beginning of the process, even though all further developments rest on this reversal or "introversion of libido," as Jung would put it. These inner developments entail both a "purification" of psychic energy—that is, its separation from the instinctive and ego drives that tend to "color" or define its expression—and structural changes in the psyche and in the energy field of the body. In psychological terms, "turning the light around," therefore, refers to the conscious introversion of libido. The rest of the practice involves the extraction of libido from the instinctive and psychological drives. This extraction is accomplished by paying close attention to sensations, emotions, and complexes. Sometimes the process actually requires deliberate stimulation of these areas. For instance, in Taoist alchemy the meditator is counseled to arouse sexual energy and then sublimate it. In tantric yoga actual sexual intercourse is used in a like manner. And in active imagination various moods, fantasies, and complexes are consciously activated through concentration. In many meditation practices, such as Zen, the released energy is then gathered into the artificially created psychic structure that I call the meditation complex. This meditation structure (analogous to the hermetic *vas* in alchemy), with its extracted and "purified" libido, is then used to activate the archetype of wholeness, the Self. This is what the text means by such images as turning the light around for a hundred days until intercourse is achieved; congealing the spirit in the lair of energy; crystallizing the energy of the combined vitalities of the sun and moon; forming the embryo; and developing the child. The archetype of the Self, therefore, is the "major medicinal ingredient" present from beginning to end in "the metal in the middle of primary water,"[54] and once it is crystalized out of the primary water, that is, out of the unconscious, it becomes the gold pill or the golden flower.

An experience of the ultimate nature of reality, no matter how profound, is not yet the crystallization of the gold pill or the golden flower. The image of crystallization, which Jung also used as an analogy for how archetypes take on manifest form, implies the establishment of the enlightened perspective as an integral part of the psychic structure. The psyche is highly mutable, and if one pursues meditation in a split-off way, in extreme cases, something like an *idiot savant* is the result: a person with an evolved spiritual perspective but essentially infantile, socially unadapted, and ruled by unconscious impulses and egoistic concerns. This is a distorted individuation or Self-realization. In such cases, only a part of the archetype of the Self has been realized. When meditation is practiced within the appropriate cultural or religious context, such distortions are avoided by preliminary and postenlightenment training. In Zen, for instance, the initial enlightenment experience is only a prelude to a koan study that may go on for decades. At the same time, the person usually lives in a community with well-defined traditions so that the personal and social aspects of the individual are also subjected to observation, modification and development. In other words, Self-realization is not to be narrowly construed, as is often the case in the West, as a mystical or transcendental experience. Self-realization or the attainment of wholeness entails a life-long process of psychological and spiritual development that aims at the gradual integration of every aspect of one's being. This is the unspoken assumption behind the meditation practice described in *The Secret of the Golden Flower*.

NOTES

All citations of CW refer to *The Collected Works of C. G. Jung,* 20 vols. (Princeton, N.J.: Princeton University Press, 1964–1979).

EPIGRAGHS

Page vii: *Milindapanha* 139–40, T. W. Rhys Davids, *The Questions of King Milinda* (New York: Dover, 1963), p. 197. I have made some editorial changes in the text.

Chapter 1: C. G. Jung, CW 11, para. 737.

Chapter 3: Andrew Wyeth, *The Helga Pictures* (New York: H. N. Abrams, 1987).

Chapter 4: Jung, CW 13, para. 335.

Chapter 5: Confucius, *Analects,* Book IV, 8. I am using the wording of Daisetz Teitaro Suzuki in his *Essays in Zen Buddhism* (First Series) (New York: Grove Press, 1961), pp. 22–23.

INTRODUCTION

1. Daniel Goleman, *The Meditative Mind: The Varieties of Meditative Experience* (Los Angeles: Jeremy P. Tarcher, 1988), pp. xxi–xxii.

2. Aryeh Kaplan, *Jewish Meditation: A Practical Guide* (New York: Schocken Books, 1985), p. vi.

3. Charles T. Tart, ed., *Transpersonal Psychologies,* (New York: Harper & Row, 1975), pp. 4–5.

4. C. G. Jung, "On the Nature of the Psyche," CW 8, para. 420.

I. JUNG, MEDITATION, AND THE WEST

1. C. G. Jung, "The Spiritual Problem of Modern Man," CW 10, para. 176. Jiddu Krishnamurti (1895–1986) was born in India and at the age of twelve was declared by Annie Besant, then head of the Theosophical Society, as the expected "World Teacher." In 1929 he broke with the organization, saying, "I maintain that the truth is a pathless land and you cannot approach it by any path what-so-ever, by any religion, by any sect." *The McGraw-Hill Encyclopedia of World Biography* (New York: McGraw-Hill Book Co., 1973).

2. Jung, CW 10, para. 176.

3. Ibid.

4. Jung, "Commentary on 'The Secret of the Golden Flower,' " CW 13, para. 83.

5. Jung, "Psychological Commentary on 'The Tibetan Book of the Dead,' " CW 11, para. 833.

6. Ibid.

7. Jung, "Yoga and the West," CW 11, para. 867.

8. Jung, "The Psychology of Eastern Meditation," CW 11, para. 920. Italics added.

9. Ibid., para. 945.

10. Ibid., para. 940.

11. Ibid., para. 939.

12. Ibid., para. 949.

13. As far as I can ascertain, three of the pictures, A3, A6, and A10, are Jung's. All of the pictures, he claims, were done independently of any Eastern influence; his own were composed before he read *The Secret of the Golden Flower*. See Jung, "Commentary on 'The Secret of the Golden Flower,' " CW 13, pp. 56ff.

14. C. G. Jung, *Memories, Dreams, Reflections* (New York: Pantheon Books, 1963), p. 196.

15. Ibid., pp. 196–97.

16. Jung, CW 13, para. 84.

17. Anna Kingsford (1846–1888) was president of the Theosophical Society in 1883 and a founder of the Hermetic Society.

Notes

18. Jung, CW 13, para. 40.

19. Ibid., para. 41.

20. Quoted in Jung, CW 13, para. 42.

21. Richard Wilhelm, trans., *The Secret of the Golden Flower: A Chinese Book of Life*, with foreword and commentary by C. G. Jung (New York: Harcourt, Brace & World, A Harvest Book, 1962), p. 22.

22. Ibid.

23. Jung, CW 13, para. 37.

24. Ibid.

25. Ibid.

26. Jung, *Letters*, vol. 2, 1951–1961 (Princeton: Princeton University Press, 1975), p. 45.

27. Jung, *Letters*, vol. 1, 1906–1950 (Princeton: Princeton University Press, 1973), p. 395.

28. Marie-Louise von Franz, *Projection and Re-collection in Jungian Psychology* (La Salle, Ill. & London: Open Court, 1978), p. 84.

29. Jung, *Letters*, vol. 1, p. 58.

30. Philip Kapleau, ed., *The Three Pillars of Zen: Teaching, Practice, and Enlightenment* (Garden City, N.Y.: Doubleday, Anchor, 1980), pp. 309 and 311.

31. Jung, CW 13, para. 43.

32. *The Hui Ming Ching or Book of Consciousness and Life* was written by Liu Hua-yang in 1794 and added to later editions of Wilhelm, *The Secret of the Golden Flower*, p. 77 and CW 13, para. 64.

33. Ibid., para. 65.

34. Ibid., para. 66. I am extending and paraphrasing Jung's argument in this entire paragraph. As can be seen from this discussion and in what follows, the Jungian definition of *projection* is much broader than the classical Freudian, which considers projection an unconscious ego defense mechanism.

35. Philip Kapleau, *Zen: Dawn in the West* (Garden City, N.Y.: Doubleday, Anchor, 1980), pp. 180–81. I have provided the English translation of the last four lines, which are usually chanted in Sanskrit: *Gate, gate, para gate, para sam gate, bodhi, svaha!* Explanatory words and phrases in brackets are mine.

36. Jung, CW 13, para. 67.
37. W. Y. Evans-Wentz, ed., *The Tibetan Book of the Dead* (New York: Oxford University Press, 1960), pp. 95–96.
38. Ibid., p. 103. Bracketed words in original.
39. Von Franz, *Projection and Re-collection*, p. 187.
40. Ibid. Italics in original.
41. Jung, *Memories, Dreams, Reflections*, p. 323.
42. Ibid.
43. Von Franz, *Projection and Re-collection*, p. 189.
44. Cited in Jung, "Synchronicity: An Acausal Connecting Principle," CW 8, para. 937.
45. Jung, CW 8, paras. 856 and 912; *Letters*, vol. I, p. 256f.
46. Von Franz, *Projection and Re-collection*, p. 193.
47. Ibid., p. 199.
48. Quoted in Heinrich Dumoulin, *A History of Zen Buddhism* (New York: Pantheon Books, 1963), pp. 253–54.
49. "The Stages of Mindfulness Meditation: A Validation Study," chaps. 6 and 7 in Ken Wilber, Jack Engler, and Daniel P. Brown, *Transformations of Consciousness: Conventional and Contemplative Perspectives on Development* (Boston & London: Shambhala Publications, 1986), pp. 161–217.
50. Ibid., p. 179.
51. Ibid., p. 187.
52. Ibid., p. 185.
53. Ibid., p. 187.
54. Ibid., p. 186.
55. Ibid.
56. Ibid., p. 188.

2 . WHAT IS MEDITATION?

1. Philip Kapleau, ed., *The Three Pillars of Zen: Teaching, Practice, and Enlightenment*, revised and expanded edition (New York: Doubleday, Anchor, 1980), pp. 10–11.
2. Patanjali, *Yoga Sutras* 1.2, in Heinrich Zimmer, *Philosophies of India*, ed. Joseph Campbell, Bollingen Series XXVI (New York: Pantheon Books, 1951), p. 284.

——— *Notes*

3. Plato, *The Symposium,* trans. Walter Hamilton (New York: Penguin Books, 1985), p. 37.
4. See Wolfgang Kretschmer, "Meditative Techniques in Psychotherapy," in Charles T. Tart, ed., *Altered States of Consciousness* (New York: Doubleday, Anchor, 1969), pp. 224–33.
5. See C. G. Jung, "Commentary," in Richard Wilhelm, trans., *The Secret of the Golden Flower: A Chinese Book of Life* (New York: Harcourt, Brace and World, A Harvest Book, 1962), pp. 105–6. Jung refers to an account by Edward Maitland, who in a state of introversion noticed a "suspension of breathing." His ordinary breathing stopped and was replaced by an internal respiration "as if by a breathing of a distinct personality within and other than the physical organism." Maitland compared this personality to the entelechy of Aristotle and the inner Christ of Saint Paul, the "spiritual and substantial individuality engendered within the physical and phenomenal personality, and representing, therefore, the rebirth of man on a plane transcending the material."
6. Kapleau, *The Three Pillars of Zen,* p. 274.
7. Jung, cw 2, para. 1352.
8. Ibid.
9. Kapleau, *The Three Pillars of Zen,* p. 238.
10. Wilhelm, *The Secret of the Golden Flower,* p. 69.
11. Ibid., p. 41.
12. Ibid., p. 22.
13. Ibid.
14. Jung, *Memories, Dreams, Reflections,* p. 199.
15. Wilhelm, *The Secret of the Golden Flower,* p. 23.
16. Ibid., p. 21.
17. Ibid.
18. Saint John of the Cross, *The Complete Works of Saint John of the Cross* (Westminster: Newman Press, 1953), vol. 1, p. 202.
19. Claudio Naranjo and Robert Ornstein, *On the Psychology of Meditation* (New York: Viking Press, 1971), p. 169.
20. Ibid.
21. Ibid.
22. See, for example, Akira Kasamatsu and Tomio Hirai, "An

Electroencephalographic Study on the Zen Meditation (Zazen)," in Tart, *Altered States of Consciousness* pp. 501–14.

23. Arthur J. Deikman, "Experimental Meditation" and "Deautomatization and the Mystic Experience," in Tart, *Altered States of Consciousness*, pp. 203–23, 25–46.

24. Kasamatsu and Hirai, "An Electroencephalographic Study."

25. Arthur J. Deikman, "Deautomatization and the Mystic Experience," in Tart, *Altered States of Consciousness*, p. 33.

26. Ibid.

27. Deikman, "Experimental Meditation," in Tart, *Altered States of Consciousness*, p. 216.

28. William Johnston, ed., *The Cloud of Unknowing and the Book of Privy Counseling* (Garden City, N.Y.: Doubleday, Image Books, 1973), pp. 48–49.

29. Kapleau, *The Three Pillars of Zen*, p. 118.

30. Jung, CW 13, para. 433.

31. Kapleau, *Zen: Dawn in the West*, pp. 70–71.

32. Ibid., p. 71.

33. Jung, CW 9, part I, para. 155.

34. Jung, CW 8, para. 388.

35. Ibid.

36. Ibid.

37. Ibid., para. 270.

38. Ibid.

39. Jung, CW 11, para. 774.

40. Wilhelm, *The Secret of the Golden Flower*, pp. 50–51.

41. Jung, *Letters*, vol. 2, p. 45.

42. Walter N. Pahnke and William A. Richards, "Implications of LSD and Experimental Mysticism," in Tart, *Altered States of Consciousness*, p. 413.

43. Marie-Louise von Franz, *On Dreams and Death: A Jungian Interpretation* (Boston & London: Shambhala Publications, 1986), p. 146.

44. Deikman "Deautomatization and the Mystic Experience," in Tart, *Altered States of Consciousness*, pp. 39–41.

45. See C. G. Jung, *Flying Saucers: A Modern Myth of Things Seen in the Skies* (Princeton, N.J.: Princeton University Press, 1978).

————— *Notes*

46. Hebrews 10:31.

47. Jung, *Letters*, vol. 1, pp. 65.–66.

3 . THE PSYCHOLOGY OF ZEN

1. Ernest Rossi, *The Twenty-Minute Break: Using the New Science of Ultradian Rhythms* (Los Angeles: J. P. Tarcher, 1991).

2. Kasamatsu and Hirai, "An Electroencephalographic Study of the Zen Meditation (Zazen)," in Tart, *Altered States of Consciousness* (Garden City, N.Y.: Doubleday, Anchor, 1972).

3. C. G. Jung, *The Vision Seminars*, book 2 (Zurich: Spring Publications, 1976), pp. 420–21.

4. Ibid., p. 421.

5. Johnston, *The Cloud of Unknowing*, p. 48.

6. Ibid., p. 56. The "cloud of unknowing" is the meditation complex, which eventually reveals its archetypal core—the Self. This is clear from the author's description: "In the beginning it is usual to feel nothing but a kind of darkness about your mind, or as it were, a *cloud of unknowing*. You will seem to know nothing and to feel nothing except a naked intent toward God. . . . Learn to be at home in this darkness. Return to it as often as you can, letting your spirit cry out to him whom you love. For if, in this life, you hope to feel and see God as he is in himself it must be within this darkness and this cloud" (pp. 48–49).

7. Kenneth Kraft, ed., *Zen: Tradition and Transition* (New York: Grove Press, 1988), pp. 42–43.

8. Quoted in Perle Besserman and Manfred Steger, *Crazy Clouds: Zen Radicals, Rebels, Reformers* (Boston & London: Shambhala Publications, 1991), p. 116.

9. Johnston, *The Cloud of Unknowing*, pp. 102–3.

10. For the complete series of ten Oxherding Pictures, see D. T. Suzuki, *Manual of Zen Buddhism* (New York: Grove Press, 1960).

11. Katsuki Sekida, *Zen Training: Methods and Philosophy*, ed. A. V. Grimstone (New York & Toyko: Weatherhill, 1985), p. 34.

12. Kapleau, *The Three Pillars of Zen*, pp. 84–85.

13. Ibid., p. 183.

14. Jung, CW 11, para. 898.
15. Kapleau, *The Three Pillars of Zen*, pp. 261, 299, 239.
16. Kapleau, *Zen: Dawn in the West*, pp. 162–63.
17. Kapleau, *The Three Pillars of Zen*, p. 302.
18. Jung, CW 14, para. 778.
19. *Meister Eckhart* by Franz Pfeiffer, trans. C. de B. Evans (London: Watkins, 1924), vol. 1, p. 221.

4 . CAN WEST MEET EAST?

1. C. G. Jung, CW 13, para. 84.
2. Ibid., para. 70. Amfortas is the fisher king of the Grail legend, who suffers from a wound in the thigh that refuses to heal. Jung felt the image was an allusion to the sexual problem left unsolved by Christianity, which is actually only one aspect of the suffering caused by the conflict between instincts and spirit.
3. Ibid., para. 69.
4. Ibid., para. 16.
5. Ibid., para. 54.
6. Ibid., para. 63.
7. Jung, CW 11, para. 825.
8. Ibid., para. 802.
9. Ibid., paras. 867–68.
10. Ibid., para. 907.
11. Ibid., para. 904.
12. Ibid.
13. Wilber, Engler, and Brown, *Transformations of Consciousness*, pp. 177 and 189.
14. Ibid., p. 27.
15. Ibid.
16. Ibid.
17. Ibid., p. 29.
18. Ibid., pp. 29–30.
19. Jung, CW 11, para. 778.
20. Zenkei Shibayama, *A Flower Does Not Talk: Zen Essays* (Rutland, Vt. & Tokyo: Charles E. Tuttle Co., 1990), p. 12.
21. Jung, *Memories, Dreams, Reflections*, p. 174.
22. Wilber et al., *Transformations of Consciousness*, p. 3.

--------- Notes

23. Jung, *Memories, Dreams, Reflections,* p. 174.

24. Ibid., p. 179.

25. Ibid., p. 181.

26. Jung, CW 13, paras. 21–23.

27. Jung, CW 14, para. 706.

28. Marie-Louise von Franz, Introduction to Barbara Hannah, *Encounters with the Soul: Active Imagination as Developed by C. G. Jung* (Santa Monica, Calif.: Sigo Press, 1981), p. 2.

29. James A. Hall and Andrew Brylowski, "Lucid Dreaming and Active Imagination," *Quadrant: The Journal of Contemporary Jungian Thought* 24, no. 1 (1991): 39.

30. Von Franz, Introduction to Hannah, *Encounters with the Soul,* p. 2.

31. Jung, *Memories, Dreams, Reflections,* p. 329.

32. Radmila Moacanin, *Jung's Psychology and Tibetan Buddhism: Western and Eastern Paths to the Heart* (London: Wisdom Publications, 1986), p. 97.

5. MEDITATION AND ALCHEMY

1. C. G. Jung, Foreword, in Wilhelm, *The Secret of the Golden Flower,* p. xiv.

2. Jung, CW 14, para. 662.

3. Ibid., para. 673.

4. Ibid.

5. Wilhelm, *The Secret of the Golden Flower,* pp. 14–15, and von Franz, *On Dreams and Death,* p. 3. The "Yellow Springs" is the land of the dead and a reservoir of life (yin) where the spirit (yang) regains its energy and prepares for a return to earthly existence.

6. Jung, CW 14, para. 673.

7. Ibid.

8. Ibid., para. 696.

9. Ibid., para. 742.

10. Ibid., para. 683.

11. Ibid., para. 681.

12. Ibid. Bracketed interpolations in original.

13. Ibid., para. 695.

14. Ibid., para. 684.

15. Ibid., para. 685.
16. Ibid. My interpolations in brackets.
17. Ibid., para. 707.
18. Ibid., para. 736.
19. Ibid., para. 705.
20. Ibid., para. 711.
21. Ibid., para. 759.
22. Ibid., para. 760.
23. Marie-Louise von Franz explores these issues further in *Number and Time: Reflections Leading toward a Unification of Depth Psychology and Physics* (Evanston, Ill.: Northwestern University Press, 1974), and *Psyche and Matter* (Boston & London: Shambhala Publications, 1992).
24. Jung, CW 14, para. 661–62.
25. Ibid., para. 762.
26. Ibid., para. 771.
27. Ibid., para. 776.
28. Ibid., para. 778.
29. Wilhelm, *The Secret of the Golden Flower*, p. 70.
30. Ibid., p. 29.
31. Ibid., pp. 29 and 22.
32. Wilhelm, *The Secret of the Golden Flower*, p. 29.
33. Ibid., p. 22.
34. Charles Luk, *Taoist Yoga: Alchemy and Immortality* (York Beach, Me.: Samuel Weiser, 1984), p. 122. Unfortunately, to make the book more comprehensible to the general public, the author has translated "lead" and "mercury" as *vitality* and *spirit*. But since the latter terms are also used to refer to other aspects of vitality (e.g., *ch'i*, soul-energy) and other aspects of spirit (e.g., *shen, yang* energy), the result is confusing.
35. Ibid., p. xii. Here is an example of the translation problems noted in note 34 above. *Vitality* here does not mean "lead" but the soul-energy (*ch'i*) transmuted or sublimated out of the lead. The lead—also referred to as the "ocean of lead" or the "cavity of the dragon"—represents the *prima materia*, in this case the instincts and emotions, and the process describes the sublimation of instinctive and emotional energy into soul-energy, i.e., into psychic energy that is no longer tied to the instincts and emotions.

Notes

36. Ibid., p. 9.
37. Ibid., p. xvii.
38. Ibid.
39. Ibid., pp. 175–76.
40. Ibid., p. 176.
41. Ibid.
42. Wilhelm, *The Secret of the Golden Flower*, p. 30.
43. Ibid., p. 75.
44. Ibid., p. 63.
45. Ibid.
46. Ibid.
47. Ibid., pp. 76–77.
48. Jung, CW 12, para. 462.
49. Jung, CW 14, para. 749. Italics added.
50. Quoted from the *Philokalia* in Daniel Goleman, *The Meditative Mind: The Varieties of Meditative Experiences* (Los Angeles: Jeremy P. Tarcher, 1988), p. 56.
51. Kapleau, *The Three Pillars of Zen*, p. 241.
52. Jung, CW 14, para. 771.

APPENDIX A: WILBER ON JUNG

1. Ken Wilber, *Eye to Eye* (Boston & Shaftesbury: Shambhala Publications, 1990), p. 255.
2. For recent endeavors that pursue this aspect of archetypes, see Charles R. Card, "The Archetypal View of C. G. Jung and Wolfgang Pauli," *Psychological Perspectives,* Part I, issue 24 (Spring–Summer 1991), and Part II, Issue 25 (Fall–Winter 1991); Victor Mansfield and J. Marvin Spiegelman, "The Opposites in Quantum Physics and Jungian Psychology, Part I: Theoretical Foundations," and Victor Mansfield, "Part II: Applications," *Journal of Analytical Psychology* 36, no. 3 (July 1991).
3. Ken Wilber, *Grace and Grit: Spirituality and Healing in the Life and Death of Treya Killam Wilber* (Boston & London: Shambhala Publications, 1991), p. 180. The statement Wilber refers to and quotes more fully in *The Spectrum of Consciousness* (Wheaton, Ill., Madras & London: Theosophical Publishing House, 1989), p. 271, is a quotation from a question-and-answer section in

The *Tavistock Lectures* (1935): "Mystics are people who have a particularly vivid experience of the processes of the collective unconscious. Mystical experience is experience of archetypes." CW 18, para. 218.

4. Wilber, *Grace and Grit*, p. 181.
5. Ibid., p. 180.
6. Wilber, *The Spectrum of Consciousness*, p. 271, and *Grace and Grit*, p. 182.
7. Wilber, *Grace and Grit*, p. 180.
8. Ibid., p. 182.
9. Wilber, *Eye to Eye*, p. 257.
10. Jung, "Archetypes of the Collective Unconscious," CW 9, Part I, para. 5.
11. Ibid.
12. Ibid.
13. Ibid.
14. Ibid.
15. Hans Jonas, *The Gnostic Religion: The Message of the Alien God and the Beginnings of Christianity* (Boston: Beacon Press, 1963), p. 60.
16. Ibid.
17. Jung, "On the Nature of the Psyche," CW 8, para. 388.
18. Ibid.
19. Jung, *Psychology and Alchemy*, CW 12, para. 462.
20. The term *collective unconscious* in this context could be misleading; one could also speak of it as collective consciousness in the sense of cosmic consciousness.
21. Marie-Louise von Franz, *Projection and Re-collection in Jungian Psychology*, p. 86.
22. Cited in Jung, "On the Nature of the Psyche," CW 8, para. 389.
23. Ibid., para. 391.
24. Ibid., para. 390.
25. Ibid.
26. Ibid., para. 392.
27. Ibid., para. 394 and n. 95.
28. Ibid., para. 394. I am using Jung's translation of the Latin motto to the edition of Nicholas Flamel.
29. Ibid.

———— *Notes*

30. Ibid., para. 395.

31. Ibid., para. 396.

32. Ibid.

33. Ibid., para. 389.

34. Ibid., para. 388.

35. Ibid., para. 395.

36. Ibid.

37. Quoted in Jung, *Psychology and Religion*, CW 11, para. 92.

38. Jung, *Psychology and Alchemy*, CW 12, para. 404.

39. Ibid.

40. Ibid. The bracketed interpolations are mine.

41. Here and in the other quotes that follow I am referring to Wilber's criticisms summarized at the start of this chapter.

42. Jung, "On the Nature of the Psyche," CW 8, para. 420.

43. Fritjof Capra, *The Tao of Physics: An Exploration of the Parallels between Modern Physics and Eastern Mysticism* (Boulder: Shambhala Publications, 1975), p. 225.

44. Jung, "Flying Saucers: A Modern Myth of Things Seen in the Skies," CW 10, para. 589.

45. Ken Wilber, *The Atman Project: A Transpersonal View of Human Development* (Wheaton, Ill., Madras & London: Theosophical Publishing House, 1989), p. 1.

46. Ibid.

47. Ibid., p. 2.

48. Ibid.

49. Jung, CW 10, para. 622.

50. Ibid., para. 779.

APPENDIX B: CLEARY, JUNG,
AND *THE SECRET OF THE
GOLDEN FLOWER*

1. Thomas Cleary, trans., *The Secret of the Golden Flower: A Chinese Book of Life,* (San Francisco: Harper San Francisco, 1991).

2. Ibid., p. 3.

3. Ibid., p. 134.

4. Ibid., p. 9.

5. Ibid., p. 73.
6. Wilhelm, *The Secret of the Golden Flower*, p. 21.
7. Ibid., p. 13.
8. Cleary, *The Secret of the Golden Flower*, p. 11.
9. Ibid., p. 77.
10. Ibid., pp. 10 and 40.
11. Ibid., p. 75.
12. Ibid., p. 58.
13. Ibid., p. 124.
14. Luk, *Taoist Yoga: Alchemy and Immortality*, p. 40.
15. Ibid., p. 190.
16. Cleary, *The Secret of the Golden Flower*, p. 76.
17. Jung, "Commentary on 'The Secret of the Golden Flower,' " CW 13, para. 39.
18. Jung, *Mysterium Coniunctionis*, CW 14, para. 296.
19. Cleary, *The Secret of the Golden Flower*, p. 79.
20. Ibid., p. 82.
21. Jung, "Commentary on 'The Secret of the Golden Flower,' " CW 13, para. 74.
22. Wilhelm, *The Secret of the Golden Flower*, p. 14.
23. Ibid., pp. 14–15.
24. Cleary, *The Secret of the Golden Flower*, p. 83.
25. Ibid., pp. 83–84.
26. Ibid., p. 85.
27. Ibid.
28. Ibid.
29. Ibid., p. 137.
30. Ibid.
31. Ibid., p. 105.
32. Ibid.
33. Flora Courtois, *An Experience of Enlightenment* (Wheaton, Ill.: Theosophical Publishing House, 1986).
34. Ibid., p. 60.
35. Cleary, *The Secret of the Golden Flower*, p. 78.
36. Ibid., p. 100.
37. Ibid., p. 105.
38. Ibid., p. 85.

─────── *Notes*

39. Ibid., p. 100.
40. Ibid., p. 101.
41. Kapleau, *Zen: Dawn in the West*, p. 187.
42. Ibid., p. 180.
43. Kapleau, *The Three Pillars of Zen*, p. 378.
44. Kogen Mizuno, *Basic Buddhist Concepts* (Tokyo: Kosei Publishing Co., 1987), pp. 148–49.
45. Jung, *Memories, Dreams, Reflections*, pp. 296–97.
46. Jung, *Mysterium Coniunctionis*, CW 14, paras. 660 and 760.
47. Ibid., para. 760.
48. Ibid., para. 762.
49. Ibid.
50. Cleary, *The Secret of the Golden Flower*, p. 142.
51. Ibid., p. 152.
52. Ibid.
53. Cleary, *The Secret of the Golden Flower*, pp. 18 and 15.
54. Ibid., p. 40.

BIBLIOGRAPHY

Besserman, Perle, and Manfred Steger. *Crazy Clouds: Zen Radicals, Rebels, Reformers*. Boston & London: Shambhala Publications, 1991.

Capra, Fritjof. *The Tao of Physics: An Exploration of the Parallels between Modern Physics and Eastern Mysticism*. Boulder: Shambhala Publications, 1975.

Card, Charles R. "The Archetypal View of C. G. Jung and Wolfgang Pauli." *Psychological Perspectives*, Part I, issue 24 (Spring–Summer 1991).

Cleary, Thomas, trans. *The Secret of the Golden Flower: A Chinese Book of Life*. San Francisco: Harper San Francisco, 1991.

The Cloud of Unknowing and the Book of Privy Counseling. Newly edited with an introduction by William Johnston. Garden City, N.Y.: Image Books, Doubleday, 1973.

Courtois, Flora. *An Experience of Enlightenment*. Wheaton, Ill.: Theosophical Publishing House, 1986.

Deikman, Arthur J. "Deautomatization and the Mystic Experience." In Charles T. Tart, ed., *Altered States of Consciousness*. New York: Anchor Books, Doubleday, 1969.

———. "Experimental Meditation." In Charles T. Tart, ed., *Altered States of Consciousness*. New York: Anchor Books, Doubleday, 1969.

———. *The Observing Self: Mysticism and Psychotherapy*. Boston: Beacon Press, 1982.

Dumoulin, Heinrich. *A History of Zen Buddhism.* New York: Pantheon Books, 1963.

W. Y. Evans-Wentz, ed. *The Tibetan Book of the Dead.* New York: Oxford University Press, 1960.

Goldstein, Joseph, and Jack Kornfield. *Seeking the Heart of Wisdom: The Path of Insight Meditation.* Boston & London: Shambhala Publications, 1987.

Goleman, Daniel. *The Meditative Mind: The Varieties of Meditative Experience.* Los Angeles: Jeremy P. Tarcher, 1988.

Hall, James A., and Andrew Brylowski. "Lucid Dreaming and Active Imagination." *Quadrant: The Journal of Contemporary Jungian Thought* 24, no. 1 (1991).

Hannah, Barbara. *Encounters with the Soul: Active Imagination as Developed by C. G. Jung.* Santa Monica, Calif.: Sigo Press, 1981.

Jonas, Hans. *The Gnostic Religion: The Message of the Alien God and the Beginnings of Christianity.* Boston: Beacon Press, 1963.

Jung, C. G. *The Collected Works of C. G. Jung.* 20 vols. Bollingen Series XX. Princeton: Princeton University Press, 1964–1979.

———. *Letters.* Selected and edited by Gerhard Adler in collaboration with Aniela Jaffé. Vol. 1: 1906–1950. Bollingen Series XCV:1. Princeton: Princeton University Press, 1973. Vol. 2: 1951–1961. London: Routledge & Kegan Paul, 1976.

———. *Memories, Dreams, Reflections.* Recorded and edited by Aniela Jaffé. Translated by Richard and Clara Winston. New York: Pantheon Books, 1963.

———. *The Vision Seminars.* Books 1 and 2. Zurich: Spring Publications, 1976.

Kaplan, Aryeh. *Jewish Meditation: A Practical Guide.* New York: Schocken Books, 1985.

Kapleau, Philip, ed. *The Three Pillars of Zen: Teaching, Practice, and Enlightenment.* Revised and expanded edition. New York: Anchor, Doubleday, 1980.

———. *Zen: Dawn in the West.* Garden City, N.Y.: Anchor, Doubleday, 1980.

Kasamatsu, Ahira, and Tomio Hirai. "An Electroencephalographic Study on the Zen Meditation (Zazen)." In Charles T. Tart, ed., *Altered States of Consciousness*. New York: Anchor, Doubleday, 1969.

Kraft, Kenneth, ed., *Zen: Tradition and Transition*. New York: Grove Press, 1988.

Kretschmer, Wolfgang. "Meditative Techniques in Psychotherapy." In Charles T. Tart, ed., *Altered States of Consciousness*. New York: Anchor Books, Doubleday, 1969.

Luk, Charles (Lu K'uan Lü), trans. *Taoist Yoga: Alchemy and Immortality*. A translation, with introduction and notes, of *The Secrets of Cultivating Essential Nature and Eternal Life (Hsin Ming Fa Chueh Ming Chih)* by the Taoist master Chao Pi Ch'en. York Beach, Me.: Samuel Weiser, 1984.

Mansfield, Victor. "The Opposites in Quantum Physics and Jungian Psychology. Part II: Applications." *Journal of Analytical Psychology* 36, no. 3 (July 1991).

Mansfield, Victor, and J. Marvin Spiegelman. "The Opposites in Quantum Physics and Jungian Psychology. Part I: Theoretical Foundations," *Journal of Analytical Psychology* 36, no. 3 (July 1991).

Meckel, Daniel J., and Robert L. Moore. *Self and Liberation: The Jung-Buddhism Dialogue*. New York & Mahwah, N.J.: Paulist Press, 1992.

Meister Eckhart, by Franz Pfeiffer. Translated by C. de B. Evans. Vol 1. London: Watkins 1924.

Mizuno, Kogen. *Basic Buddhist Concepts*. Tokyo: Kosei Publishing Co., 1987.

Moacanin, Radmila. *Jung's Psychology and Tibetan Buddhism: Western and Eastern Paths to the Heart*. London: Wisdom Publications, 1986.

McGraw-Hill Encyclopedia of World Biography. New York: McGraw-Hill Book Co., 1973.

Naranjo, Claudio, and Robert Ornstein. *On the Psychology of Meditation*. New York: Viking Press, 1971.

Odajnyk, V. Walter. "Gathering the Light: A Jungian Exploration of the Psychology of Meditation." *Quadrant: Journal of the C. G. Jung Foundation for Analytical Psychology* 21, no. 1 (1988).

———. *Jung and Politics: The Political and Social Ideas of C. G. Jung*. New York: Harper Colophon Books, 1976.

———. "Meditation and Alchemy: Images of the Goal in East and West." *Psychological Perspectives,* issue 22 (Spring 1990).

———. "The Political Ideas of C. G. Jung," *American Political Science Review* 67, no. 1 (March 1973).

———. "Zazen: A Psychological Exploration." *Psychological Perspectives,* issue 25 (Fall–Winter 1991).

Patanjali. "Yoga Sutras." In Heinrich Zimmer, *Philosophies of India,* edited by Joseph Campbell. Bollingen Series XXVI. New York: Pantheon Books, 1951.

Phanke, Walter N., and William A. Richards. "Implications of LSD and Experimental Mysticism." In Charles T. Tart, ed., *Altered States of Consciousness.* New York: Anchor, Doubleday, 1969.

Rossi, Ernest. *The Twenty-Minute Break: Using the New Science of Ultradian Rhythms.* Los Angeles: Jeremy P. Tarcher, 1991.

Saint John of the Cross. *The Complete Works of Saint John of the Cross.* Westminister: Newman Press, 1953.

Sekida, Katsuki. *Zen Training: Methods and Philosophy.* Edited with an Introduction by A. V. Grimstone. New York & Tokyo: Weatherhill, 1985.

Shibayama, Zenkei. *A Flower Does Not Talk: Zen Essays.* Rutland & Tokyo: Charles E. Tuttle Co., 1990.

Spiegelman, J. Marvin, and Mokusen Miyuki. *Buddhism and Jungian Psychology.* Phoenix: Falcon Press, 1987.

Suzuki, Daisetz Teitaro. *Essays in Zen Buddhism.* First Series. New York: Grove Press, 1961.

———. *Manual of Zen Buddhism.* New York: Grove Press, 1960.

Tart, Charles T., ed. *Transpersonal Psychologies.* New York: Harper & Row, 1975.

von Franz, Marie-Louise. *On Dreams and Death: A Jungian Interpretation.* Boston & London: Shambhala Publications, 1986.

———. *Projection and Re-collection in Jungian Psychology.* La Salle, Ill. & London: Open Court, 1978.

Wilber, Ken. *The Atman Project: A Transpersonal View of Human Development.* Wheaton, Ill., Madras & London: Theosophical Publishing House, 1989.

———. *Eye to Eye.* Boston & Shaftesbury: Shambhala Publications, 1990.

———. *Grace and Grit: Spirituality and Healing in the Life and Death of Treya Killam Wilber.* Boston & London: Shambhala Publications, 1991.

———. *The Spectrum of Consciousness.* Wheaton, Ill., Madras & London: Theosophical Publishing House, 1989.

Wilber, Ken; Jack Engler; and Daniel P. Brown. *Transformations of Consciousness: Conventional and Contemplative Perspectives on Development.* Boston & London: Shambhala Publications, 1986.

Wilhelm, Richard, trans. *The Secret of the Golden Flower: A Chinese Book of Life.* With a Foreword and commentary by C. G. Jung and part of the Chinese meditation text *The Book of Consciousness and Life* with a Foreword by Salome Wilhelm. New York: Harcourt, Brace and World, A Harvest Book, 1962.

Zimmer, Heinrich. *Philosophies of India.* Edited by Joseph Campbell. Bollingen Series XXVI. New York: Pantheon Books, 1951.

INDEX

"Absolute knowledge," 40–42
Active imagination, 111, 131, 206
  danger of, 126–27, 128
  effectiveness, 127–28
  as gateway to unconscious, 121–25
  Jung's development of, 120–24
  as meditation, 48, 71, 76, 124, 131–32
  techniques and guidelines, 124–26, 128–32
  See also Passive imagination
Affirming Faith in Mind, 204–5
Aion (Jung), 167, 186
Alaya-vijñana, 61–64
Albedo, 89, 162–63
Alchemy
  albedo (illumination), 162–63
  compared with psychology and meditation, 160
  Eastern, 116–17, 137, 144–49
  Eastern and Western compared, 152–59
  goals, 10–11, 52–54, 136, 145, 164, 177
  golden flower, 52–54, 145, 163
  as internal process, 144–52
  lapis, 163–64, 182–83

as means of liberation, 209–10
and meditation complex, 89, 159–67
nigredo, 59–60, 138, 157, 183
prima materia, 60, 63, 180, 182–83, 184
scintillae, 177–78, 180–82
and the Self, 182–83
unio mentalis, 157, 161
unus mundus, 142, 153, 163, 207
vas, 161–162
Western, 52–54, 116–17, 133–34
See also Coniunctio; Secret of the Golden Flower, The
Altered States of Consciousness (Tart), 6
Amitāyurdhyāna Sūtra, 18
Answer to Job (Jung), 186
Archetypes
and "absolute knowledge," 40
and archetypal images, 173–74, 204
as energetic structures, 186–87
and instincts, 174
Jung's definition, 173–74
and mysticism, 175–76, 184
numbers as, 79
of paradise, 71–73, 97–98

Index

Index

Index

You might also enjoy reading:

The Guilt Cure
by Nancy Carter Pennington & Lawrence H. Staples
ISBN 978-1-926715-53-7

The Creative Soul: Art and the Quest for Wholeness
by Lawrence H. Staples
ISBN 978-0-9810344-4-7

The Cycle of Life: Themes and Tales of the Journey
by Erel Shalit
ISBN 978-1-926715-50-6

Eros and the Shattering Gaze: Transcending Narcissism
by Kenneth A. Kimmel
ISBN 978-1-926715-49-0

Divine Madness: Archetypes of Romantic Love
by John R. Haule
ISBN 978-1-926715-04-9

Farming Soul: A Tale of Initiation
by Patricia Damery
ISBN 978-1-926715-01-8

The Sister From Below: When the Muse Gets Her Way
by Naomi Ruth Lowinsky
ISBN 978-0-9810344-2-3

Becoming: An Introduction of Jung's Concept of Individuation
by Deldon Anne McNeely
ISBN 978-1-926715-12-4

Resurrecting the Unicorn: Masculinity in the 21st Century
by Bud Harris
ISBN 978-0-9810344-0-9

Phone Orders Welcomed—Credit Cards Accepted
In Canada & the U.S. call 1-800-228-9316
International call +1-831-238-7799
www.fisherkingpress.com

Fisher King Press Presents:

The Dairy Farmer's Guide to the Universe
Jung, Hermes and Ecopsychology in Four Volumes

We keep forgetting that we are primates and that we have to make allowances for these primitive layers in our psyche. The farmer is still closer to these layers. In tilling the earth he moves around within a very narrow radius, but he moves on his own land. —C.G. Jung

Volume I: *Jung and Ecopsychology* presents the main premises of Jungian ecopsychology, offers some of Jung's best ecopsychological quotes, and provides a brief overview of the evolution of our dysfunctional Western relationship with the environment. **—ISBN 978-1-926715-42-1**

Volume II: *The Cry of Merlin—Jung, the Prototypical Ecopsychologist* makes the basic premises of Jungian ecopsychology more convincing and understandable by illustrating how they evolved out of Jung's lived experience. **—ISBN 978-1-926715-43-8**

Volume III: *Hermes and the Cows—Hermes, Ecopsychology and Complexity Theory* is an exegesis of the myth of Hermes stealing Apollo's cattle to be used as a mythic foundation for Jungian ecopsychology with Hermes' wand as its symbol. **—ISBN 978-1-926715-44-5**

Volume IV: *An Archetypal View of the Land, the Seasons, and the Planet of the Insect* explores the environment, with the Midwest as an example, using traditional Jungian and Hillmanian approaches to deepen our connection with the land, the seasons, and insects. The Dalai Lama said how we relate to insects is very important for it reveals much about a culture's relationship with the psyche and nature. **—ISBN 978-1-926715-45-2**

Dennis Merritt, Ph.D., LCSW, is a Jungian psychoanalyst and ecopsychologist in private practice in Madison and Milwaukee, Wisconsin. Dr. Merritt is a diplomate of the C.G. Jung Institute, Zurich and also holds the following degrees: M.A. Humanistic Psychology-Clinical, Sonoma State University, California, Ph.D. Insect Pathology, University of California-Berkeley, M.S. Entomology, University of Wisconsin-Madison, B.S. Entomology, University of Wisconsin-Madison. Over twenty years of participation in Lakota Sioux ceremonies have strongly influenced his worldview.

Phone Orders Welcomed—Credit Cards Accepted
In Canada & the U.S. call 1-800-228-9316
International call +1-831-238-7799
www.fisherkingpress.com

Made in the USA
Lexington, KY
10 July 2012